KV-191-804

METALWORKING
for Schools, Colleges and Home Craftsmen

Oscar Almeida

Senior Lecturer in Handicraft
Trent Park Training College

MILLS AND BOON LIMITED, LONDON

First printed 1967

Second (Metric) edition 1971

Reprinted 1974

ISBN 0 263 51583 4

PUBLISHED BY MILLS AND BOON LIMITED
17-19 FOLEY STREET, LONDON, WIA IDR.
**MADE AND PRINTED IN GREAT BRITAIN BY
THE GARDEN CITY PRESS LIMITED
LETCHWORTH, HERTFORDSHIRE**

Contents

Acknowledgements

I wish to thank the many friends who have helped me with this book.

Special thanks to Mrs I. Smith who typed and put the manuscript in order and to my colleagues Mr W. Alton, Mr T. R. Bennett and Mr S. H. Glenister for general advice and encouragement. Thanks also to the lecturers from the Central School of Arts and Crafts: Mr F. Beck, Mr J. E. Stapley and Mr Brooker for their help with the chapter on decorative processes: Mr W. E. King, from Hornsey College of Art, for his kind advice on silversmithing: Mr Clayton-Cave who made extensive corrections to the chapter on Heat Treatment and Mr T. Deeley for his help with the section on Metals (both from the British Iron & Steel Research Association): the Aluminium Development Association, Copper Development Association, and Tin Research Institute for help in their respective fields.

I wish also to thank the numerous engineering firms who supplied drawings and photographs which are acknowledged under each illustration, where appropriate.

(*The drawings are by the author and the articles are made by the author unless otherwise stated.*)

I

Design

Everything designed to be made in metal should have a purpose. The designer must understand this purpose and know the materials and processes used in the carrying out of his design. He must design within his knowledge and experience.

Even purely decorative work must perform its function, i.e., to be decorative. Apart from decorative work, providing your design functions, the simpler it is the better. There is a tendency among students to make designs much too involved. This tendency can be rectified, once having made your design, by asking yourself can I simplify it? This often leads to a more efficient design.

Efficient things must be made from the materials best suited for the purpose. For instance: stainless steel for kitchen utensils and cutlery; mild steel for tools which have to be case hardened; aluminium where lightness is required; gilding metal, nickel silver and brass for decorative work, and so on. This choice of materials must take into account cost, methods of joining the metals, ease of fabrication, strength, weight, etc.

The dreadful moment comes in designing when you sit down with a large piece of blank paper in front of you. Perhaps one of the best ways to start is by making a number of small sketches of the thing you are designing, then developing your best design. This calls for practice. The ability to draw is not heaven-sent: it comes only by hard work.

However, hard work on its own is not enough. You must keep abreast of the latest developments because we live in a changing living world in which many forces influence the shape and the kind of things we use. If you are wise you keep up to date, if you are a genius you are ahead of your time.

Time permitting, it is often advisable, once having completed your design on paper, to make a model of the thing you have designed. This is known as a "mock-up". By doing this you learn a lot about the design which it is not possible to learn from the drawing. "Mock-ups" can be made from any suitable material that comes to hand and they are not necessarily made the same size as the finished work, although this is advisable wherever possible.

When your design is finished you wonder, quite naturally, whether it is good or bad. Listen to the opinion of people who know, but ultimately the best test is time. By this we mean that a good design survives all the changes of fashion and taste. This is a rare quality.

2

Metals

Before considering particular metals and alloys there are terms applied to all metals which should be understood.

Brittleness. The tendency of a metal to break with little deformation and under low stress. Cast iron is brittle.

Compression. The opposite of tension. It is the ability to stand pressure. Metals such as cast iron which are strong in compression are known as "good load carriers".

Conductivity. The ability to allow the passage of electricity or heat. Silver and copper are very good conductors of heat and electricity.

Creep. This is the slow yielding of metals under a load. This yielding may take months or years as in furnace and steam boiler parts. Creep takes place more often at high temperatures, but soft metals such as lead, tin and zinc suffer from creep at room temperatures. The lead sheets on church roofs thicken towards the eaves.

Ductility. The property which enables a metal to withstand mechanical deformation without cracking particularly when being stretched as in wire drawing.

Fatigue Failure. Metals which have withstood all the normal tests under heavy stress have been known to fracture when a much lighter intermittent stress is applied millions of times. Over one hundred years ago Sir William Fairbairn found that a wrought iron girder would stand a single load of up to 12 tonnes, but if a load of little more than 3 tonnes was applied 3,000,000 times the girder would break.*

Impact Resistance. This is the ability of metal to withstand a severe impact without failure. A machine developed by Edwin G. Izod is much used in Britain for testing this kind of resistance. On this machine, a notched metal test piece is broken by a heavy swinging pendulum and the amount of energy required to break it is measured.

Malleability. The property enabling a metal to be hammered or rolled into thin sheets or similar forms. Gold is the most malleable metal as it can be hammered to 0·0000063 mm thick. In this form it is translucent and is known as gold leaf which is used for applying to surfaces for decoration such as in sign writing.

Shear Strength. The ability of a metal to withstand the action of two parallel forces acting in opposite directions as in a guillotine.

Specific Gravity. The ratio of the weight of a substance to the weight of the same volume of water.

Tensile Strength. The maximum pulling stress which a metal can withstand before breaking. A test piece of a known cross-sectional area is stretched until it breaks and the power needed is recorded. Tensile strength is stated in Newtons per square millimetre (N/mm^2). The tensile strength of a piece of metal is known as its tenacity.

Toughness. This denotes a condition intermediate between brittleness and softness. Or it can be said to be a combination of strength and ductility.

Stress. The term is used to denote the intensity of load applied to a material in relation to the area of its cross section.

* From *Metals in the Service of Man* by W. Alexander and A. Street.

IRON AND STEEL

More than any other metal steel has made our present technological age possible. From the finest hypodermic needle used by the dentist to the heaviest industrial machinery, steel is predominant. Steel is an alloy of iron and carbon. In fact steel is composed mainly of iron with, in some cases, only as little as 0·1% carbon. There are many kinds of steel consisting of iron alloyed with carbon together with other metals such as chromium, nickel, molybdenum, silicon, manganese, vanadium and cobalt. Iron, however, remains the basis of all steels.

The modern steelmaking processes can be grouped as follows:

1. The converter processes.
2. The open-hearth process.
3. The electric furnace processes.

In considering these processes we must also take into account some of the early achievements which led to the development of the present industry and we start with ironmaking.

The Production of Iron

At the beginning of the seventeenth century Dud Dudley made the first improvement in iron smelting. By using coal as a fuel he was able to produce about 3 tons of pig iron in one week. However, the first big improvement was brought about by Abraham Darby in 1709 when he used coke for smelting. This was the beginning of the iron and steel industry as we know it now. In those early days the iron was smelted from ores found locally, but now much of it is imported.

The best ores for iron making in order of quality are magnetite, haematite and limonite. About half the ore used in Britain is obtained in this country. The rest is imported from Canada, the United States, U.S.S.R., Brazil, Sweden and Venezuela. Some ores lie within 100 feet of the surface and can be mined by open-cast working, but haematite often requires deep mine working.

Magnetite ores contain the mineral magnetite. It is grey-black in colour, magnetic and is the richest ore, containing up to 65% iron as mined. Haematite is reddish brown and contains between 20% and 60% iron. Limonite ores contain between 20% and 55% iron.

Iron ores are known as "acid" or "basic" which are terms derived from the type of furnace lining used. The slag made in each process is consequent on the kind of ores used.

Basic or high phosphorous ores, with up to about 2·5% phosphorus, are the kind usually found in Britain. These are often mixed with imported ores of the haematite group to improve them. Acid, or haematite (low phosphorous), ores contain up to about 0·04% phosphorus and have a relatively high silicon content. In Britain the greater tonnage of iron is basic.

Here are some typical analyses of irons made from British ores.

	Basic	*Haematite* (*Acid*)
Carbon	3·5	3·75
Silicon	0·85	2·0
Sulphur	0·08	0·04
Phosphorus	1·6	0·045
Manganese	1·0	0·5

Before the ores are used in the blast furnace they are treated to remove some impurities. They are then mixed with coke breeze (fine coke dust) and limestone and roasted to produce sinter, or made into high iron content pellets and charged into the furnace with the coke and limestone. The coke used in the blast furnace is produced in coke ovens which are adjacent to the blast furnace. Limestone is used as a flux and is usually quarried near the blast furnace site.

Smelting in the Blast Furnace

A large furnace is about 30 metres high and over 10 metres in diameter at its widest part (fig. 1). The fire brick lining can be almost 1 metre thick and the outside plates are 38 mm thick.

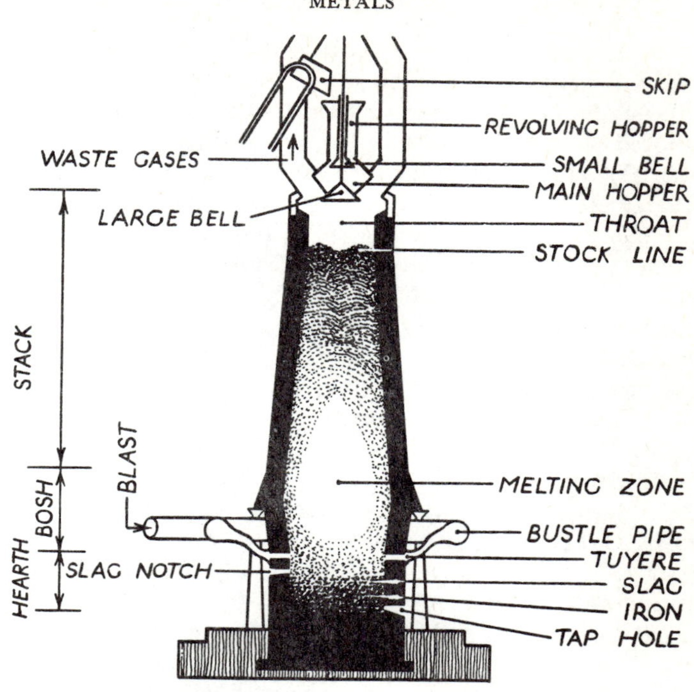

FIG.1. DIAGRAM OF BLAST FURNACE

The prepared ore, coke and limestone, known as "the charge", are put into the blast furnace by means of the skip.

The coke, in addition to producing heat and the reducing agent (reducing iron oxide to iron), combines with the iron to make a lower melting point alloy.

A preheated air blast passes through the large bustle pipe, which encircles the base of the furnace, and is blown into the charge through the tuyères (pronounced "tweers"). The oxygen of the air blown in at the bottom causes the coke to burn fiercely. This generates heat and large columns of reducing gas. As the coke burns away the charge descends in the furnace against the stream of gas rushing upwards. The gas and heat act on the ore and together with the limestone bring about the extraction of the iron and its separation from the earthy matter. The hot gases which cannot escape, because the double bell cones are never both open at the same time, are collected at the top of the furnace and pass through the exhaust ducting to the down pipes and thence, after cleaning, to the coke ovens and cowper stoves. The chequered brick lining of these is heated by the gas and later used to preheat the cold air on its way to the furnace. Each furnace has three stoves one being "on blast" and giving up heat whilst the others are "on gas" and receiving heat.

On the bend of each tuyère there is a small piece of blue glass; by looking through this the interior of the furnace can be inspected.

The smelting process is continuous. Once the furnace is lit it is kept going for months or even a year or more and normally is only stopped when the refractory lining needs attention.

The limestone produces a liquid slag which floats on top of the iron. When the slag has risen almost level with the tuyeres it is tapped off through the slag notch. This slag is used for railway track ballast or coated with tar and used for road making. Some basic slag is used for fertiliser.

The iron is tapped four or five times per day by breaking through the clay plug of the tapping hole thus allowing the molten metal to gush out. The impure iron-carbon alloy is either cast into metal moulds or it is cast into moulds of sand which originally looked like pigs feeding from a sow. For that reason the iron at this stage was called pig iron. (This term now applies to all the iron as it comes from the blast furnace.) Often however the pig iron is run into large refractory lined ladles which take the iron in the molten state to the steel making plant.

Recently the efficiency of blast furnaces has been improved by the injection of oil, fine coal, oxygen or steam into the blast.

Cast Iron

Cast iron is usually made from pig iron in a foundry where it is remelted and refined in a small furnace, not unlike a blast furnace, but which is only about 6 metres tall. A general characteristic of cast iron is that it is brittle and cannot be forged into shape. However there are various kinds of cast iron.

Grey Cast Iron. This is the commonest form of cast iron. When fractured it has a grey appearance. The properties of this iron are regulated to suit various requirements. The higher grades are used for machine beds and other machine parts, and the lower grades for grates, drainpipes, guttering, etc.

White Cast Iron. Is very hard and brittle and is difficult to machine. It has a white appearance when fractured. It is used for machine parts, such as those found in cement works, which have to stand great pressure and often rough usage.

Malleable Castings. These are produced by packing white cast iron components in an oxidising material and heating to red heat for several days and allowing to cool slowly. This causes some of the carbon to be removed by oxidation.

Malleable castings are tougher than ordinary iron castings. They can be machined and are used for machine parts which have to withstand shock.

Wrought Iron

Wrought iron is probably the oldest and, at its best, the purest form of iron. It was produced long before the Christian era and in its purest form contains only a very small amount of carbon and fibrous slag.

Primitive furnaces are still in existence in Africa which reduce iron ore to iron using charcoal as a fuel and goatskin bellows for the air blast. Most of the carbon is removed by oxidation thus raising the melting point of the iron which remains in the pasty stage. The almost pure iron which is obtained is hammered into the desired shape. Before the eighteenth century iron was made in this way in Sussex and the Forest of Dean in furnaces known as bloomeries. Wood charcoal was used as fuel.

In 1794 the puddling furnace, which provided a much cheaper way of producing iron, was introduced by Henry Cort. The small amount of wrought iron produced today is made in furnaces similar to the one used by Henry Cort, (fig. 2). It is a reverberatory type furnace and unlike the blast furnace the metal is not mixed with the fuel. The furnace is charged with pig iron and flux. The fuel is burned in a grate at one end of the furnace and only the hot fumes are in contact with the charge. The heat is reflected from the roof on to the charge to melt it.

Soon after the metal melts the carbon monoxide gas burns on the surface and it appears to boil. It is stirred or puddled by men with long heavy iron bars. The almost pure iron rises to the top and because of its higher melting point remains pasty and separates from the slag. The puddler manipulates the iron and unavoidably some of the slag, into blooms on the end of the iron bar. These weigh about 36 kilogram. After removal from the furnace the blooms are rolled then wired together in a faggot and brought to welding heat and re-rolled so that they are united. This disperses the slag throughout the metal and gives it its characteristic fibrous structure.

Wrought iron resists corrosion well and for this reason it is used in boiler making. It has also a good resistance to fatigue and sudden shock and is thus used for chains, hooks and haulage gear. Only a limited quantity of wrought iron is made today having been largely superseded by mild steel.

Mild Steel

In 1856 Sir Henry Bessemer introduced the Bessemer Converter which could make steel quickly and cheaply. The converter is shown in figure 3. The outside casing is made of steel and the whole furnace can be tipped on trunnions through which the air pipe, which is connected to the air holes at the bottom passes.

The refractory lining is either "acid", made from silica bricks, or "basic", made from crushed dolomite rammed with tar.

The original converters had only acid linings, until in 1878 Sidney Thomas and Percy Gilchrist introduced the basic lining thus making it possible to use high phosphorous ores.

A known amount of molten pig iron which may contain 3%–4% carbon is poured into the converter together with some

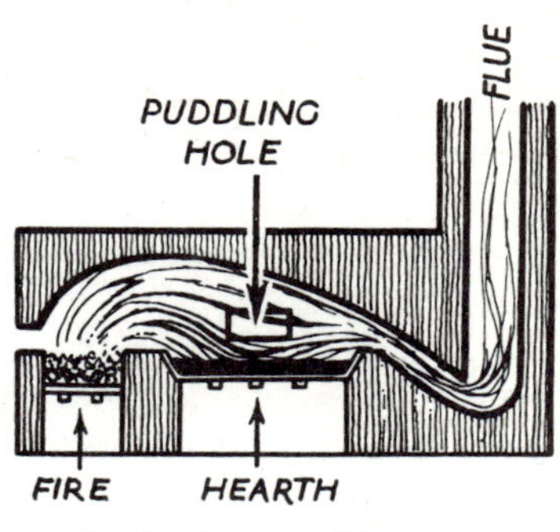

FIG.2. PUDDLING FURNACE

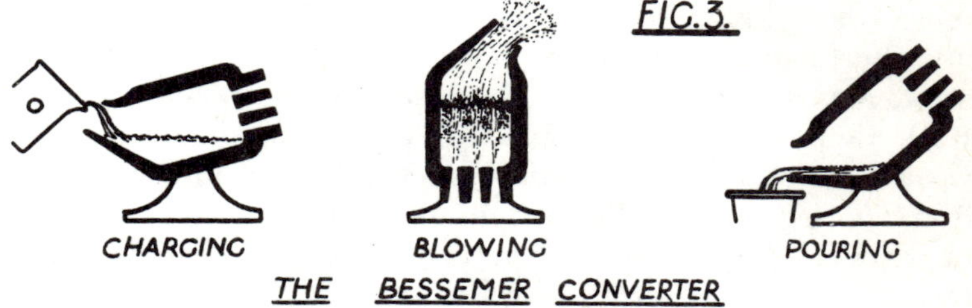

THE BESSEMER CONVERTER

limestone. The air blast is then turned on at low pressure. As the converter is turned on its trunnions to the upright position, the air pressure is increased. This prevents the steel from going into the holes.

The air blowing through the steel burns out the carbon and the other impurities. This is known as "the blow". It causes a spectacular show of sparks which lasts about 20 minutes. When the flame drops it means there is no carbon left, but the blast is kept on to burn out the phosphorus and the flame becomes a dense brown smoke. This stage is known as the "afterblow" and lasts for two or three minutes. The carbon has been eliminated from the metal but it contains oxides and gases which have been formed during the blow and which must be removed. The inclusion of the necessary carbon and the de-oxidation are accomplished by the addition, at the end of the blow, of a calculated quantity of ferro-manganese, an alloy of iron, manganese and carbon. The converter is rotated and the steel poured into ladles and then cast into ingots. Mild steel contains less than 0·25% carbon.

The Cementation Process

This is the oldest known method of making steel. It was probably first used in India about 1400 B.C. Bars of wrought iron were packed with charcoal in sealed crucibles and kept at red heat for several days. In this process the carbon in the charcoal combines with the iron to form cementite at the surface of the bars; for this reason it is called the cementation process. The bars were then bundled together and reheated to welding heat and forged together into a single bar to obtain a more even distribution of carbon. The bar could then be cut into short lengths and welded together again. This was repeated as often as desired. The steel thus obtained was known as shear steel. Small quantities of shear steel are still made. This process was quite good for small articles such as knives and shears, but it was not possible by this method to obtain an even distribution of carbon for large work. The cementation process is similar to the present-day case hardening process (see Chapter 7).

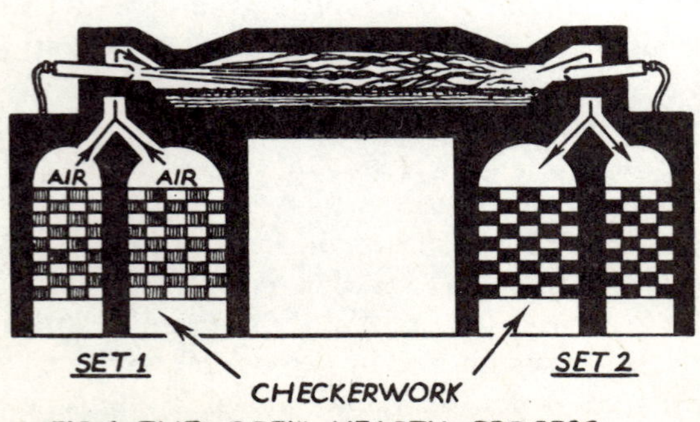

FIG.4. THE OPEN HEARTH PROCESS

The Crucible Process

Benjamin Huntsman who was a clock maker realised that to make good clock springs he needed steel in which the carbon was evenly distributed. In 1740 he developed a method of introducing the carbon to the iron when it was molten. This was done in small quantities in a crucible (because this steel was poured into moulds it was known as cast steel). It is actually an alloying process and is similar in principle to the modern induction process.

Open-Hearth Process

This was developed in 1867 by Charles W. Siemens in co-operation with Pierre Martin, by whom it was first patented.

Today more steel is produced by this method in Britain than by any other.

Figure 4 shows the open-hearth furnace. This is a reverberatory furnace in which the heat from the burning fuel, after passing over the charge, heats the chequered brickwork of one set of preheating chambers. When this set of chambers is hot the passage of gas and air is reversed so that it now passes through the hot bricks and becomes itself preheated and, after passing over the charge, heats the other set. The direction of the flow of gases is reversed periodically. This is known as the regenerative principle, and by this means a sufficiently high temperature is obtained to treat large quantities of metal and to keep it molten throughout the process.

The furnace is charged with pig iron and steel scrap. When this is melted, iron or millscale is added mainly to remove carbon by oxidation. During this process samples are taken from the furnace and analyses are made of the metal and slag. When the refining is complete either the tapping notch is broken or the furnace is tilted, depending on the type, and the steel is tapped into a ladle. The steel is then teemed from the ladle into ingot moulds. The furnace is tapped about every 12 hours. Some furnaces charged with hot metal are ready for tapping after 8 hours.

By using either a basic or acid lining, according to the type of charge, this furnace produces low and medium carbon steels. The average capacity of these furnaces is 250 tonnes and they are fired by gas or fuel oil.

Electric Furnaces

These are either electric arc (fig. 5), in which the heat is generated by an arc between graphite electrodes and the metal, or induction furnaces.

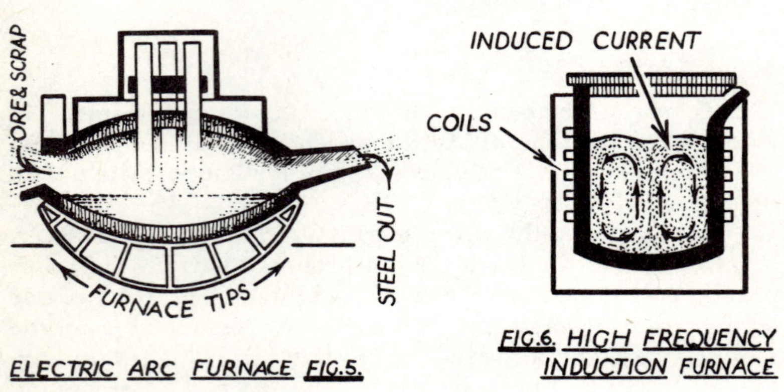

ELECTRIC ARC FURNACE FIG.5.

FIG.6. HIGH FREQUENCY INDUCTION FURNACE

The high frequency induction furnace (fig. 6) is a hollow vessel with a refractory lining round which is wound a water cooled coil of copper wire. The charge consists of carefully selected scrap to which the necessary alloys are added. When the coil is energised with an electric current an induced current in the charge causes it to heat up and melt. There is very little slag in this process.

Both processes are used for making high grade alloy-steels including stainless steel. For these high grade steels the temperature must be carefully controlled and impurities kept to a minimum.

Since the cost of electricity has not risen as rapidly as the cost of other fuels electric arc furnaces, with a capacity up to 100 tonnes, are being used on a large scale. One steelworks in Britain is now making 1·35 million tonnes of ingots in one year with six high powered arc furnaces which in the past it took 21 openhearth furnaces to make.

Modern Converter Processes

Since Bessemer introduced his converter in 1856 and thereby started the "Steel Age", improvements have been made notably by the introduction of oxygen to the process. By injecting oxygen and air, or steam, or carbon dioxide, a greater proportion of scrap can be added to the charge: up to 15% as against a maximum of 5%.

The most recent converter processes are known as the L.D. process, the Kaldo and the rotor.

The L.D. process is named after the initial letters of the Austrian towns Linz and Donawitz where it was first developed. In this process oxygen is blown on to the top of the molten pig iron in the converter, which is vertical (fig. 7). This process is mainly used on pig iron with a low phosphorous content.

The Kaldo process is so named from Professor Kalling its inventor and Domnarvet, the Swedish steel works where it was

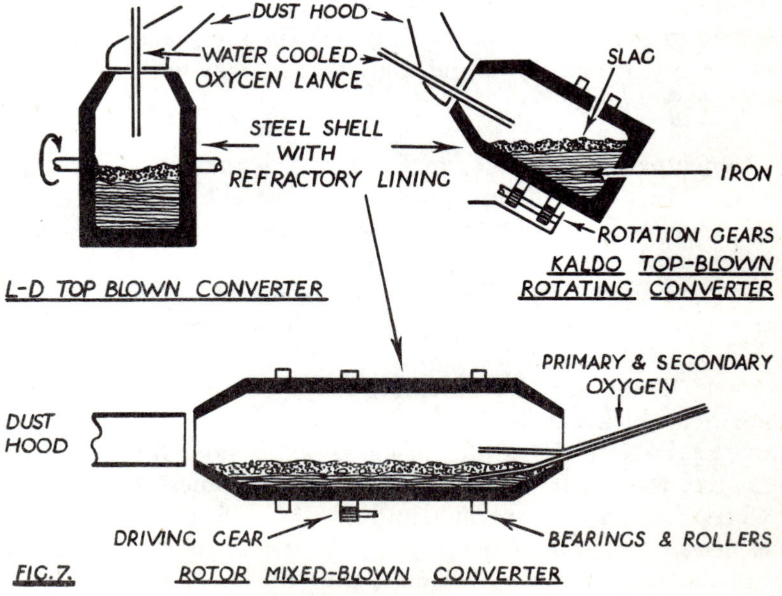

FIG. 7. ROTOR MIXED-BLOWN CONVERTER

developed. It is a basic process. The converter, which is inclined at an angle of 20° to the horizontal, slowly revolves about its axis whilst a jet of oxygen is directed on to the surface of the molten metal through a lance (fig. 7). This process takes about 90 minutes and irons with up to 2% phosphorus are used. The rotation of the converter allows the heat to be evenly transmitted to the charge and the quality of the metal obtained can be more closely controlled than by other converter methods. A fairly high percentage of scrap can be used in this process and a wide range of steels obtained.

The rotor process was developed in Germany. It uses a horizontal converter with two nozzles. One jet of oxygen blows into the molten metal as the vessel slowly revolves, and the other jet blows on to the surface of the metal (fig. 7).

Alloy Steel and Alloying Elements

Plain carbon steels have certain limitations such as lack of strength, hardness and high ductility, also non-retention of hardness at temperatures developed in metal cutting.

By using alloying elements special qualities have been imparted to steels to suit them for specific uses. Here are some of the important alloys and alloying elements and the effects they have on steel.

Chromium. This is the chief alloying element in all stainless steels. These contain between 12% and 30% chromium. One of the best known groups of stainless steel is the austenitic, which is generally known as 18/8 stainless steel, because it contains approximately 18% chromium and 8% nickel with additions of titanium, molybdenum and copper. Austenitic stainless steel cannot be hardened by heat treatment but can be work hardened. There are two other groups of stainless steel namely ferritic, which can be hardened only to a small extent, and martensitic, which can be hardened and tempered in a similar manner to carbon steels. A wide variety of stainless steels is used where resistance to corrosion and strength at high temperatures is needed, such as in jet engines. It is also used for surgical instruments, cutlery and kitchen utensils.

Cobalt. It is highly magnetic and is used in cutting tools to increase their hot hardness and in heat resisting nickel base alloys.

High Speed Steel. In 1868 Robert Mushet discovered that certain tungsten alloy steels could "self harden". Later, in 1900, he produced high speed steel which contained between 14% and 18% tungsten. This steel keeps its hardness at high temperatures; for this reason it is used in cutting-tool steels and for hot dies used for hot working of metals.

Manganese. It is usually added to steel in the form of ferromanganese, an alloy of iron, manganese and carbon. Above 10% added to steel makes it very difficult to machine. Small additions to steel improve the elasticity.

Molybdenum. It has a very high melting point—2,625°C which is exceeded only by four other metals: tungsten, rhenium, tantalum and osmium. It is used in heat resisting steels and where 18% tungsten is used in high speed steel it can be replaced by 9% molybdenum—it is said to have twice the "power" of tungsten.

Nickel. Alloys of iron and between 36% and 50% nickel are used for length standards, pendulum rods and measuring tapes, because they expand and contract very little at room temperatures. It is used in nickel chrome steel which has approximately 4·4% nickel, 1·2% chromium, 0·5% manganese, 0·3% carbon and 0·2% molybdenum and a tensile strength of up to 100 tons per square inch.

Silicon. It is a non-metal. When used in conjunction with manganese it makes excellent steel for car springs and bridges. Silicon improves the elasticity of steel. When up to 4% is added to steel it greatly increases its magnetic permeability.

Tungsten. It has the highest melting point of any metal—3380°C. It is used in steels which need to keep their hardness at high temperature such as high speed steel.

Vanadium. This is used as a de-oxidising agent in steel manufacture. It also gives steel grain refinement. 0·5% vanadium added to chromium steel makes it easier to forge and stamp and more resistant to shock.

Two metals which are neither iron nor steel but which are so much used in engineering that they must be mentioned are: cemented carbides and stellite.

Cemented Carbides. These are very hard and brittle. They are used as tips on cutting tools which are brazed on to carbon steel shanks. Cemented carbides consist of particles of tungsten carbide in a matrix of metal with a lower melting point; this matrix metal is usually cobalt. Cemented carbides are classified as:

1. Tungsten carbides which are used for machining highly abrasive metals such as irons and bronzes.
2. Titanium tungsten carbides which although less hard than tungsten carbides are used to machine steels because they resist the tendency for "chips" to become welded to the tip.

Stellite. This is an alloy of cobalt, chromium and tungsten. It is produced in an electric furnace and cast into shape; it cannot be forged into shape. Since it will retain its hardness and cutting edge even at red heat, it is used for rapid machining of hard metals. Stellite contains about 50% cobalt, up to 33% tungsten and 3% carbon. As it contains no iron it is not a steel and is non-magnetic.

METALS AND THEIR PROPERTIES

Non-Ferrous Metals

Aluminium. It is extracted from bauxite, an ore rich in aluminium oxide, which derives its name from Les Baux near Arles in France, where it was first worked commercially. Although aluminium is the most plentiful metal in the earth's crust (of which it forms 8%) it does not occur in its metallic

WORKSHOP DISTINGUISHING TESTS FOR FERROUS METALS

Test	*Mild Steel*	*Carbon Steel 0·4% C to 1·5% C*	*Cast Iron*	*High Speed Steel*	*Wrought Iron*
Grind on emery wheel	Bright yellow sparks with a few star-like sparks	Streams of bursting star-like sparks	Non-bursting dull red sparks close to wheel	Dull red sparks, some cling to the wheel	Bright non-bursting sparks
Sound—drop on anvil	Medium pitch metallic sound	Ringing high pitch sound	No ring dull note	Ringing sound not as high as carbon steel	Almost no ring. A little higher than cast iron
Make red hot and hammer	Works readily	Not as malleable as mild steel	Breaks up under the hammer	Does not work readily	Works readily
Make red hot and cool slowly	No effect	May become softer	No effect	May become brittle (depends on kind of steel)	No effect
Make red hot and quench	No effect	Becomes hard and brittle	May crack otherwise little change	Becomes hard and brittle	No effect
File	Files easily	Difficult	Filings dark, skin hard	Difficult	Files easily
Nick thin bar and hammer in vice	Bends then breaks. Grey crystalline fracture	Bends little then breaks. Fine silver crystalline fracture	Breaks easily. Light grey crystalline fracture	Bends little then breaks. Fine blue grey crystalline fracture	Bends well. Coarse grey fibrous fracture
Turn in lathe	Turns well. Swarf long and curly	Less easy than mild steel. Swarf breaks into short chips	Under hard skin, turns well. Chips crumble	Less easy than mild steel. Swarf long	Turns easily but finish is poor. Swarf long and curly

state, and only within the last hundred years has its production been developed.

Napoleon III of France had spoons and forks made from aluminium. The King of Siam, when he visited the French court, was delighted to receive a watch charm made from this rare metal, which was considered more precious than gold. At that time aluminium could only be manufactured by costly and laborious methods from bauxite and other salts of aluminium.

Bauxite ore is usually found near the surface and is mined in large quantities by open-cast working in Jamaica, U.S.S.R. France, Surinam, U.S.A., Guinea, Guyana, Greece, India and Australia.

Before smelting, the ore is refined by the concentration process devised by Karl Josef Bayer in 1890. In this process the almost pure aluminium oxide is dissolved in hot caustic soda while the impurities in bauxite are insoluble and are left behind. After drying the pure aluminium oxide is then converted into aluminium by electrolysis.

The electrolytic process requires a powerful electric current: for this reason aluminium reduction plants are often situated near fast flowing rivers where cheap hydro-electric power is developed. The electrolytic method was developed by Charles Hall in America and Paul Heroult in France. Although they worked independently they both arrived at the same solution to their problem.

They found that a mixture of 10% to 15% alumina in a mineral known as cryolite would become molten at 1,000°C when an electric current was passed through it. When the mixture was kept molten by the heat from the electric current the aluminium oxide split into aluminium and oxygen.

Cryolite is mined in Ivigtut in south-western Greenland. In recent years cryolite has been made synthetically.

Figure 8 shows an aluminium furnace.

Aluminium is an important engineering material. It is light and will not easily corrode in the atmosphere. This resistance to corrosion is due to the oxide film that rapidly forms on the surface so that the aluminium becomes insulated from further attack. Commercially pure aluminium is relatively soft but this lack of strength is overcome by alloying.

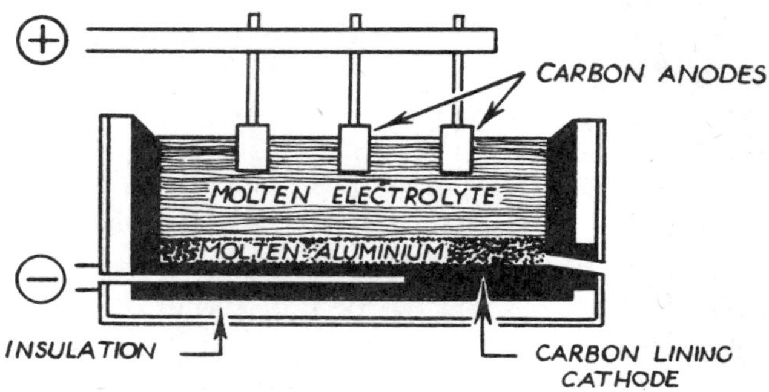

FIG. 8. EXTRACTING ALUMINIUM BY ELECTROLYSIS

Aluminium Alloys. Many alloys have been developed but they are used in two forms—wrought and cast. The wrought forms are those that have been forged, rolled, extruded, pressed or drawn. The cast form is made by gravity or pressure casting the molten metal in steel moulds or alternatively the metal can be poured into sand moulds which can only be used once.

Most of these alloys are classified by the British Standards Institution. They are referred to by code letters and numbers. A popular casting alloy used in the motor industry contains 7% copper, 3% zinc and 3% silicon. Another much used alloy contains 3% copper, 5% silicon and about 0·5% manganese.

Wrought components are made from an alloy containing small quantities of manganese or magnesium or magnesium and silicon, or for high strength they may contain copper or zinc.

Some alloys, containing approximately 4·25% copper and 0·5% magnesium, after heating and quenching in water will become harder and stronger after a few days. This is known as age hardening. Age hardened aluminium alloy is used in large quantities in the aircraft industry but because these alloys are not good corrosion resisters they are covered on each side with a thin layer of pure aluminium. This is known as cladding.

Cladding is performed by rolling a thin sheet of pure aluminium in each side of the alloy sheet. The total thickness of the pure aluminium front and back is about 10% of the thickness of the sheet.

Copper. Copper is almost without doubt the first metal to have been used for everyday articles. It is thought to have been first smelted in 3500 B.C., but even before this the metal, which can be found in the pure state (native), was hammered into useful shapes.

Copper has a reddish-gold appearance; it is malleable; it can be drawn into wire as fine as 0·0254 mm diameter and rolled into thin sheets, forged, pressed, beaten or spun. It is an excellent conductor of heat and electricity and can be readily soldered, brazed or welded and it is resistant to many forms of corrosion.

Copper is crushed from ores which contain no more than 4% copper. These are ground to a fine powder and the copper bearing grains are separated by the flotation method. The flotation process is worthy of note, not only because it is widely used, but because it is unusual in that the dense metal compounds are caused to float in a bath of frothed-up liquid, while the unwanted minerals are wetted and sink to the bottom. A reverberatory furnace is then used to remove more of the impurities. This leaves a mixture of copper and iron sulphide known as the matte. This is heated in a converter, which is similar to the Bessemer converter, to remove the iron and sulphur and then it is finally refined either by fire refining or by electrolytic refining.

Fire refining is a process whereby the impure copper is melted and some impurities burnt by oxidation. After the slag has been removed, hardwood poles are forced into the molten metal to remove the oxygen by combustion. This is known as poling; the copper is then poured into moulds.

Electrolytic refining produces high purity copper. In this process large pieces of impure copper (anodes) are suspended in dilute sulphuric acid. These are interleaved with thin cathodes of pure copper. By electrolytic action copper from the anodes is deposited on to the cathodes and the impurities go to the bottom of the bath.

Brass. This is the best known copper alloy consisting of copper and up to 40% zinc. Apart from zinc some brasses may contain small quantities of aluminium, lead, manganese, silicon and tin.

Cartridge Brass or Best Brass, from which cartridges and shells are made, contains 70% copper and 30% zinc (usually referred to as 70/30 brass) and is the most ductile of the cold working brasses.

Admiralty Brass is similar to cartridge brass except that it contains up to 1% tin which increases its corrosion resistance.

Gilding Metal contains copper and between 20% and 5% zinc. It derives its name from its golden colour. It is used for decorative work on buildings and for jewellery and beaten metalwork.

Muntz Metal or Yellow Metal contains 40% zinc. It is used for casting and for hot working operations such as rolling and extrusion and as a brazing alloy for steels.

Bronze. Properly speaking it is an alloy of copper and tin, but it has come to include alloys such as silicon bronze and aluminium bronze which contain no tin and others such as manganese bronze which contain only a small amount. Bronze was used for weapons as long ago as 2000 B.C. In parts of the world where tin and copper ores exist together it was probably first smelted by accident. Later copper and tin ores were smelted together in varying proportions to produce bronze for particular purposes. Bronze is harder than copper, it casts well, has good corrosion resisting qualities and good wearing qualities.

Phosphor Bronze contains 3·75% to 12% tin and between 0·1% to 0·5% phosphorus. This is a good bearing material but as the phosphorous content increases so the ductility decreases.

Lead Bronze containing about 30% lead has been used with great success on aero engines. The lead in the bearings acts as a metallic lubricant when the oil film breaks down. Small amounts of lead (about 1%) are added to bronze to improve its machinability.

Aluminium Bronze, containing 5% to 10% aluminium, is produced in strip, wire, rod and tube forms. This alloy is used as a substitute for steel where strength and non-magnetic properties are required. It is also used for ships' fittings and components which need to be corrosive resistant.

Gunmetal was used, in early times, for casting cannon. It is a bronze which contains a small amount of zinc and is excellent for casting. Admiralty gun metal contains 88% copper, 10% tin and 2% zinc and is widely used for marine purposes. A gun metal which contains 85% copper and 5% each of tin, zinc and lead (85–5–5–5) is a much used casting material in foundries.

Tin. It is smelted from cassiterite which is a tin oxide known also as tinstone. It is mined in Malaya, Indonesia and Bolivia. The tin ore is washed out from the tin deposits, most of which are alluvial. The ore is then crushed and roasted in a reverberatory furnace to remove the sulphur and arsenic present. Then it is washed and mixed with slaked lime and anthracite and smelted in a reverberatory furnace. The crude tin is then poured into moulds. Later this is purified in another reverberatory furnace in which most of the impurities are skimmed off as slag.

Tin is a shiny white metal which is very soft and weak and has a low melting point (232°C) and has excellent corrosion resisting properties. The "cry of tin" is the name given to the sound a piece of tin makes when it is bent backwards and forwards.

The most common use of tin is in tinplate, which consists of steel sheets coated on each side with a thin layer of tin from which containers are made to store food, paints, lubricants and many other commodities.

Almost 50% of the tin produced goes into the making of tinplate. The mild steel sheets before being coated with tin are hot rolled to 1·8 mm thick, then cleaned by pickling in dilute sulphuric acid, then cold rolled to about 0·26 mm thick. After annealing it is rolled again which gives the sheet the correct surface finish and degree of hardness. The prepared sheet is then tinned either by electro-deposition or by hot dipping. The former process accounts for about three-quarters of the world production.

The electric process is carried out in large automatic plants which can make tinplate at an average rate of 300 metres per minute; the tin being in long strips which are coiled. In the hot dipping process the sheet steel is cut into small pieces which are passed through a bath of molten tin equipped with rollers which remove the excess tin on the surface. The thickness of the tin coating by this process is approximately 0·002 mm and by the electric process approximately 0·001 mm.

Tin Lead Solders (see Chapter 4 on joining metals).

White Metal Alloys. These are alloys chiefly of tin, lead, copper and antimony. The best known white metal is Babbits metal which consists of 88% tin, 4% copper and 8% antimony. This is used for bearings. Apart from bearing metal the term white metal includes pewter, printers' alloys and solders.

Type Metal is an alloy used for printing type and consists of 50% to 85% lead, up to 25% tin and between 10% and 30% antimony. This has the unusual property of expanding on cooling, thus it forces itself into every corner of the type mould giving an excellent casting.

Pewter is a white metal and consists, today, of approximately 94% tin, 4% to 5% antimony and 1 to 2% copper. This alloy is also known as Britannia metal. It can be cast, rolled or spun and is suitable for food vessels. Ancient pewter was composed of lead and tin and was used for utensils and coins. Between the fourteenth and eighteenth centuries it was widely used for plates and other vessels. In this country the pewterers had their own guild and "touch mark", which was a hallmark and ensured a certain standard of workmanship and quality of material.

Zinc. This is a blue-grey metal which is obtained from zinc blend (a sulphide) mined chiefly in North America and Australia. The metal does not occur in its native state but is obtained either by electrolysis or distillation. Zinc was first made in Sumatra and China and was not commercially produced in England until 1740.

In the electrolytic process concentrates of zinc are dissolved in sulphuric acid and after purification deposited electrolytically on aluminium sheets from which it is later stripped and cast into slabs. This method produces an almost pure metal. The distillation or thermal process is one in which a briquetted mixture of roasted ores and bituminous coal is heated in a vertical retort made from silicon carbide bricks, in which reduction can proceed continuously. The zinc forms as a vapour and is caught as a liquid metal in condensers.

A large proportion of zinc produced is used for making brass. Another important use is for coating iron—galvanising—which gives excellent protection against rust. It is also used in the form of zinc-base alloys for die casting.

Lead. It is a heavy bluish-grey metal (specific gravity 11·3) which is easily fusible and lacks strength. It is obtained chiefly from the lead ore, galena. After the ores are crushed they are separated from the impurities by the flotation process and after roasting they are reduced in a blast furnace.

Lead was used in antiquity; the Romans made extensive use of it for lining baths and making water pipes, the seams of which they fused together by pouring hot lead along the prepared joint. This was known as "lead burning". "Plumbum" was the name they used for lead and our present-day workers in lead are known as plumbers. Lead has a low melting point (327°C) and casts easily from the molten state. It is used for roof covering and water pipes and for fonts and rainwater heads. It resists acid well and is used for containers for these corrosive liquids. A more recent use is for shielding against radiation in atomic energy establishments. It is estimated that at present 15,000 tonnes of lead per year are used for this purpose in Britain.

Nickel. This is a silvery white metal which takes a good polish and is resistant to corrosion and is magnetic. It can be cast, forged, welded, brazed and hard soldered; and it is strong both at low and high temperatures. Its melting point is 1,454°C, nearly as high as iron. Eighty-five per cent of the world's output of nickel is obtained from ores mined in Sudbury, Ontario.

The ores usually contain copper and iron and sometimes precious metals. The name "nickel" is German and is derived from "Kupfer-Nickell" which might be translated as "devil's copper". It was so called by miners in the Hartz Mountains when they produced a nickel-copper alloy when struggling to obtain copper. The original process for separating nickel from its ores was developed in 1751. This process consisted of melting metallic sulphides with nitre cake which, when cooled, formed two separate layers, the top one containing copper and the bottom nickel. Since then nickel production has been greatly improved.

Nickel is used chiefly as an alloy in ferrous and non-ferrous metals and as a pure metal in plating.

Nickel Silver. In China, two thousand years before nickel was isolated, an alloy called "paktong" was made by melting a mixture of copper-nickel ore and zinc ore. A number of alloys of this type were made in Europe in the early part of this century and were known as German silver.

Nickel silver with 5% to 35% nickel, 50% to 60% copper and 15% to 35% zinc is used, because of its colour and resistance to corrosion, for tableware which is silver plated and known as E.P.N.S. (Electro Plated Nickel Silver). It is widely used for contact springs in telephone exchanges.

Gold. This is the precious metal of antiquity. Its malleability has been mentioned, but it is also the most ductile metal: one grain Troy can be drawn into wire 2·4 kilometres long. The pure metal is too soft for general use so it is hardened by alloying. The term "carat" used in connection with gold means a 24th part: e.g., 18 carat gold has 18 parts by weight pure gold and 6 parts alloying elements. The alloying elements are often 3 parts copper and 1 part silver.

Silver. It is the best conductor of heat and electricity; it is malleable and ductile and its pleasant white colour makes it a pleasure to handle. Sterling or standard silver has contained, since 1696, 92·5% pure silver. Silver can be cast or wrought and it is available in sheet, strip and tube form. Apart from its use in silversmithing it is used in large quantities for making silver solders.

Platinum. This is white in colour and is malleable and ductile. It is superior to gold in its resistance to corrosion. Because of its colour and strength it is used for making the fine settings in jewellery for precious stones, particularly diamonds.

3

Fitting

MEASURING, MARKING-OUT AND TESTING

Accuracy is the word that comes to mind when we mention engineering. On bench work this accuracy is ensured by careful measuring, marking-out and testing.

The Rule. The most common measuring tool is the steel rule. These are available in lengths from 100 mm to 2 metres. They are divided into mm and cm.

Scribers. The scriber (fig. 1) is the marking-out tool most used with the steel rule. It is made of hardened and tempered carbon steel. It should be ground to a point in such a way that the lines of the grindstone are in line with the axis as shown, otherwise the tip will break off more easily.

FIG.1.

To ensure that scribed lines show clearly it is usual to clean the metal and then colour it with copper sulphate or some proprietary marking-out fluid. Castings can be rubbed with white chalk or given a coat of whitewash.

Dot Punch. Some engineers like to dot punch the lines after marking-out so that the scribed lines are not "lost" when further work is being done on the workpiece. Dot punching is done with a sharp centre punch (fig. 2). The dot punch mark should be heavy enough to be seen, but not so large that it disfigures the work.

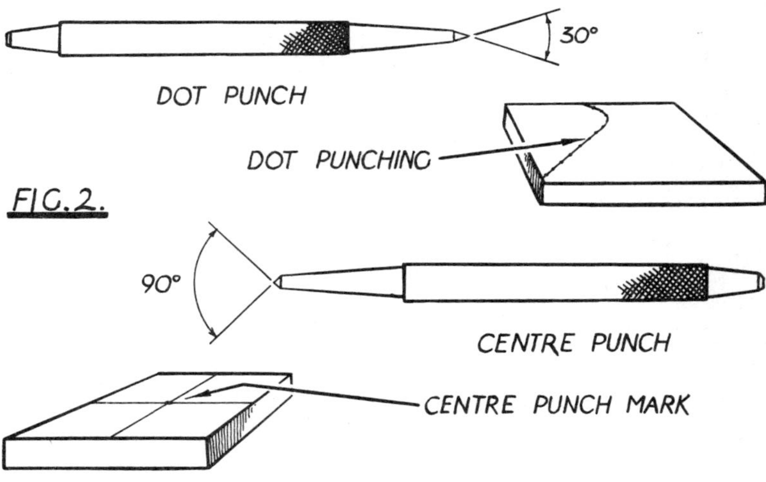

Centre Punch. Before a hole is drilled the exact centre must be centre punched (fig. 2).

Dividers. Spring dividers, trammels, odd-leg calipers (also known as jenny calipers or hermaphrodite calipers) are used for marking-out (fig. 3).

Calipers. Calipers are used to facilitate measuring, both for outside work such as checking the diameter of a rod, or for internal work, e.g. checking the diameter of a bored hole. These are shown in figure 4. Both spring type and firm joint calipers

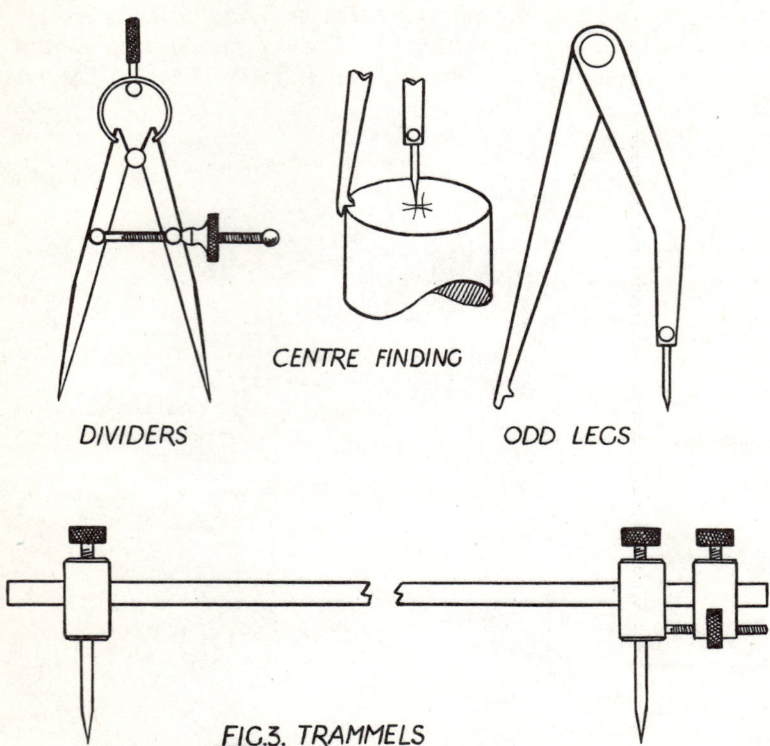

FIG.3. TRAMMELS

are available for internal and external use. Spring calipers are used in schools more than the firm joint kind because they are easier for a beginner.

Firm joint calipers are sometimes known as "tap" calipers because many engineers tap them to open and close them (fig. 4). By tapping a very fine degree of accuracy is obtainable.

Try Squares or Engineers' Square. Testing or "trying" a right angle is done with a try square. These are precision tools and should never be dropped or otherwise misused. They are

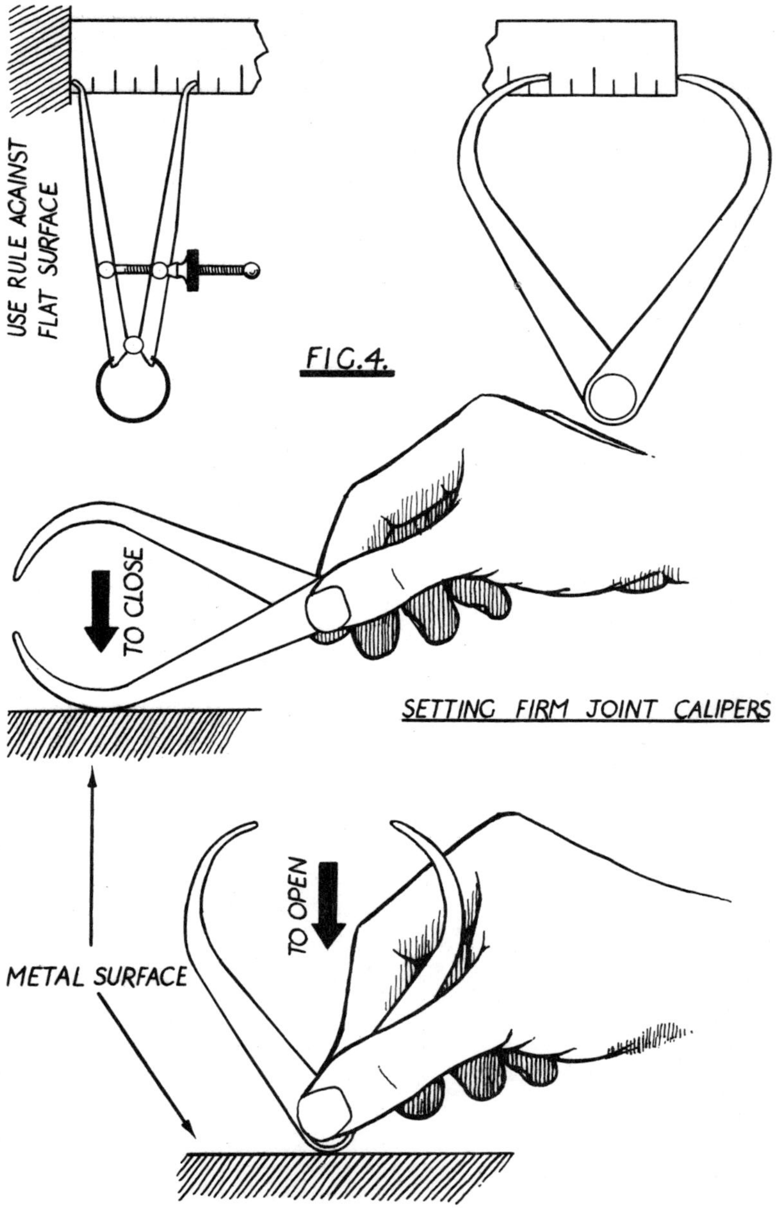
USE RULE AGAINST
FLAT SURFACE
FIG.4.
TO CLOSE
SETTING FIRM JOINT CALIPERS
TO OPEN
METAL SURFACE

available in many sizes from those with a 50 mm blade up to very large ones with 1 metre blades. Various qualities are obtainable: a good one for workshop use has a 125 mm hardened and tempered blade and a case-hardened stock. Figure 5 shows one method of using a try square. It is important that the stock be kept firmly pressed against the work.

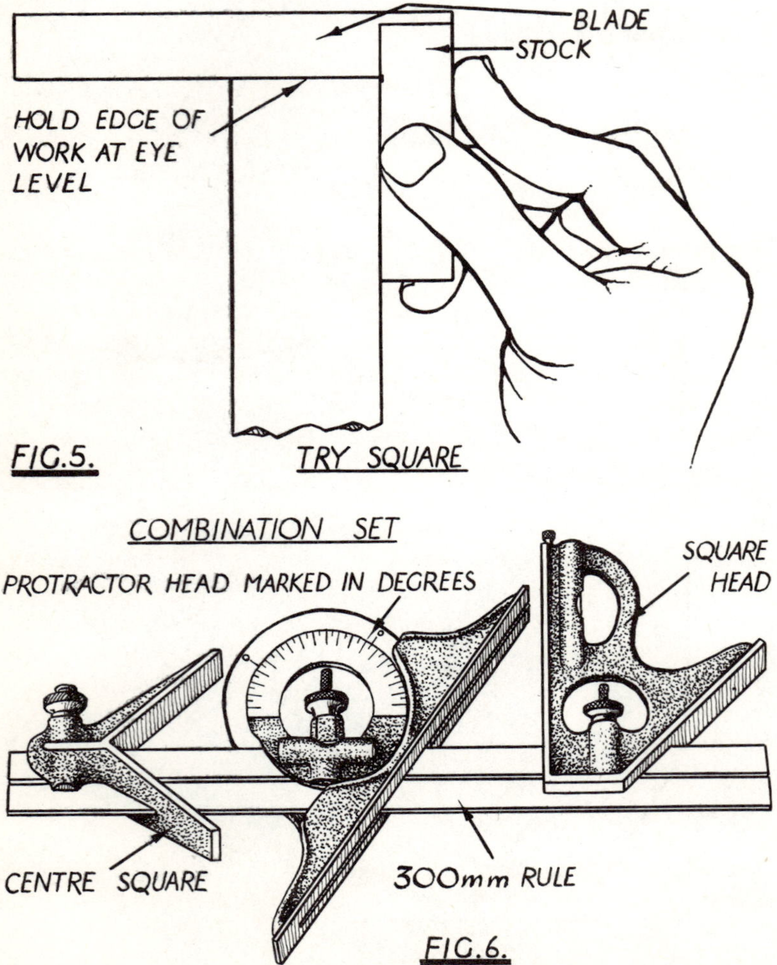

Combination Set. A combination set is shown in figure 6. It comprises a rule which is usually 300 mm long, a centre head or centre square which can be used to find the centre of circular work, a square head with which angles of 90° and 45° can be set out, and a protractor head for obtaining angles which can be read direct from the scale.

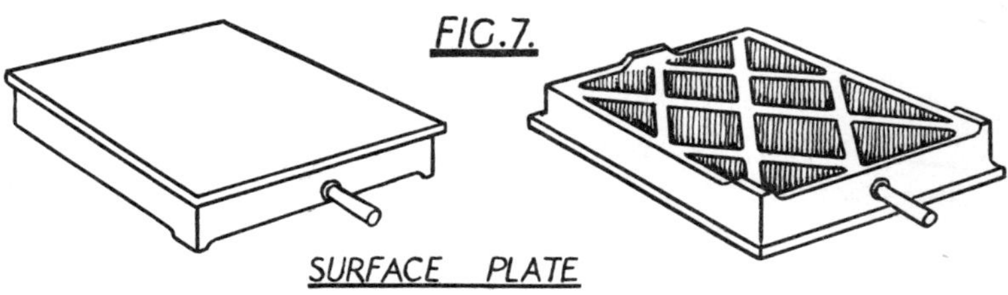

Surface Plate (fig. 7). Surface plates provide an accurate flat surface from which to mark out work. They are made of fine grained cast iron with a thick top and heavy ribbing underneath to resist distortion. They stand on three legs for stability. The surface is planed and on the best plates it is hand scraped. A wooden cover into which a piece of thin felt is stuck should be used for protection when the plate is not in use. The felt inside the cover should be soaked in oil to prevent rust on the plate.

Surface Gauge or Scribing Block. The surface gauge is used on the surface plate for marking-out lines parallel to the surface of the plate (fig. 8). The height of the point is set against a rule which is stood vertically on the plate or against the rule of the combination set held upright in the square head. The fine adjusting screw allows the point to be raised or lowered fractional amounts. The base of the scribing block is vee-shaped so that it can rest on round sections. Often there are two small pins which can be pushed to protrude below the bottom surface. These are used in special circumstances such as in figure 8a.

Vee-Blocks. Vee-blocks are useful for holding round work for marking-out on the surface plate, as shown in figure 9.

Vee-blocks are made in pairs and each block of the pair is stamped with the same number. They should always be used as

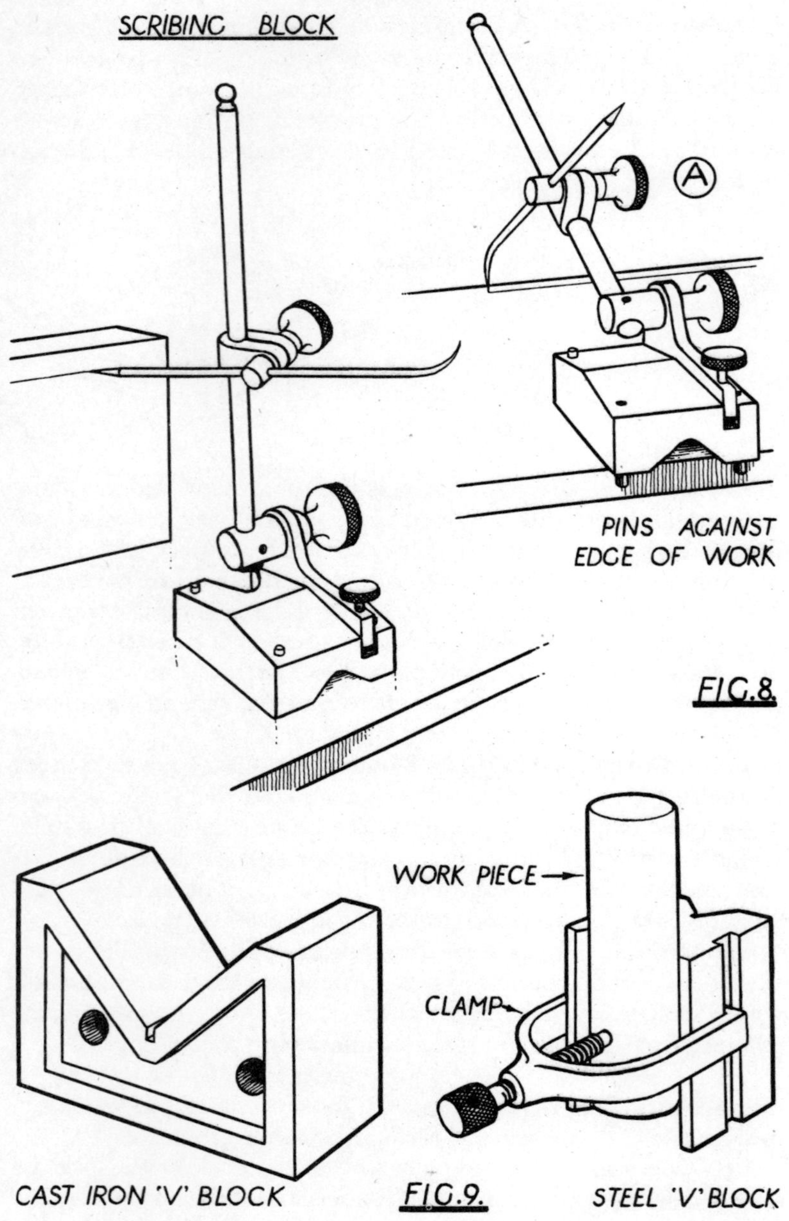
SCRIBING BLOCK
A
PINS AGAINST EDGE OF WORK
WORK PIECE
CLAMP
CAST IRON 'V' BLOCK
STEEL 'V' BLOCK

FIG.8.

FIG.9.

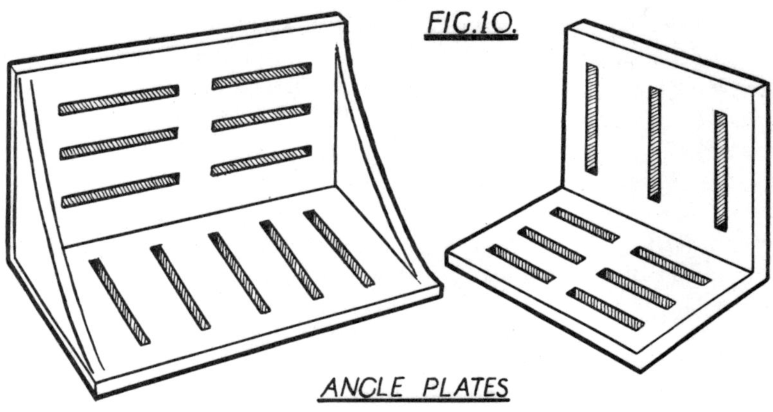

a pair unless only one block is required. The larger blocks are usually made of cast iron, but the smaller, more accurate, vee-blocks are made of mild steel, case hardened and accurately ground. These are made with grooves along the side for clamps which secure the work as shown in figure 9.

Angle Plates. Angle plates are made from fine grained cast iron. They are available in a large variety of sizes and qualities. Small ones are about 75 mm long and the largest ones take two men to lift them. They are made either machined all over or with webbed ends (fig. 10). Large irregular shaped work pieces can be clamped against them for marking-out. The ends of the angle plates are machined so they can be stood on end if required.

Micrometer Caliper. This is an almost indispensable precision measuring instrument in the Metalwork Room. They are available in sizes ranging from 0-25 mm 25-50, 50-75 and so on. Figure 11 shows a 0-25 mm micrometer.

In principle they are simple. One end of the spindle is threaded and this screws into the sleeve. The thread has a pitch of 0·5 mm which means that each revolution of the spindle opens or closes the gap between the anvil and the spindle space 0·5 mm. The spindle and the thimble move together. The thimble is divided into 50 so that each division is 1/50 of 0·5 = 0·01 mm. The sleeve is marked off on either side of the datum line. The major divisions represent millimetres on one side and the minor divisions on the other side are placed between the numbered ones to give half millimetres. The micrometer in figure 11 shows a reading of 7 mm. Figure 12 shows a reading of 10.66 mm i.e.

Major divisions	= 10 × 1·00 mm	=	10·00 mm
Minor divisions	= 1 × 0·50 mm	=	0·50 mm
Thimble divisions	= 16 × 0·01 mm	=	0·16 mm
	Reading	=	10·66 mm

Figure 11 shows a part section of a micrometer. (1) the hardened faces of the anvil and spindle (2) spindle (3) lock nut (4) sleeve (5) main nut (6) screw adjusting nut (7) thimble adjusting nut (8) ratchet (9) the thimble (10) frame (11) cut away on frame (to allow measurements to be taken in restricted spaces).

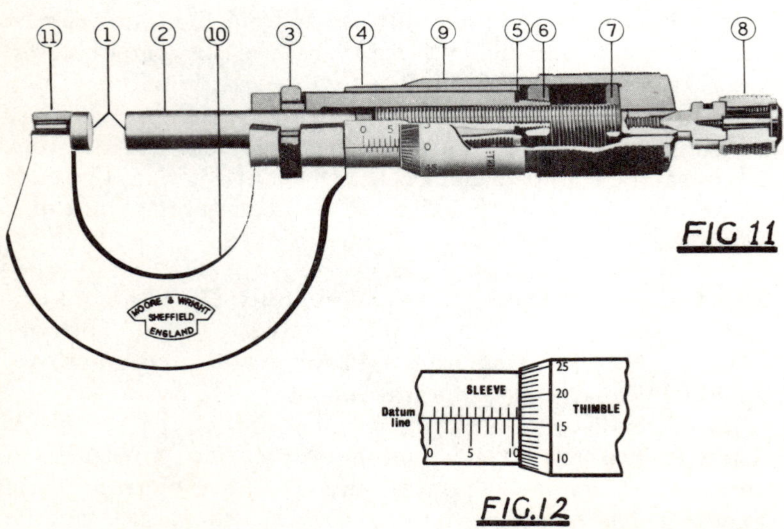

FIG 11

FIG.12

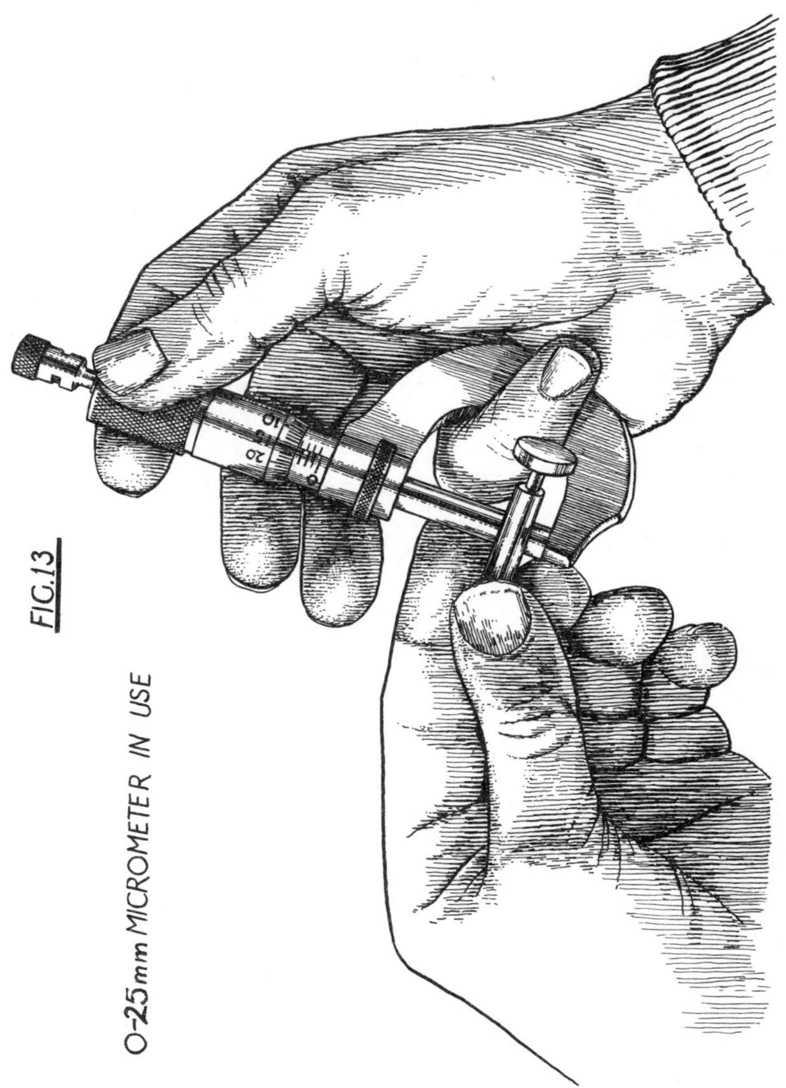

FIG.13

0-25mm MICROMETER IN USE

The ratchet at the top is provided so that the same pressure will be applied whoever uses the instrument. However, most engineers know when they are exerting the right pressure by "feel" so that they seldom use the ratchet. The locknut sets the instrument at a given reading, but this can cause damage if used by beginners because so often they try to force it over the work being measured. The locknut is useful when large numbers of components of similar size are being checked. Figure 12 shows the best way of holding the micrometer. It takes a little practice to learn the knack of holding the micrometer in one hand, but it is invaluable because it leaves the other hand free to hold the component to be measured.

Vernier Caliper Gauges. These are precision instruments used for taking internal and external measurements to within 0·02 mm. Figure 14 shows a vernier caliper. For normal workshop use they are 150 mm long, although much larger ones are available.

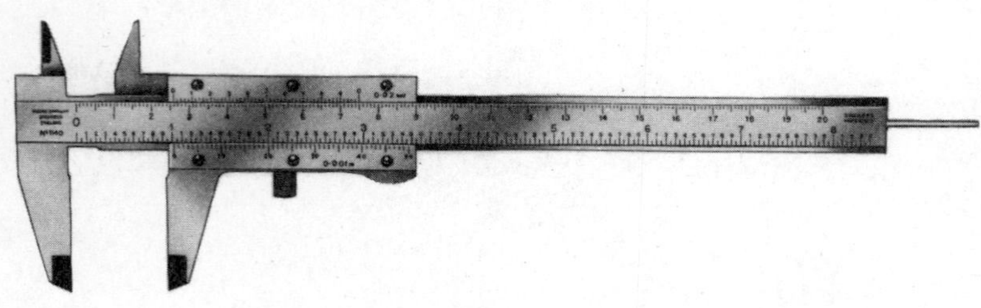

FIG. 14—VERNIER CALIPER GAUGE WITH INCH AND METRIC READINGS
Courtesy of Moore & Wright (Sheffield)

VERNIER SCALE

MAIN SCALE

a.	53 MILLIMETRES	53·00
b.	8 TENTHS	0·80
c.	2 HUNDREDTHS	0·04
		53·84 mm.

FIG 15

How to read the Vernier Caliper. Figure 15. Metric reading —0·02 mm. The Main Scale is graduated in millimetres and the Vernier Scale is divided into 50 divisions over a distance of 49 mm, each division equalling 49/50ths of a millimetre (0·98 mm). The difference between a division on the Main Scale and the Vernier Scale is 1/50th mm (0·02 mm).

Main Scale:

a	Each large number	= 10·00 mm
b	Each division	= 1·00 mm
	Vernier Scale	
c	Each number	= 0·10 mm
d	Each division	= 0·02 mm

(a)	5 × 10·00 mm	= 50·00 mm
(b)	3 × 1·00 mm	= 3·00 mm
(c)	8 × 0·10 mm	= 0·80 mm
(d)	2 × 0·02 mm	= 0·04 mm

Caliper reading = 53·84 mm

To read the vernier it is helpful to use a magnifying glass to check the coincidence of the line on the fixed scale with the one on the sliding scale.

Screw Pitch Recognition Gauge. This is used for checking the pitch of a thread. It is also useful for checking the radius at the crest and the root of the threads when screwcutting on the lathe. The pitch of the thread is clearly marked on each blade and they are available with blades ranging from 0·25 mm pitch to 7·0 mm pitch. Figure 16 shows one of these gauges.

Radius or Fillet Gauge. Radius gauges are used to check radii on internal and external work. These are bought in sets and are available in decimal, fractional or metric radii. Figure 17 shows a radius gauge which has 20 blades.

Feeler Gauge. These are in sets as shown in figure 18. The thickness of the blades ranges from 0·03 mm to 1·0 mm. They are used for checking narrow gaps.

Thread Angle Gauge. These are used for checking the angle when grinding a tool for screw cutting and for setting the tool in correct relationship to the axis of the work on the lathe (fig. 19).

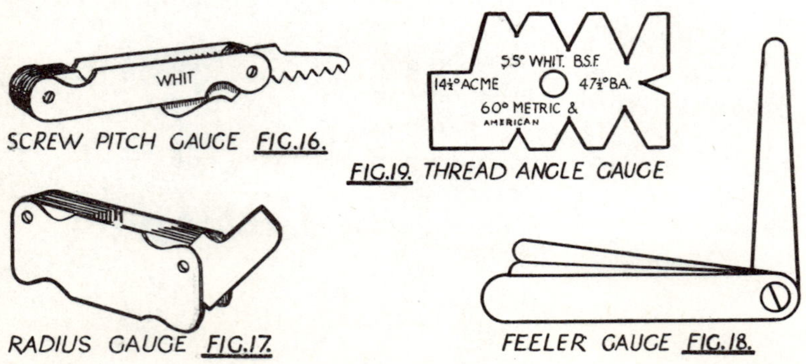

SCREW PITCH GAUGE FIG.16.

FIG.19. THREAD ANGLE GAUGE

RADIUS GAUGE FIG.17.

FEELER GAUGE FIG.18.

BENCH WORK

The bench vice is the important holding device at which most of the bench work is done. Usually each pupil in the metalwork room has a vice place.

Engineers parallel jaw vices (fig. 20) are usually made of cast iron with inset steel jaws. These may or may not have a quick release mechanism. This is for quick opening and closing of the vice and it is operated by a lever which lifts and lowers a half nut which engages on a buttress thread. Heavy hammering or bending should be done on the leg vice (Chapter 6, fig. 3) not on the bench vice. The roughened surface of the jaws is sometimes covered with vice clamps to protect the work. These are made of some soft metal such as copper, aluminium or lead.

Hand Vices (fig. 21). These are useful for holding thin pieces of metal when using the drilling machine. Hand vices are made of drop forged steel. The jaws are roughened to improve the grip, but for this reason it is advisable to use two pieces of thin cardboard as temporary vice clamps to prevent damage when holding non-ferrous sheet metal.

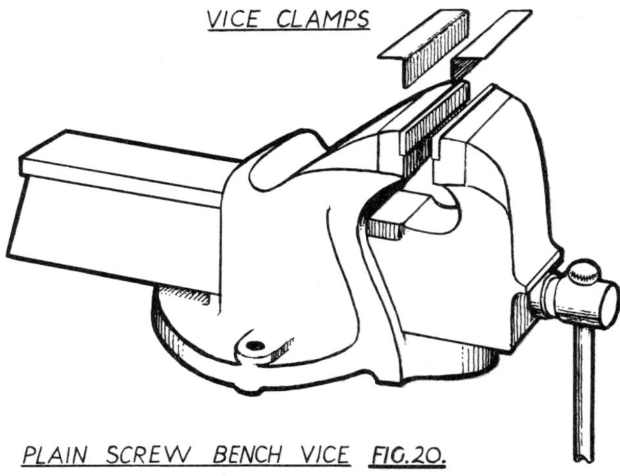

PLAIN SCREW BENCH VICE FIG.20.

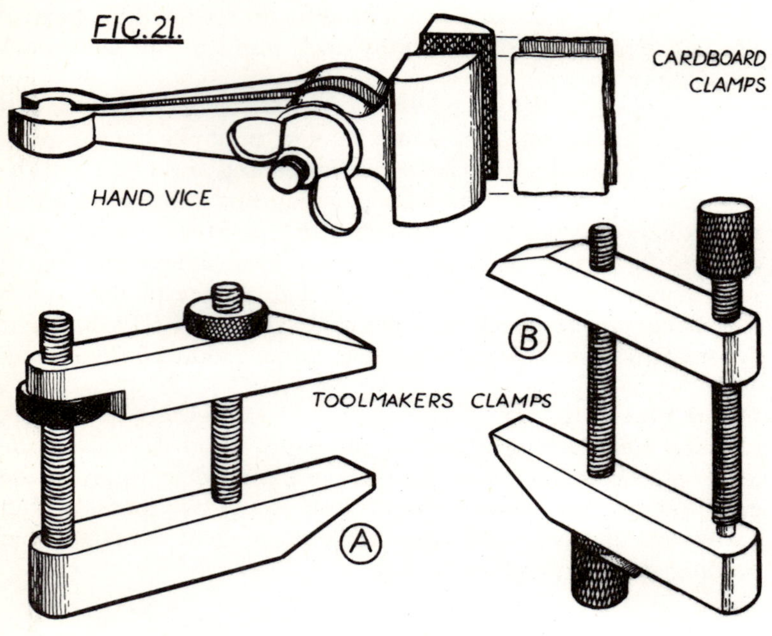

Tool Makers Clamps. As the name suggest, these are much used by toolmakers who often make their own. Many toolmakers prefer the kind shown in figure 21A to those at B. because they have one jaw uninterrupted by the head of a screw. This plain jaw can be rested on a flat surface such as a drilling machine table. When gripping work the jaws should be adjusted so that they are parallel.

Toolmakers clamps are made of case hardened mild steel. It is a mistake to make these from small square section stock because the strength is required in one direction which is better obtained using oblong section stock.

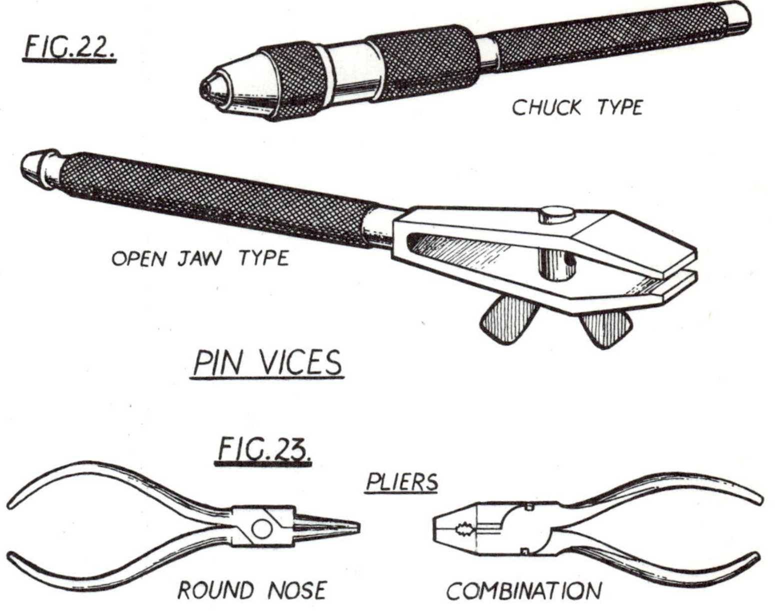

Pin Vices (**fig. 22**). They are used for holding small work. The handle is hollow to allow long lengths of metal to be held. Pin vices will hold work up to 2 mm diameter.

Pliers (**fig. 23**). Some of these can be used as holding devices, although many pliers, such as side cutting and round-nosed, have other uses.

Hack Saws (**fig. 24**). The illustration shows a tubular frame hack saw, but there are other types available. In principle they are all similar. There is always provision for adjusting the frame to suit the length of blade, and for turning it axially through 90° as shown. The blade is always held in tension.

The adjustment for length on the saw shown is provided by the tubular frame which slides through the top of the handle and is locked in place by a knurled set screw.

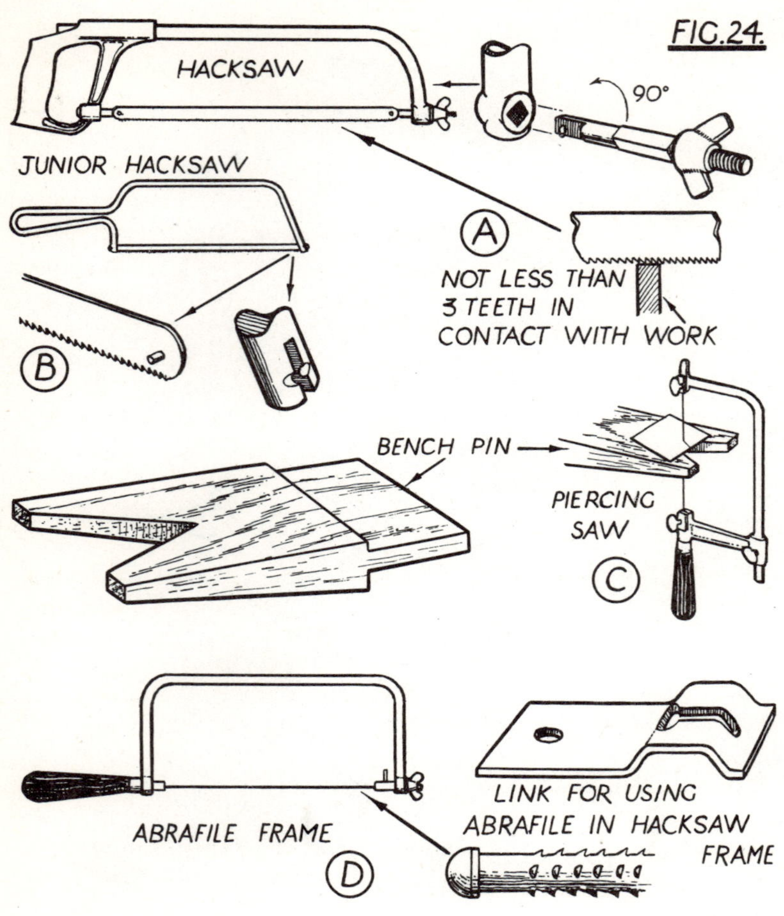

The blades are usually 254 mm or 304 mm long, 12 mm deep and 0·6 mm thick. The pitch of the teeth varies between 0·8 mm pitch to 1·5 mm pitch. Note the length of a hacksaw blade is measured from the outside edges of the holes. These are made of either high speed steel, which is more expensive but will last longer and cut harder metals, or of low tungsten steel. Low tungsten steel blades are made either as "flexible", which have teeth hardened but the back soft and are very tough, or "all hard" type blades, which are hard throughout. These are preferred by skilled men because they are more rigid.

When choosing a blade it is important to select one which will have a minimum of 3 teeth always in contact with the work (fig. 24A) otherwise "chatter" will result and teeth will start to break off. When inserting a blade in the hacksaw frame, the teeth must always point forward, i.e. away from the operator. Remember to use the full length of the blade when hacksawing and to take about one second for each cut, i.e. don't try to cut too quickly because this often causes the blade to twist or brake and results in bad work.

Junior Hacksaws. These are useful for smaller work (fig. 24B). The blade, which is 150 mm long, is held in tension by the spring of the frame itself. The blades have a small pin inserted at each end by which they are held in the frame.

Piercing Saws (fig. 24C). These are for very fine work such as that done by jewellers and silversmiths, but they are sometimes useful in the school workshop for piercing out motifs in sheet metal.

For piercing the saw should be used in the upright position and the work held by hand on a bench pin which is made of wood as shown. The teeth of the blade should point downwards, i.e. towards the handle.

"Abrafile" Tension File. This is really a file but it is used as a saw. The blade which is like a thin round file is held taut in the frame (fig. 24D).

Tension files are available in lengths from 150 mm to 275 mm approximately 2 mm diameter. Special links are made for using these blades in a hacksaw frame.

Power Hacksaws (fig. 25). These are used in workshops where a lot of sawing is necessary. The machine might be a small bench model with a jaw capacity of 50 mm by 50 mm, or a heavy duty type with a capacity of 250 × 250 mm. Special large blades are made for these machines.

FIG. 25—POWER HACKSAW
Courtesy of Edward G. Herbert Ltd.

Chisels. These are usually called cold chisels because they are used for cutting cold work. The flat chisel is the most used.

Cold chisels can be made from hardened and tempered carbon steel or bought made from "non-temper chrome alloy steel". These are extremely tough and yet can be sharpened with a file. Flat carbon steel chisels should be ground as in figure 26. The lines left by the grinding wheel should be as shown, i.e. they should be in line with the axis thus helping to prevent the extreme edge from breaking off. The cutting edge is ground in a slight arc so that when cutting the main thrust is taken in the centre. The top of the chisel which is soft will become "mushroomed" with continued use unless ground off from time to time. If this mushroom is not ground off it can be dangerous because a glancing blow from the hammer might cause a piece to fly off.

Flat chisels are useful for shearing thin stock as shown in figure 26A, or for cutting out sheet metal on a chipping block as shown at B.

Half round chisels are often used for cutting oil grooves and "cleaning up" corners as shown at C.

Cross cut or cape chisels are used where a narrow groove is required such as a key-way (D).

The diamond chisel can be used for cutting into sharp internal corners. A typical example is shown at E.

Hammers. The engineer's ball pein hammer is the type most used in the metalwork room. The heads are made from hardened and tempered carbon steel. Popular weights in the workshop are 0·2 kgm, 0·3 kgm and 0·4 kgm. The handle is of hickory or ash. The hammer head is made fast on the handle by a wood wedge which is often firmly held in place by a metal wedge. The section in figure 26F shows how the hole is tapered both ways.

Files. The file is the most used hand cutting tool in the engineering workshop. It is made of hardened and tempered high carbon steel but the tang is left soft. The length of a file is measured from the tip to the shoulder and does not include the tang. Files are available from 100 mm to 400 mm long in a var-

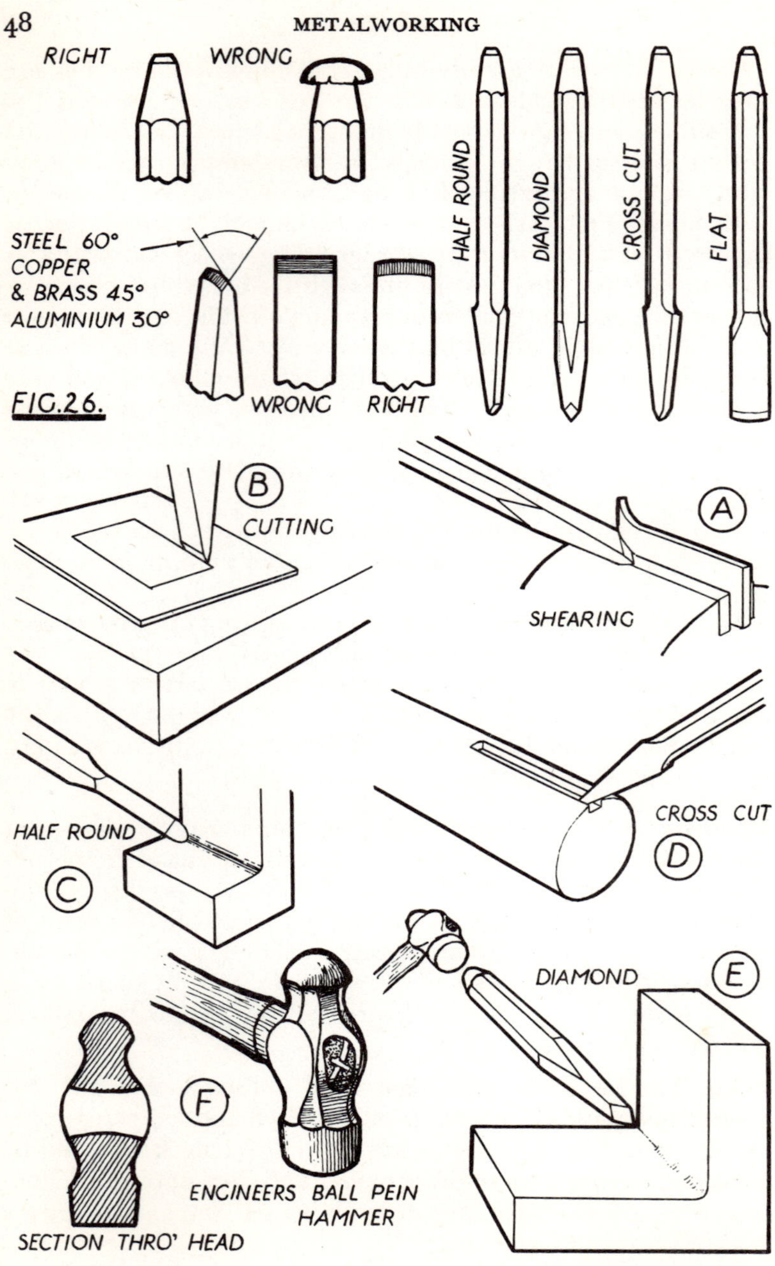
RIGHT
WRONG
STEEL 60°
COPPER
& BRASS 45°
ALUMINIUM 30°
WRONG
RIGHT
HALF ROUND
DIAMOND
CROSS CUT
FLAT
FIG.26.
B
CUTTING
A
SHEARING
HALF ROUND
C
CROSS CUT
D
DIAMOND
E
F
ENGINEERS BALL PEIN
HAMMER
SECTION THRO' HEAD

iety of sections and are available either single or double cut. The grades of cut range through: bastard, second cut, smooth and dead smooth. To prevent clogging of the teeth (pinning) it is best to cut soft metals with the coarser grade of files. Special files known as "Dreadnought" and "Millenicut" are used when a lot of filing on soft metal is done. Non-ferrous metals require new files for best results. The files can afterwards be used on steel.

File handles are bought separately and various sizes are available. To prevent splitting, a steel ferrule is fitted. It is usual to fit these by heating the tip of the file tang to red heat and then forcing it into the handle. Care must be taken to keep the file handle in line with the file. Figure 27 shows some of the more common kinds of file.

Flat files can be used on a wide variety of work. These are available in lengths from 100 to 400 mm in grades of cut: bastard, second cut, smooth and dead smooth.

Hand files are available from 100 to 400 mm long in all grades of cut. This file is parallel in width but it tapers in thickness towards the end. One edge has no teeth (safe) so that it can be used against shoulders or in corners where another type of file might cause damage.

Round files are 100 to 400 mm long, available in all cuts. They are often used to enlarge holes and to file radii. The smaller sizes are sometimes known as rat tail files.

Half round files are 100 to 400 mm long, available in all cuts. Used for filing concave surfaces and inside large holes.

Three square files are 100 to 400 mm long, are available in all cuts, and are used for filing sharp corners and vees,

Square files are 100 to 400 mm long, available in all cuts. Often used for filing drilled holes square and for filing slots.

Warding files are 100 to 200 mm long, available in all cuts. They are parallel in thickness but taper in width. They are useful for filing narrow slots such as are found on keys and inside locks.

FIG.27. TYPES OF CUT

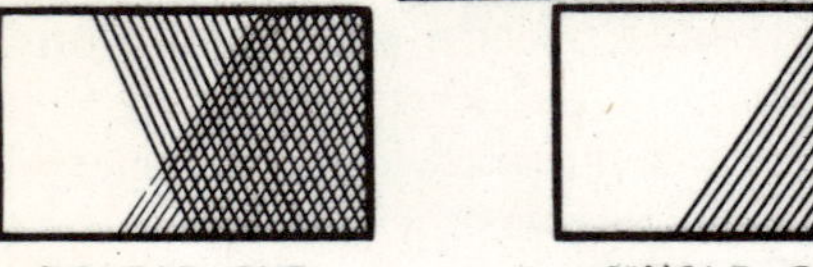

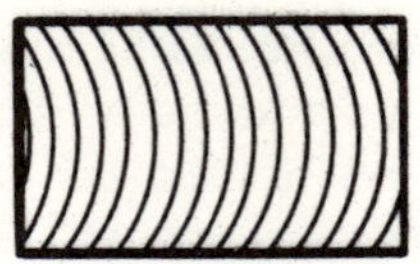

Knife files are 100 to 300 mm long, available in all cuts, and are used for filing into sharp corners etc.

Needle or Swiss files are for fine work. These vary in length from 100 to 175 mm. They do not need a handle: the shaft is knurled to provide a grip. Finer cuts than smooth and dead smooth are made. A large number of shapes are available, one of which is shown (fig. 28).

Rifflers are used by engravers, die makers and silversmiths. They are usually double ended and scores of different shapes are available. One of these is shown (fig. 29).

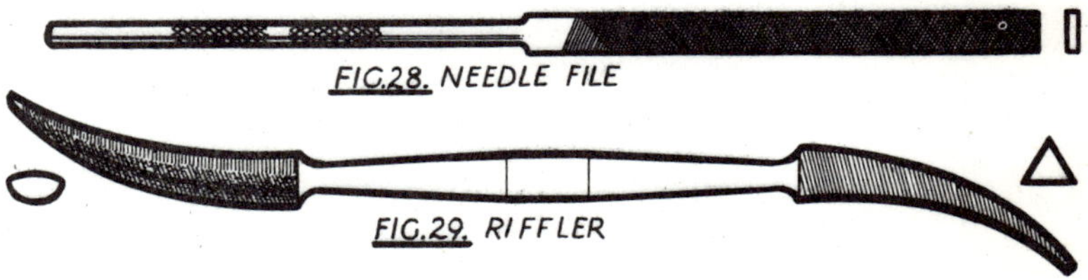

FIG.28. NEEDLE FILE

FIG.29. RIFFLER

Filing. Before commencing to use a file, make sure it is clean. This is best done by pushing a file pricker (fig. 30) a number of times across the teeth until it takes up the shape of the teeth and removes all the dirt and metal particles. The file pricker can be made from a thin piece of mild steel filed to a chisel end. Some people use a file card for this, but continued rubbing of the hard steel bristles on a file tends to spoil the edge of a file particularly when this is done almost as a habit in the school workshop.

The workpiece should be held securely and as low as possible in the vice and the edge to be filed held horizontally. The work should be at a comfortable height, but of course it is not possible to make the height of the vice suitable for all people. A right handed person should stand at the vice with feet apart—left foot foremost—more or less in the stance of a boxer. The file handle is held in the right hand with the right elbow close to the body. The tip of the file is held with the left hand. The weight of the body should supply the force and weight should be transferred from the right foot to the left on the forward stroke. It must be remembered that a file cuts only on the forward stroke.

On the return stroke the pressure is taken off the file, but it is not lifted from the work. Use the full length of the file and don't try to rush. The aim usually is to prevent rocking and to obtain a flat surface. For heavy filing more weight is put on the end of the file and the file is pushed diagonally across the work, first from one side and then from the other, thus removing the crests of the ridges made by the previous stroke. For light filing the tip is held lightly between the thumb and forefinger of the left hand.

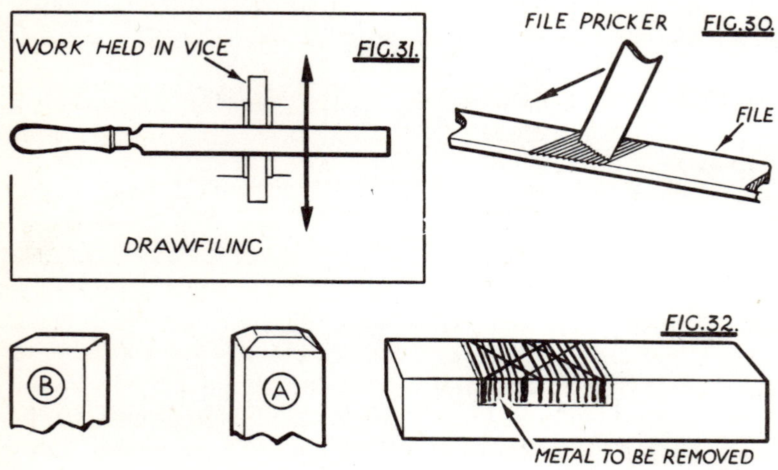

Drawfiling (Fig. 31) is a finishing process and if done properly gives a smooth flat surface. Chalk rubbed on the file helps to prevent pinning (the clogging of the teeth by small particles of metal) and gives a better finish to the work. Any oil or grease on the surface being filed makes the file cut less efficiently. Even perspiration from the fingers, when taking the last fine cuts, tends to make the file skid. For this reason avoid, as far as possible, touching the surface being filed. As the work nears completion it should be taken out of the vice and checked frequently with a try square or a rule, or both.

If a lot of metal has to be removed by filing, it is an aid to make criss-cross cuts in the metal first (fig. 32) either with a hacksaw or the edge of a file. Another method is to rough chamfer the work first as shown in figure 32A and then to file flat as at B.

Care of files. 1. Don't knock or rub files together. Remember they are hard and will damage each other.

2. Keep them in a rack slightly apart from each other.

3. Don't attempt to file hardened steel.

4. Avoid using a new file on the hard sandy skin of a casting—old files will do for this.

5. Don't throw away old files, they make good scrapers and hand turning and wood turning tools, but must be properly tempered otherwise they might break and cause injury to the user.

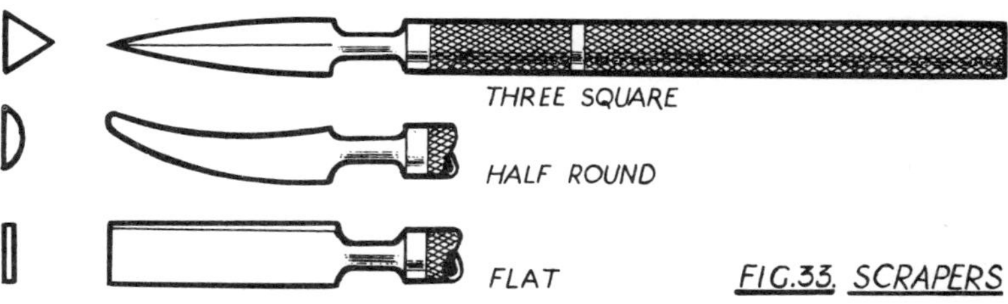

FIG.33. SCRAPERS

Scraping. Scrapers are made from hardened and tempered carbon steel and the edges are sharpened, after grinding, on a fine oil stone. Three scrapers are shown in figure 33. These are used for removing small amounts of metal usually when working on something which has to be accurate, e.g. when making a surface plate or scraping a bearing.

When scraping a flat surface it is usual to lightly coat a master flat surface, such as a good surface plate, with a thin coat of engineers blue. The work is then rubbed on the master surface or the master surface rubbed on the work, and any high spots which show blue scraped off. This is repeated as often as required until all the high spots are removed. Scraping, however, is a slow and therefore expensive process which has been largely superseded by surface grinding.

Taps and Tapping. Taps are used for making internal threads They are available in sets of three (fig. 34) made from high speed steel or carbon steel.

Before tapping a suitable hole must be drilled which is usually a little larger than the core diameter of the tap. (See chart at back of book.)

Start tapping with the taper tap which is held in either a bar or a chuck type tap wrench (figs. 34A and 34B). It is important to keep the tap in alignment with the hole and once the tap has started to cut it is advisable to reverse it a fraction of a turn periodically to break the chips. This tap is then followed by the second tap and then by the plug. If a shallow open ended hole is being tapped the taper tap alone will do the work. When tapping a blind hole the plug tap must be used finally and the chips knocked out of the hole from time to time. Taps are brittle and will break off in the hole if too much pressure is applied. To reduce the friction when tapping it is advisable to use a lubricant on all metals except brass and cast iron.

LUBRICANTS FOR THREADING

Material to be threaded	*Lubricant*
Aluminium	Paraffin
Brass	None
Bronze and copper	Paraffin or lard oil
Cast iron	None
Mild steel	Sulphur base oil

Broken Taps. A lot of time can be wasted in trying to remove a broken tap from a piece of work. Often it is quicker to discard the part and start again. However, there are several methods used for the removal of broken taps.

1. Use a tap extractor. These work better on the larger sizes. They have three or four prongs, according to the kind of tap being removed, which fit into the flutes of the broken tap.

2. Break out the tap using a small chisel and a hammer.

3. On an open ended hole it is sometimes possible to drive the tap out with a punch from the back.

4. If a carbon steel tap is broken in the hole it is possible to heat the tap and the surrounding metal with a blow pipe flame to cherry red and allow to cool slowly then centre punch and drill out. This is not possible with high speed steel taps because the temperature required is too high to be obtained with the blowpipe.

5. If the tap is broken in a blind hole, build a small wall of plasticine about 12 mm high all round the broken tap and carefully pour in concentrated nitric acid. This will etch away a little of the workpiece as well as part of the tap. Wash away every trace of the acid and unscrew the broken tap with a hammer and a small punch.

After a tap has been removed by any of these methods it is often necessary to drill and tap a size larger.

Dieing. Stocks and dies are used for cutting external threads. These are shown in figure 35. The dies are made from hardened and tempered steel and may be of the circular split die pattern or loose dies.

The circular split die is the one popularly used in school. There are three adjusting screws but the adjustment is only slight. The middle screw, which is pointed, forces the split open and the two side screws are for closing the die.

When starting to cut an external thread the die should be "open", i.e. with the centre screw tight; also the side screws must be screwed down to prevent any tendency for the die to twist. The end of the rod to be threaded should be slightly tapered to allow the die to start. The taper can be filed. Use a lubricant as for tapping and keep the die "square" to the rod. Reverse the die a little from time to time to break the chips. After the first cut try the thread in the tapped hole. If it is too tight take another cut with the dies after slackening the centre screw and tightening the outside ones.

Riveting. Rivets are mentioned in the chapter on joining metals and the more common kinds are shown there.

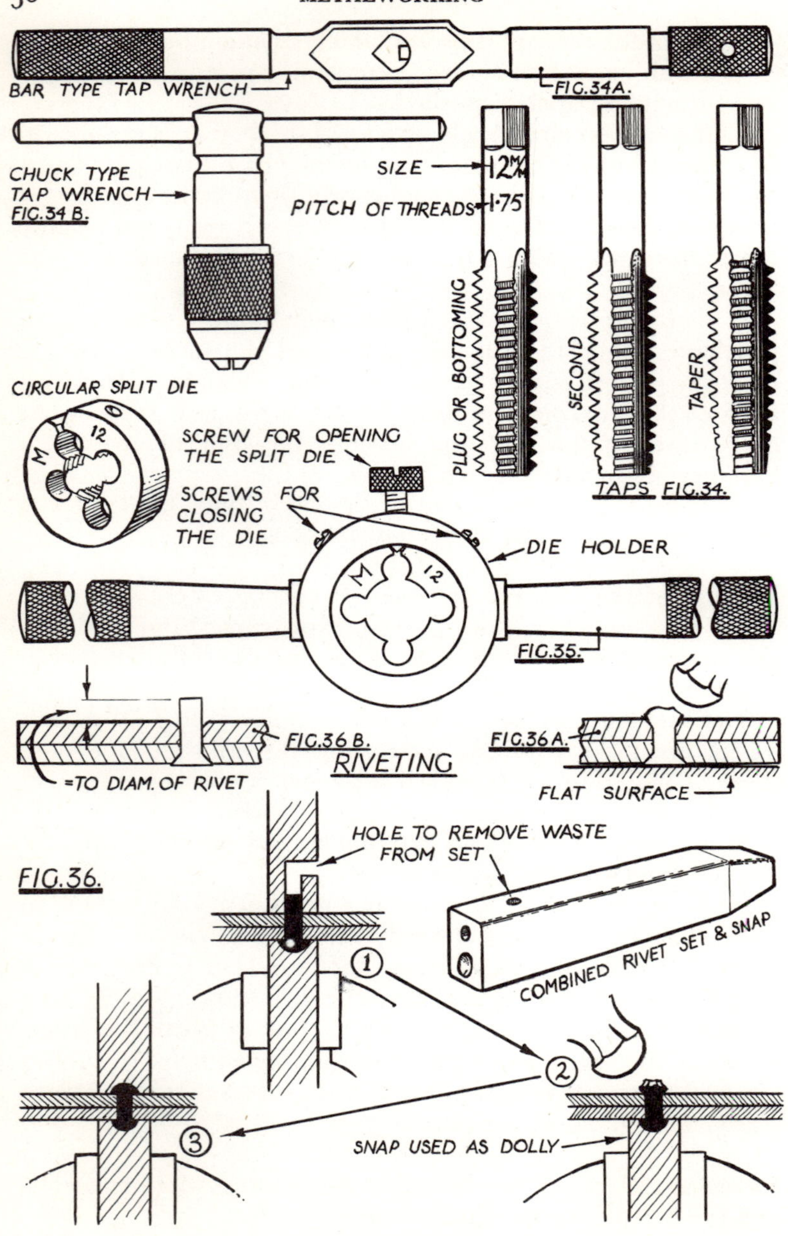
BAR TYPE TAP WRENCH
FIG.34A.
CHUCK TYPE
TAP WRENCH
FIG.34 B.
SIZE
12M/M
PITCH OF THREADS
1·75
PLUG OR BOTTOMING
SECOND
TAPER
TAPS FIG.34.
CIRCULAR SPLIT DIE
M
12
SCREW FOR OPENING
THE SPLIT DIE
SCREWS FOR
CLOSING
THE DIE
DIE HOLDER
FIG.35.
FIG.36 B.
RIVETING
FIG.36 A.
=TO DIAM. OF RIVET
FLAT SURFACE
HOLE TO REMOVE WASTE
FROM SET
FIG.36.
COMBINED RIVET SET & SNAP
1
2
3
SNAP USED AS DOLLY

Riveting in school requires a ball pein hammer, a dolly and a set and snap (fig. 36). Before riveting the parts must be drilled with the right size drill. It is important that the rivet be a good fit in the hole otherwise it might bend when being hammered.

Countersunk-head rivets are often used in school work because they can be filed flush and make a clean job. When using a countersunk rivet, support the head on a flat surface such as the face of the anvil (fig. 36A). The length of the rivet depends on the depth of the countersink, but usually if the amount left for riveting is equal in length to the diameter of the rivet an adequate head can be formed leaving enough to clean off with a file (fig. 36B).

Snaphead rivets are supported underneath with a rivet snap held in a vice, which acts as a dolly (fig. 36 (1)). First the two pieces are set down to make sure the plates are properly together. This operation is important on large sheets which might be distorted. The head is first formed with a ball pein hammer (fig. 36 (2)) and finished off with the snap (fig. 36 (3)). The amount of rivet above the hole required for forming a snap head is usually equal to slightly more than the diameter of the rivet.

For special riveting jobs such as we meet when making model steam engines it is often necessary to make up special dollies.

Spanners and Screwdrivers (fig. 37). Nuts and bolts are loosened or tightened with a spanner. These are made to suit the various sizes of nuts and bolts available. It is important to use the right size spanner otherwise the nut or bolt head soon becomes badly worn at the corners. When using an adjustable spanner be sure that it is properly tight. Many kinds of spanners are available but the most popular ones are those shown

Screw Threads. I.S.O. (International Standards Organization) has recommended that British industry should adopt metric screw threads by 1975. This provides a 'coarse' and 'fine' series of screws, bolts and nuts (see table at back). However, the existing standard threads shown here will inevitably be still in use for some years.

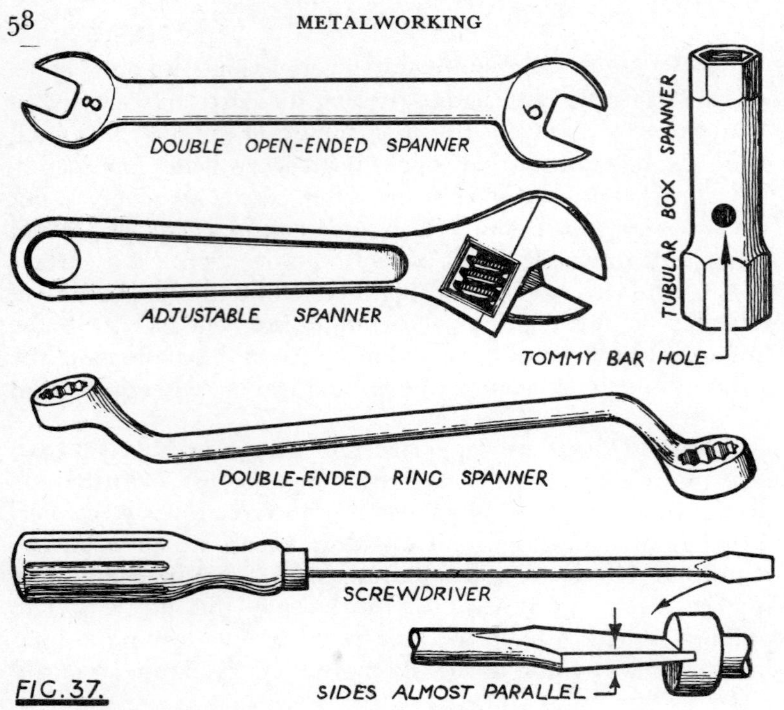

FIG. 37.

British Standard Whitworth (*B.S.W.*) The BSW thread form was devised by Sir Joseph Whitworth and first used in 1841. This thread has been widely used since it was first introduced, but as engineering work has become more and more varied other standard threads have been introduced such as British Standard Fine and British Standard Pipe.

British Standard Fine (*B.S.F.*) and *British Standard Pipe* (*B.S.P.*). These both use the Whitworth thread form but have a finer pitch. In the B.S.F. thread this fine pitch gives a larger core and thus more strength, except that the thread is a little weaker. But the nut is less likely to be loosened by vibration. For pipe work the thread needs to be fine otherwise it would break through the wall of the pipe.

British Association (*B.A.*). This is used often on threads below a quarter of an inch diameter. These threads have a fine pitch

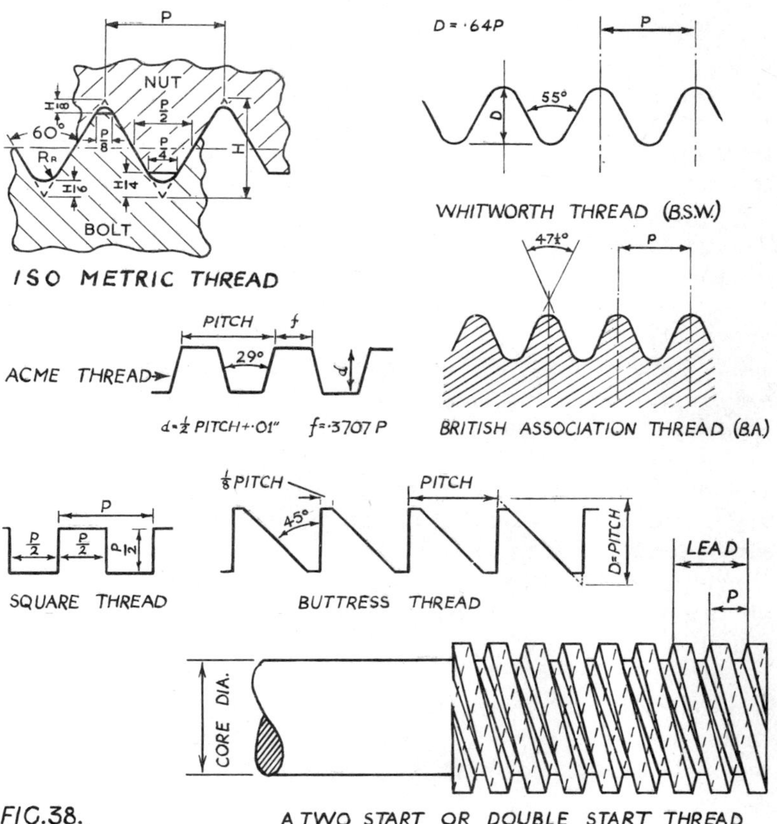

FIG.38.

(metric) and the sizes are closely graded starting from O.B.A. which is the largest (see table at back). B.A. threads are used for delicate work.

Square Thread. This is used for transmitting motion in either direction such as on the cross slide of a lathe. There is less friction on this kind of thread than on the vee threads.

Acme Thread. This is often used on the lead screws of lathes because it is easier to engage the split nuts on this slightly vee'd thread than on a square thread. It transmits motion in both directions and is easier to cut than the square thread.

Buttress Thread. Wherever the thrust is required in one direction, as on some screw jacks, this thread is used. It combines the easy transmission qualities of the square thread with the strength of the vee thread.

Terms Used for Threads *Pitch.* The pitch of a thread is the distance between two threads measured axially; for convenience, it is the distance between the crests of adjacent threads.

Lead. The lead of a screw is the distance it advances in the nut in one revolution. This is only the same as the pitch on single start threads, but on a double start thread it moves twice the pitch and on a treble start thread it moves three times and so on. It is possible to see how many starts a thread has by looking at the end of the bolt. A double start thread has two threads of the same depth running round the cylinder and a three start thread, three. Multi-start threads, as these are called, are used on machinery where quick axial movement of the thread is required.

Core Diameter. The core diameter of a thread is the outside diameter minus twice the depth of the thread. It must be measured at right angles to the axis.

Outside Diameter. The outside diameter is the diameter measured over the crests of the threads. Screws, bolts etc. are known by this dimension, e.g. an M12 bolt has an outside diameter of 12 mm.

4

Methods of Joining Metals

Probably the oldest method of joining metals is by riveting. Over 4,000 years ago vessels were made by riveting together copper and bronze plates.

The craftsman of long ago must have worked under great difficulty using a very primitive drill to make his holes for riveting (fig. 1). Later when iron was used they found that joints could be made by forge or fire welding.

Joining metals by forge welding has been done for thousands of years but we are not sure when this method was first used. The swords used by the Vikings were made of plaited or twisted strips of metal which were heated to white heat and then hammered together, that is, they were forge welded (fig. 2).

The method of obtaining the heat was probably similar to that used today by the primitive Kikuyu people of Kenya. The

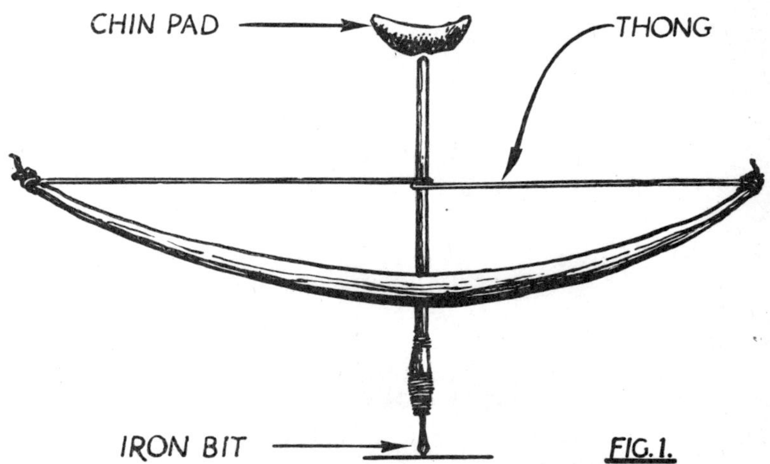

FIG. 1.

furnace is a shallow hole in the ground lined with clay. A charcoal fire is started and kept going with plentiful supplies of charcoal. The blast comes from two bellows which consist of "baggy" goat skins tied over specially made earthenware pots. The loose skins are gathered up in the centre and bound on to stocks in such a way that they can be moved up and down thus increasing and decreasing the volume of air trapped inside. At the bottom edge of each pot there is a tube which takes the air

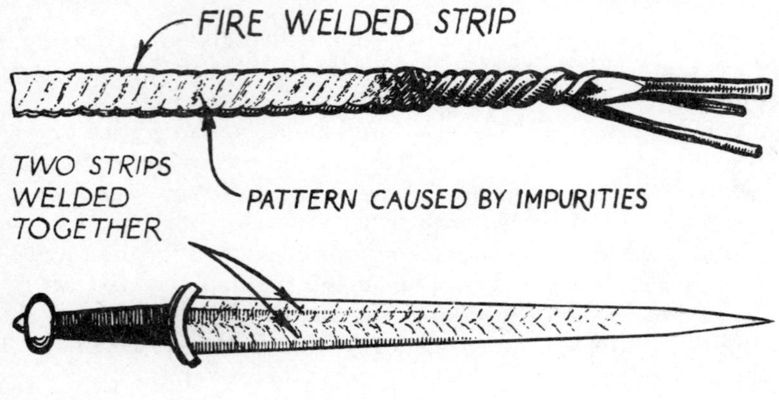

FIG.2.

FIG.3

to a tapered fireclay funnel (*tuyère*) which leads into the heart of the fire. There are no valves in these bellows. As one bellow is pumped down forcing the air into the fire, the other is brought up and the air comes in at the place where the tube enters the tapered funnel (fig. 3).

Today work is much easier for a craftsman and we have more methods of joining metals than were known by the ancient metalworkers. For convenience we can divide the methods of joining metals into two groups: 1. using heat, 2. working cold.

In group 1 we have:
- soft soldering
- silver soldering
- brazing
- welding

In group 2 we have:
- screws (this includes bolts, studs and nuts)
- rivets.

SOFT SOLDERING

This method of joining metals does not require a lot of heat nor expensive equipment. The solder is an alloy mainly of tin and lead.

Lead melts at 327°C and pure tin melts at 232°C but when they are alloyed together they start to melt, i.e. they become pasty, at about 183°C. The range of temperature over which they are pasty depends on the proportion of tin to lead, e.g. plumber's solder (tin 30% and lead 70%) has a long pasty range—necessary for wiping a joint—whereas tinman's solder (tin 65% and lead 35%) passes quickly from a liquid to solid state (see fig. 4). Solders with lower melting points are made by adding bismuth to the tin/lead alloy. These are often termed Low Melting Point (L.M.P.) solders.

Preparation of Joint

Before two surfaces are joined together by solder they must be cleaned mechanically, e.g. by filing, wire brushing, scraping

SOLDERS AND FLUXES FOR SOFT SOLDERING VARIOUS METALS

Work to be soldered	*Flux*	*Type of solder*
Brass Gilding metal Copper Gun metal	Zinc chloride. Paste flux. Resin. Solder paint (contains its own flux).	Any solder can be used but the choice of solder will depend on the type of work being done.
Electrical work	Resin cored solder. Resin.	Tin 60%, lead 40%.
Galvanised iron Zinc	Zinc chloride or very weak diluted hydrochloric acid.	Any solder with 40% or more tin.
Pewter Britannia metal	Glycerine to which one or two drops of hydrochloric acid is added. Resin, tallow, resin cored solder.	65% tin, 35% lead or pewter wire. For amateur use LMP solder = tin, leadand bismuth.
Lead	Tallow.	Tin 30%, lead 70%.
Aluminium	Cannot be soldered in the usual manner but there are many kinds of special aluminium solders and fluxes available. The difficulty is in removing the oxides, which form rapidly, from the surfaces of the metal. This is often done by melting the solder on to the fluxed surface and then scratch brushing underneath the layer of molten solder so that the solder can "take" without the aluminium being exposed to the air.	Proprietary brands usually containing only tin (no lead) with some zinc. Typically 90% tin, 10% zinc.
Cast iron	Tinning is slow: afterwards any flux can be used.	50% tin, 50% lead.
Chromium steel	Difficult to "tin" except by methods similar to those used on aluminium.	Any solder with 45% tin or more if pre-tinning has been successful.

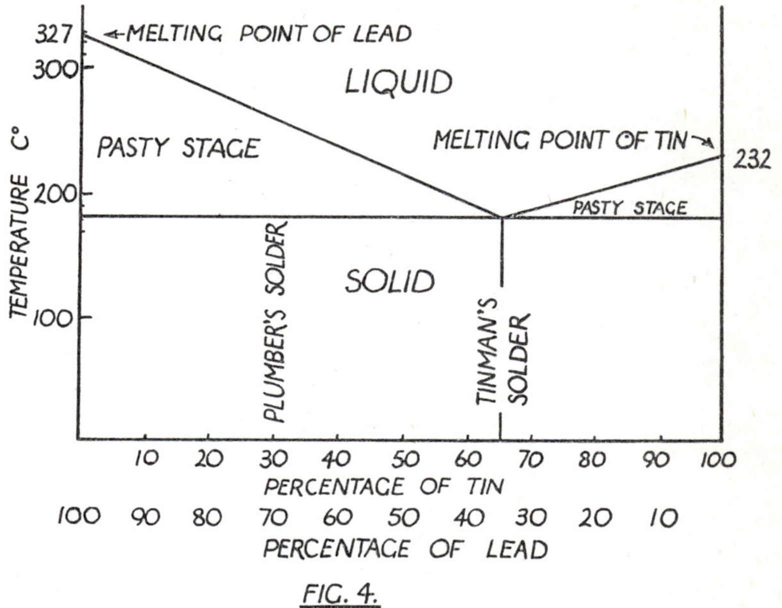

FIG. 4.

etc., but this is not enough. The remaining thin film of oxides must be removed chemically by using a flux.

Fluxes for Soft Soldering

The fluxes are divided into two groups: active and safe.

Active fluxes. 1. Zinc chloride, also known as "killed spirit" is popularly used in workshops. It is made by adding scraps of zinc to hydrochloric acid until all the bubbling has stopped. It should be made in an earthenware or lead vessel in a place where the fumes are readily taken away, such as on a window sill. Then it should be filtered and about 50% water added. If necessary it can be cleared by adding a few drops of concentrated hydrochloric acid.

2. Paste fluxes containing either zinc chloride or ammonium chloride in petroleum jelly.

3. Ammonium chloride (Sal ammoniac).

Safe Fluxes. 1. Tallow
2. Resin
3. Oleic acid.

There are also many proprietary brands available, not all of them good.

Usually solders will "take" much more readily with active fluxes because they are slightly acid and tend to clean the joint by their etching action. The joint should be thoroughly washed after soldering to remove the corrosive flux residue. For this reason active fluxes should never be used on electrical work.

1. Soldering Iron Method

The soldering iron method is the most popular. Copper is used for the bit because it is a very good conductor of heat (fig. 5).

A soldering stove is often used to provide the heat for the soldering iron (fig. 5).

The soldering iron is heated in the stove until a green flame shows that it is hot enough. It should now be removed from the flame if not required for immediate use and rested close to the flame but not actually touching it. Oxides form very readily on the heated copper bit so it must be tinned before use. Once it has been tinned properly it should not need re-tinning for a long time. The common fault in schools is overheating. This results in the bit being burned. Directly after each heating the iron should be fluxed and given a fresh coat of solder. It is important to heat the whole of the bit not merely the tip otherwise it will not hold the heat long enough to do a satisfactory job.

Tinning is done by heating the bit in the stove until a green flame shows. Remove from the stove and briskly file the faces with a file which should be kept for this purpose. Don't overdo the filing. Now put the tip into a hollow in a sal ammoniac block in which there are small pieces of solder. By this method the whole of the tip can be covered with an even layer of solder at once. It is now tinned.

When the parts to be soldered have been properly prepared and fluxed the tinned soldering iron is taken from the stove, fluxed and recharged with solder. The flux can be in a small tin lid and the solder in another. The charged iron should be held against the pieces to be soldered for a moment to allow the heat to be transferred from the bit to the work and then gently moved along the joint. Often it is best to use the edge of the bit as this allows more heat to get to the work. Surplus solder can be picked up with the tip of the soldering iron.

Figure 5A shows a small electric soldering iron. Electric soldering irons are usually used for electrical work but can also be used where the ordinary soldering iron is used.

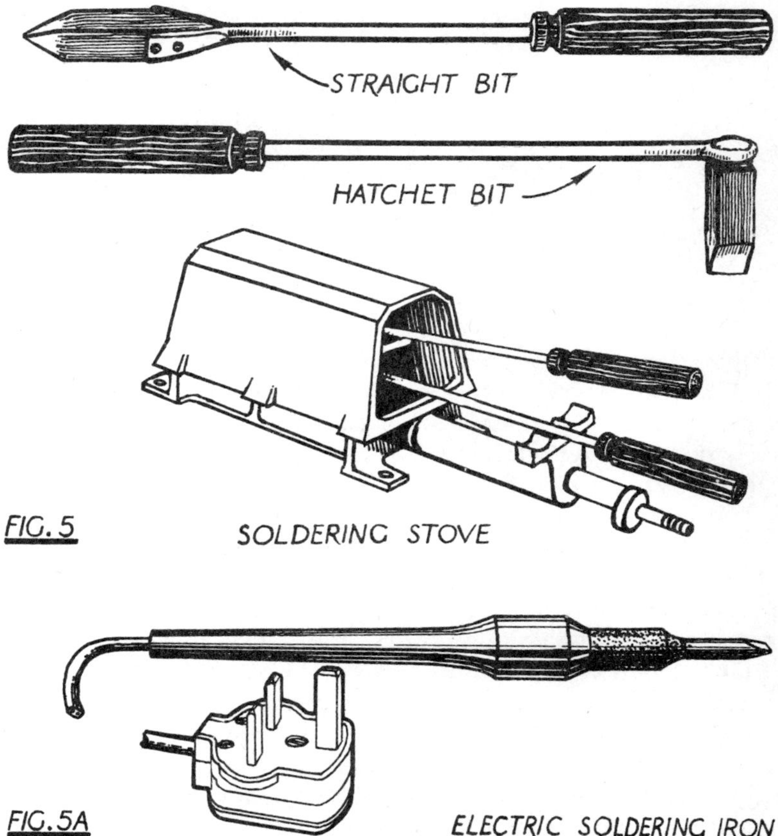

FIG. 5

ELECTRIC SOLDERING IRON
FIG. 5A

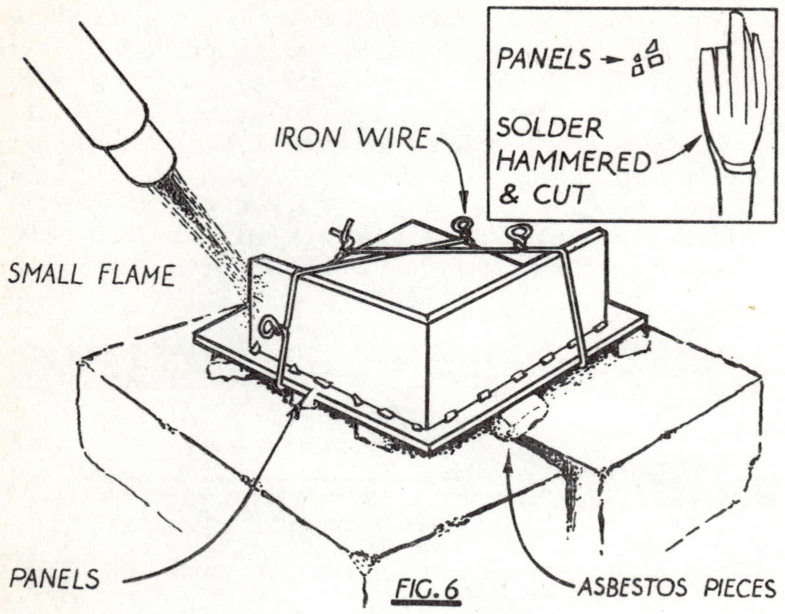

FIG. 6

2. Blowpipe Soldering

This is a reliable method, particularly on heavy gauge metal and on large work where a soldering iron would be inadequate. It is not to be recommended for tin plate work because the tin surface can be damaged by the flame.

The method often used is to cut small pieces or panels of solder from the strip which has been hammered and cut as shown (fig. 6).

Lay these small panels of solder along the edges of the prepared joint. Usually killed spirits is used as a flux. The flame, which should be small, must be kept moving. First the flux will bubble and usually in doing so it will displace some of the panels. If any of the panels move too far they can be gently pushed back into place with a thin pointed rod—a pointed rod will not conduct too much heat away from the work (fig. 6A).

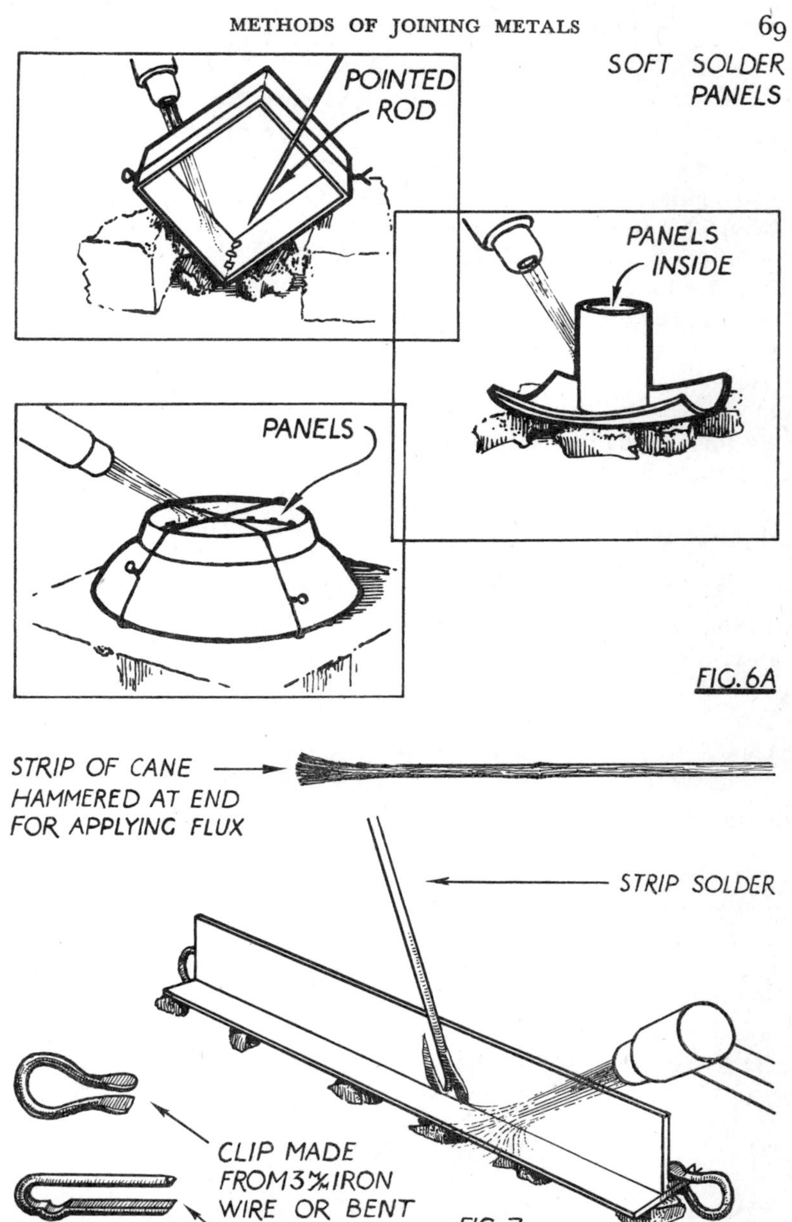
SOFT SOLDER PANELS
POINTED ROD
PANELS INSIDE
PANELS
FIG. 6A
STRIP OF CANE HAMMERED AT END FOR APPLYING FLUX
STRIP SOLDER
CLIP MADE FROM 3/64 IRON WIRE OR BENT SPLIT PIN
FIG. 7

When the melting point of the solder is reached, the solder will run into the joint. If the solder does not run into every part of the joint as required, it can be helped by quickly applying a little more flux to the parts where the solder has not run. This is best done with a small piece of cane which has been hammered to make the end fray (fig. 7).

Notice that flat work should never be laid flat on a fire brick or asbestos sheet, if it is it will take too long to heat up because the surface on which it is lying has to be brought up to the same heat as the rest of the work.

It is a good plan to support it either on a bed of small pieces of broken fire brick, or asbestos cubes, or small pieces of coke. By this means the flame can get under the work.

Panels of solder need not always be used. The strip of solder which has been suitably hammered at the end can be "fed" into the joint as the required heat is reached (fig. 7).

3. Solder Paint Method

Solder paint is available in small jars and contains its own flux. The parts to be joined should be clean and well fitting. The solder paint is then applied to both pieces before they are positioned. Heat is then applied either with a small flame from the blowpipe or if convenient by pressing the flat face of a soldering iron against them until enough heat is transferred to make the solder paint melt.

4. Sweating

By this method the parts to be joined are cleaned and fluxed and each surface is then tinned. These tinned surfaces are then put together and gently heated either by a soldering iron or the blowpipe. Sweating usually works better if slight pressure is applied to the parts to be joined. When a stronger joint than we can make with soft solder is required we use silver solder.

SILVER SOLDERING OR HARD SOLDERING

Silver solder is available in different grades. The temperature at which these melt can vary between 630°C and 830°C. Most silver solders are made from alloying silver copper and zinc. Here are some from the wide range available:

Easy-Flo melts at approx.	630°C
Easy Solder melts at approx.	723°C
Medium melts at approx.	765°C
Hard melts at approx.	778°C
Enamelling melts at approx.	800°C

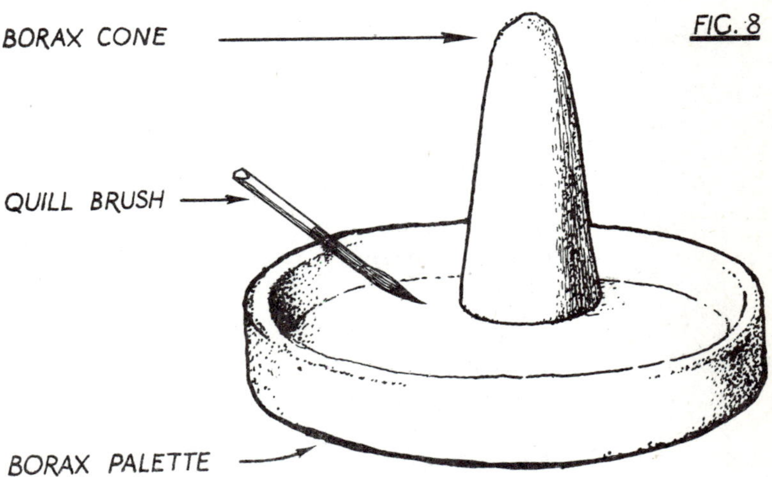

FLUXES FOR SILVER SOLDERS

Most silver soldering can be done by using borax as a flux. Borax may be bought in lump form (borax cone) (fig. 8) or in powder. If the borax cone is used it is usual to use it in conjunction with the borax palette and a little water. The cone is gently rubbed in the palette into which a few drops of water have been placed. Soon the water will become cloudy and then after a little more rubbing it will have the consistency of thin cream. It is now ready for use as a flux.

If powdered borax is used it can be made into a thin paste and then applied.

Other proprietary fluxes in powder form are available. In many cases these are more suitable than borax particularly when the makers of the solder make a flux to be used specifically with the solder.

SILVER SOLDERING METHOD

1. The parts to be joined must be well fitting and clean.

2. These parts must be fluxed properly particularly where you want the solder to run.

3. The parts must be secured.

4. Heat the work with the torch and when hot enough apply the solder strip. When the work is hot enough the solder will run right along the joint. If panels or filings of solder are being used, these must be applied before heating commences. Both parts of the work to be joined must be at the same temperature, i.e. they must both be at the melting point of the solder.

5. Do not quench a soldered joint if it can be avoided because this causes undue stresses owing to the different rates of cooling of the parts.

6. Remove binding wire or clips etc. after cooling.

7. Pickle to remove oxides and flux residue. This is done by warming the article in a solution of 1 part sulphuric acid to 10 parts water, i.e. the pickle, in a copper pan. Large articles can be heated to black heat, i.e. not red hot, and then immersed in the pickle which is usually kept in an earthenware vat. Do not leave soldered articles too long in the pickle because it attacks the zinc in the solder and makes the joint porous.

Sometimes it is necessary to silver solder a small part on to a much larger one. Owing to the length of time required to bring the larger part to the right temperature the flux is burnt away at the edges of the joint. This prevents the solder from running. One way to overcome this is to prepare the parts by drilling holes as shown in figure 9.

When the panels of solder and flux are in the hole the boss can be secured in its place with clips. Take care to properly flux the place where you want the solder to run. Now heat the work until the solder melts and you see the fine silver line of molten solder all round the joint. Allow to cool and clean in usual manner.

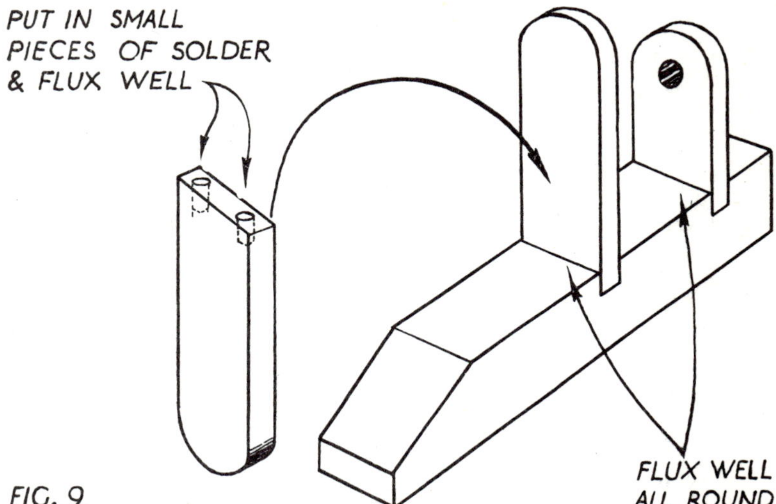

FIG. 9

How Solder Joins Metals

When sufficient heat is applied to the solder it melts and combines at the point of contact with the metals it is joining. This of course applies only to well-fitting, properly cleaned and fluxed metal (fig. 10).

This combining of the solder and the metals to be joined happens not only in soft soldering but also in silver soldering and brazing. The intermetallic compound is usually only a few thousandths of an inch deep.

BRAZING

This is similar to silver soldering: in fact silver soldering is sometimes known as silver brazing. To be precise brazing is the joining of metals with brass. Brass is an alloy of copper and zinc.

A higher temperature is required and a stronger joint is made by brazing than by silver soldering.

The brazing alloy is called brazing spelter. Spelter is obtainable in rod, powder, granulated or in ribbon form. If used in

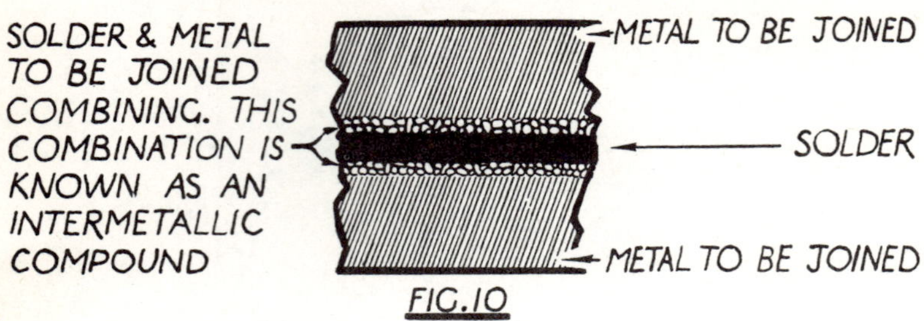

FIG. 10

powder or granulated form it is usually mixed with flux and water to make a paste.

There are several grades but these are three popularly used and known as:

Soft	50% copper	50% zinc	melts at approx. 870°C
Medium	54% copper	46% zinc	melts at approx. 880°C
Hard	60% copper	40% zinc	melts at approx. 900°C

Flux for Brazing

Borax can be used for most purposes but there are several made up powders available.

Brazing Method

Prepare as for silver solder. In the school workshop the biggest enemy to brazing is heat loss. This causes the operator to take too long on the work and this in turn causes excessive oxidation. Often this is owing to insufficient care being taken in packing firebricks or asbestos round the parts to be joined. Also brazing is reserved for the larger pieces which conduct the heat from the joint very readily. Figure 11 shows a well packed joint to be made on a gate frame.

If a brazing rod is being used it helps if the tip of the rod is heated and then dipped in the tin of dry flux. This causes the flux to adhere to the end of the rod. When the parts to be brazed are hot enough, this flux on the end of the rod will help the flow of molten brass when it is touched on to the joint. Remember the heat to melt the rod must come from the work

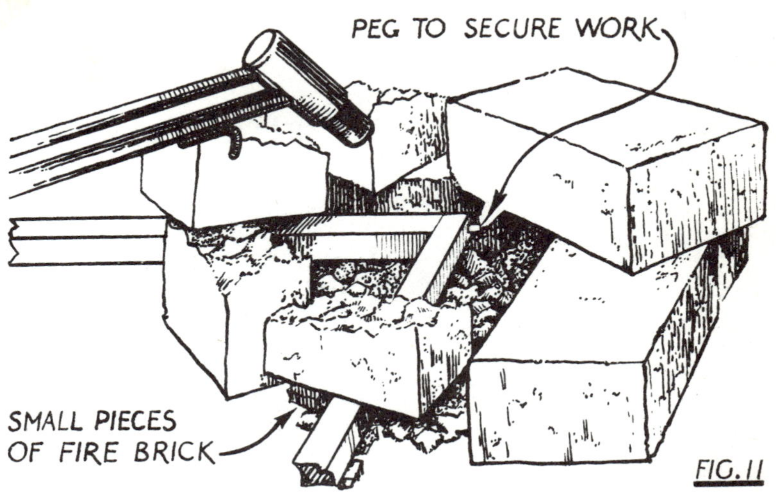

and not the flame. Important too is the fact that brazing should be done at one heat, i.e. the torch should not be taken off the work once having started until the brazing operation is completed; otherwise excessive oxidation takes place.

For circular work a rotary table is very useful. This can be used for soldering as well as brazing (fig. 11A).

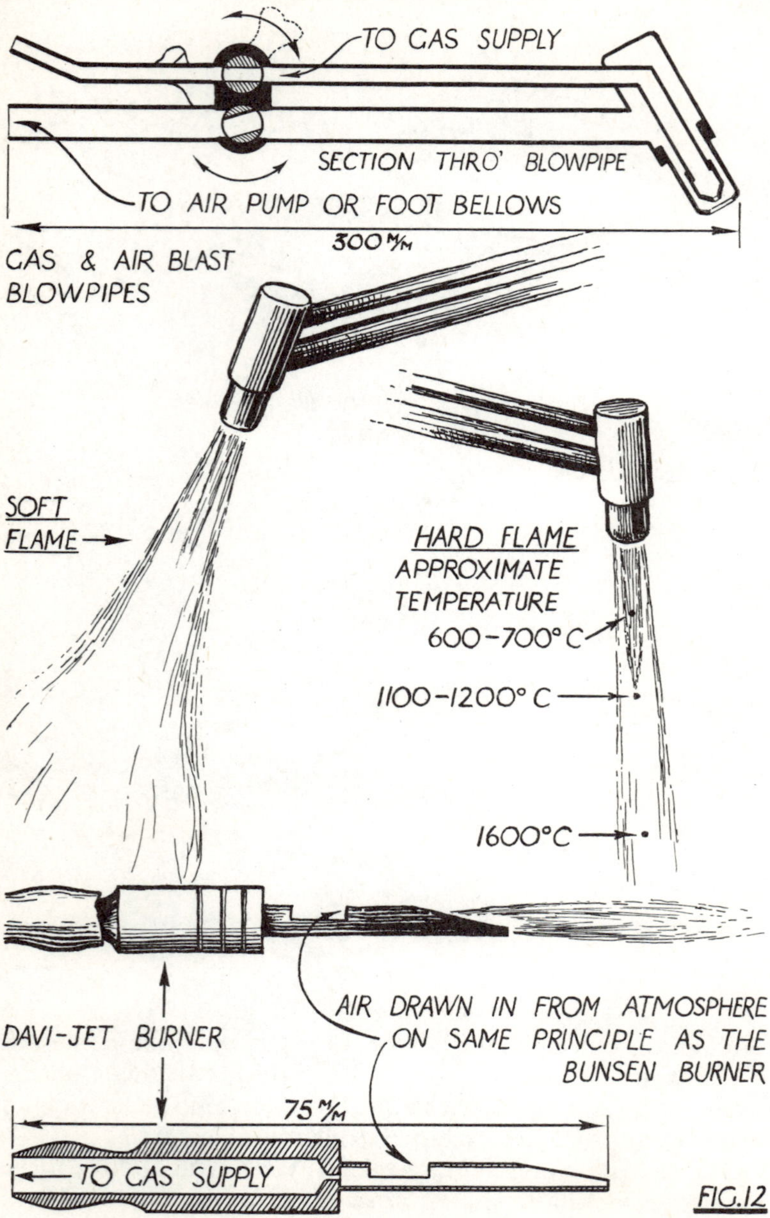

TO GAS SUPPLY

SECTION THRO' BLOWPIPE

TO AIR PUMP OR FOOT BELLOWS

300 M/M

GAS & AIR BLAST BLOWPIPES

SOFT FLAME

HARD FLAME

APPROXIMATE TEMPERATURE

600–700° C

1100–1200° C

1600°C

DAVI-JET BURNER

AIR DRAWN IN FROM ATMOSPHERE ON SAME PRINCIPLE AS THE BUNSEN BURNER

75 M/M

TO GAS SUPPLY

FIG. 12

Cleaning the Joint After Brazing

The makers of the flux will usually give their recommendations. Hot water is often mentioned for the removal of flux residue. Small work can be boiled in a solution of water and alum.

Figure 12 shows a blowpipe in section. The soft flame shown is used for obtaining an "all over" heat on a piece of work. It is made more fierce (hard flame) by either increasing the air blast or cutting down the gas for the purpose of concentrating the heat on a smaller area.

At the bottom of figure 12 is shown a Davi-jet burner. This is useful for soft soldering particularly on pewter ware. The intensity of the flame is adjusted merely by turning the gas tap.

WELDING*

Electric Arc and Resistance Welding

Arc welding is done by using a coated metallic electrode, which makes an electric arc with the job being welded, or two carbon electrodes. The parts are joined by fusion. The metallic electrode is actually a metal filler rod coated with a fluxing agent. This coating also contains a material which gives off a gas as it burns therefore excluding the atmosphere from the joint being made.

Resistance welding is not unlike the old process of forge welding. A heavy electric current is passed (by means of two electrodes) between the parts to be joined until the fusion temperature is reached. These parts are then held under pressure for a brief moment until fusion at that point is complete.

* The interested student can read fully on welding from the book: ***Welding*** by A. C. Davis.

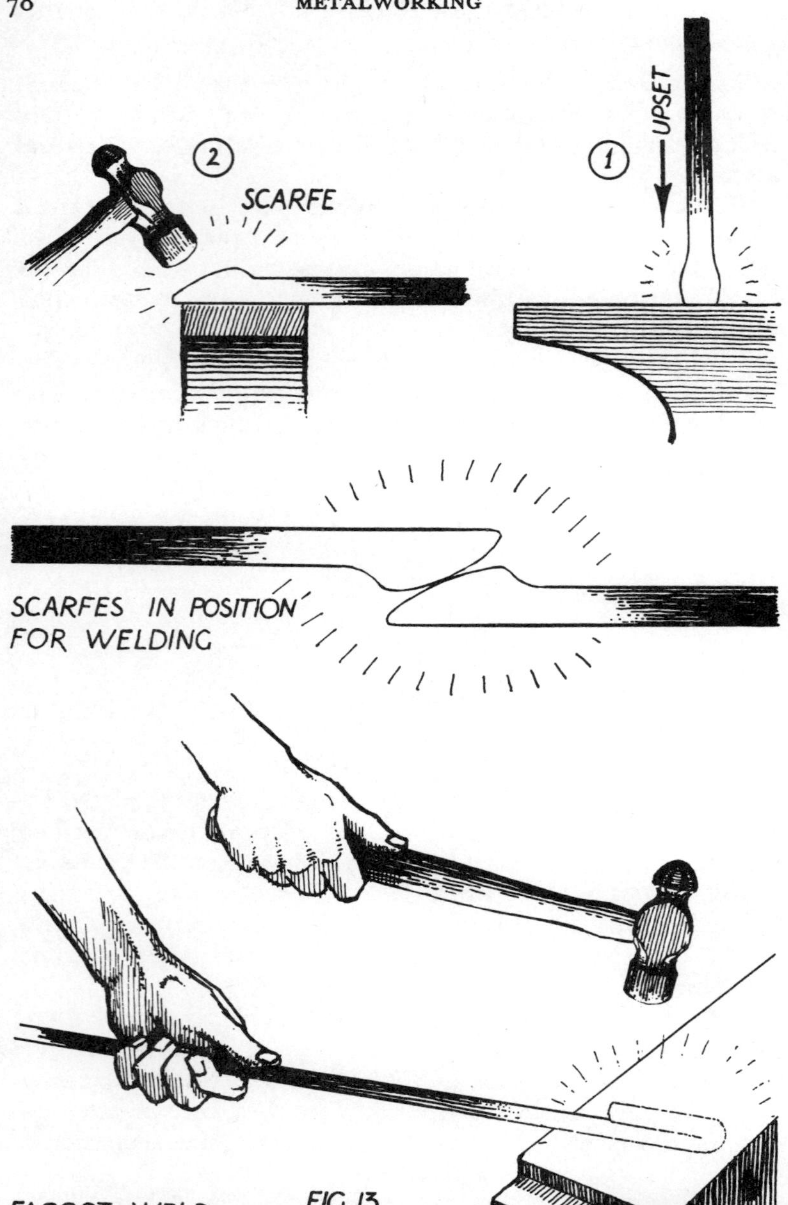
UPSET
2
1
SCARFE
SCARFES IN POSITION FOR WELDING
FAGGOT WELD

FIG. 13

Oxy-acetylene Welding

In this process, unlike silver soldering and brazing, the parent metals are melted. The oxy-acetylene flame melts the edges of the parent metal into pools to which a filler rod of the same material is melted.

Forge Welding

Forge welding, or fire welding, uses the blacksmith's hearth. Before a fire-welded joint can be made it is essential to have a clean clinker-free fire and the parts to be joined must be upset and scarfed (fig. 13). The scarf must have rounded faces so that they touch in the centre; thus the molten scale is driven out during hammering. It is usual to have an assistant for fire welding. The parts to be joined are heated to a creamy white heat and removed from the fire and tapped on the edge of the anvil to shake off the dirt. Care must be taken to ensure that the scarfs are in proper relationship to each other before the first blow is struck in the centre of the work. It must now be repeatedly hammered, working from the centre, to drive out the molten scale. It may be necessary to reheat for the weld to be completed.

A properly fire-welded joint cannot be detected from the parent metals. A beginner will do well to start by making a faggot weld as an exercise. This does not require an assistant nor a pair of tongs (fig. 13).

Some skilled blacksmiths can fire weld* without using any flux but others always use a flux. Silver sand, burnt borax, laffite welding plate or a powder sold by The Amalgam Co. of Sheffield can be used.

SCREWS

This is a broad term which includes: bolts, studs, set screws, grub screws, thumb screws, socket head cap screws, Phillip screws etc.

* Full details regarding fire welding may be obtained from The Rural Industries Bureau publications on forge work.

Usually these are used to secure two or more pieces together except where a bolt or screw is used as a hinge pin.

Bolts

These are as shown. They always have a nut and usually a washer too (fig. 14).

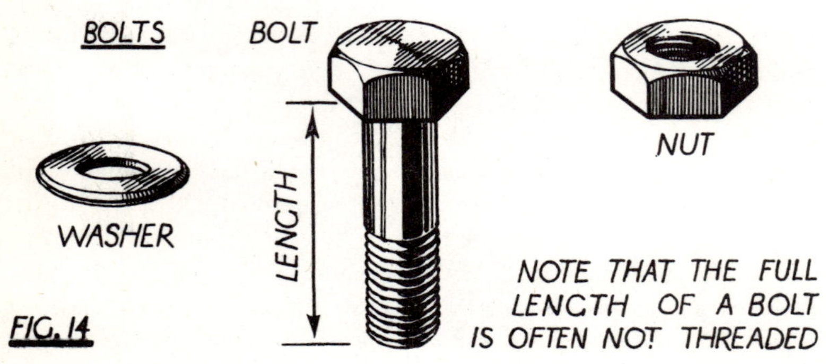

FIG. 14

Screws

These have no nut (see top of fig. 15).

Grub Screws or set Screws

Often used to secure pulleys to shafts (bottom of fig. 15).

Thumb Screws

These are used where easy removal is desired (bottom of fig. 15).

Studs

They have no head and no nut. They are sometimes used in place of bolts. It is easier to replace a worn stud than to re-drill and tap a hole after the thread is worn or stripped. A good example of the use of studs can be seen on the cylinder block of a car (fig. 16).

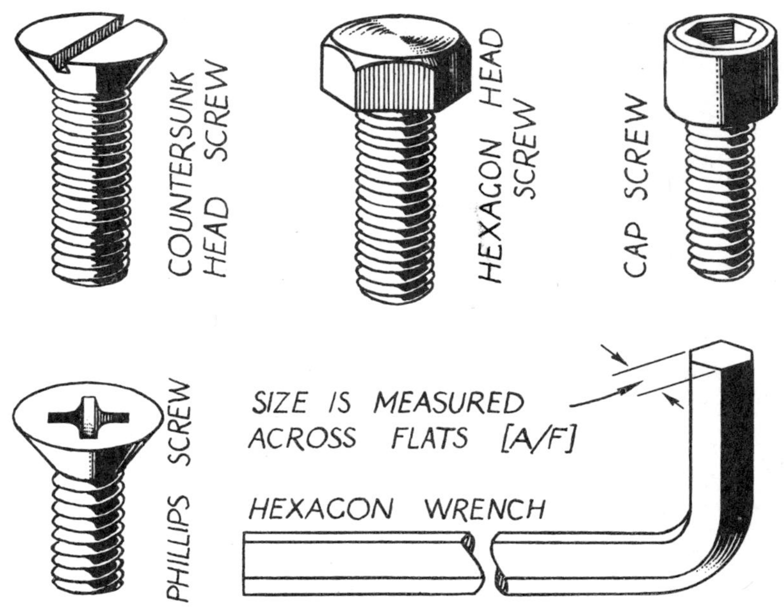
COUNTERSUNK HEAD SCREW
HEXAGON HEAD SCREW
CAP SCREW
PHILLIPS SCREW
SIZE IS MEASURED ACROSS FLATS [A/F]
HEXAGON WRENCH

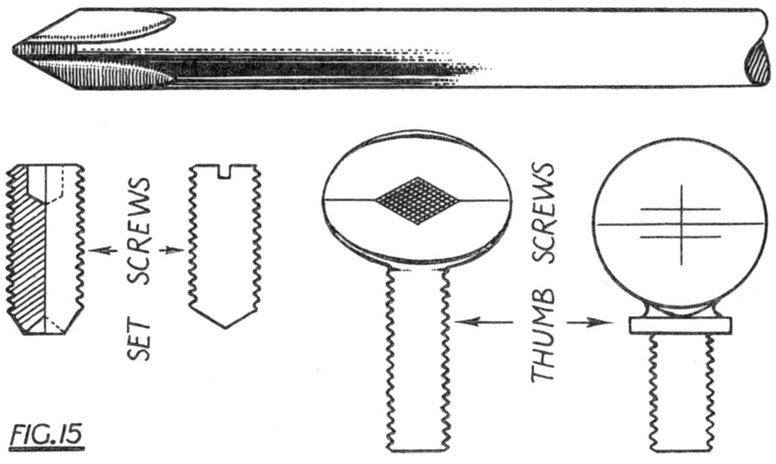
END OF PHILLIPS SCREW DRIVER. AVAILABLE IN FOUR SIZES
SET SCREWS
THUMB SCREWS

FIG. 15

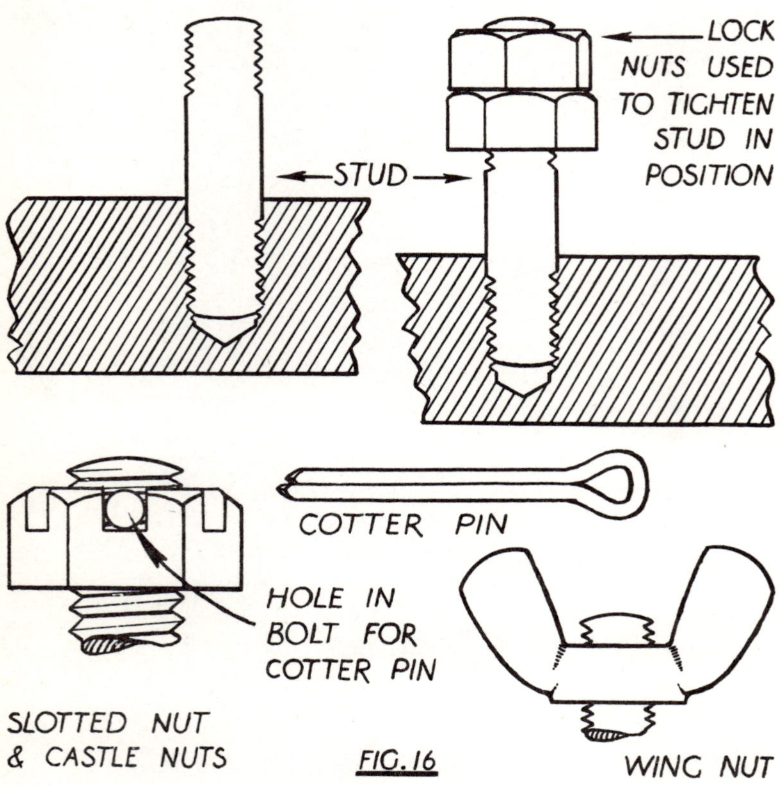

FIG. 16

NUTS

They include wing nuts, hexagon-headed nuts and castellated nuts (fig. 16). Lock nuts are often used where vibration might loosen a single nut. A castle or slotted nut secured by a cotter pin is similarly used to prevent loosening by vibration.

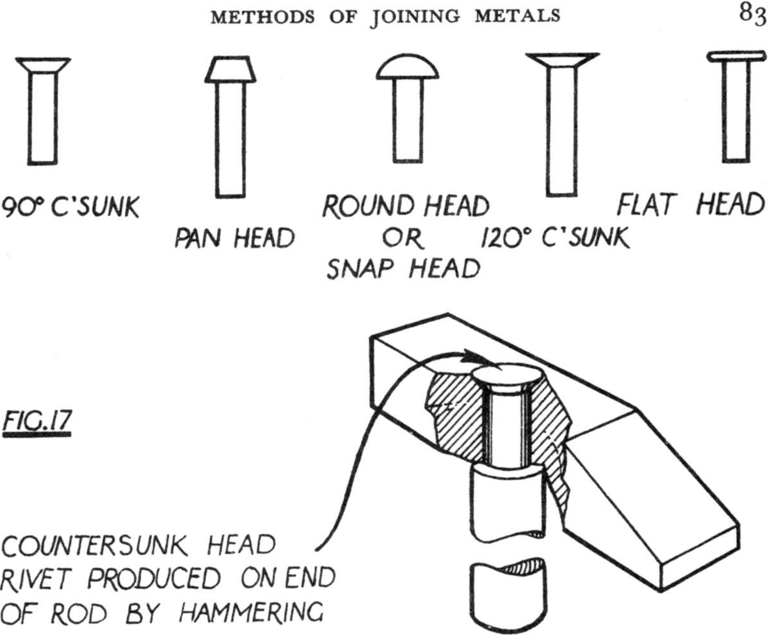

RIVETS

Metal parts or plates can be joined by rivets to make a permanent joint or, if a single rivet is used it can be as a pivot or hinge.

Those commonly used are shown in figure 17.

Rivets are classified by the shape of the head, their length, diameter and the metal from which they are made.

The diameter of the rivet used must be related to the thickness of the plates being riveted. In school we often use our own judgement when selecting rivets for a piece of work, but it is common practice when riveting plates between 1.5 mm and 12 mm thick to use a rivet the diameter of which equals twice the thickness of the plates being riveted. Plates thicker than 12 mm should have a rivet $1\frac{1}{2}$ times the thickness of the plate. When riveting plates of unequal thickness the calculation is based on the thinner plate.

The distance between the centres of two rivets in the same row (pitch) should not be less than 2 × diameter of rivet and the centre of the rivet should not be closer to the edge of the metal than $1\frac{1}{2} \times$ diameter of rivet. It is usual to have the rivets and the parts to be joined of the same material.

On large work the rivets are often made red hot before being inserted into the hole. This makes a better joint because as the rivet cools it contracts and pulls the plates together. Also the rivet is easier to work as it is more plastic when red hot.

Rivets are often made as spigots on the ends of rods which are hammered over as shown (fig. 17).

5

Casting

Casting is done in a foundry where molten metal is poured into cavities in sand left by a pattern. Foundry work in school is usually done in a part of the workshop set aside for this purpose.

The metal is melted in a crucible pot which is heated in an insulated crucible furnace. Crucibles are made of plumbago but zinc-based alloys and aluminium alloys can be melted in a cast iron pot (fig. 1).

The patterns are popularly made of soft close-grained wood, a good example being jelutong which is close-grained and easy to work. Wherever possible internal corners are radiused by applying wax or leather fillets or by using plastic wood so that no fragile corners will be left in the sand when the pattern is removed. The pattern is also suitably tapered or drafted. $\frac{1}{8}''$ per foot is sufficient, but for school work a greater draft is often allowed. This drafting is to facilitate easy removal from the sand. The pattern is finished with glass paper and varnished or painted. Figure 2 shows the pattern for a small vice. Allowance must be made for machining and for the metal shrinking when it cools.

Patterns which do not have one large face, as in figure 2, can be made as split patterns. These are often easier to manage if mounted on a board as in figure 3. If a board is not used, the halves of the pattern can be accurately located by dowel pins as shown in figure 4. When a pattern is made for use by an outside foundry, the various parts must be coloured to indicate to the foundryman where to allow the better metal to be for subsequent machining. These colours are specified in the British Standards No. 467: 1957. Red, for parts to be left as

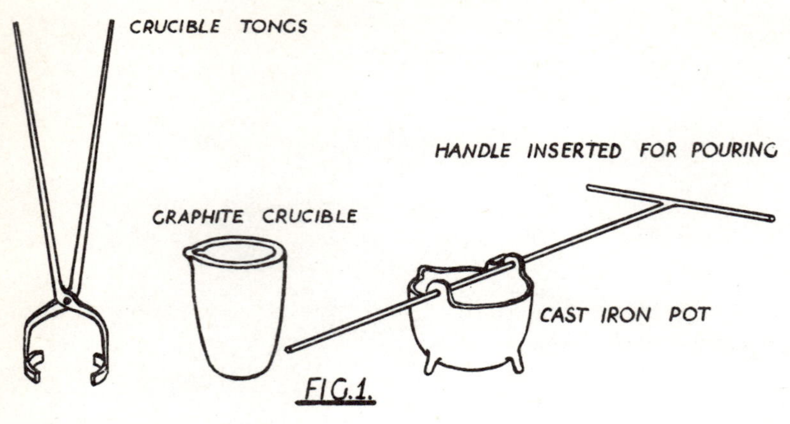

CRUCIBLE TONGS
HANDLE INSERTED FOR POURING
GRAPHITE CRUCIBLE
CAST IRON POT

FIG.1.

FIG. 2.

FIG.3.

FIG.4.

COPE
DRAG
HANDLES CUTAWAY TO SHOW LOCATING PINS

FIG.5.

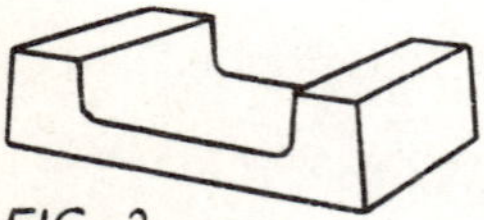

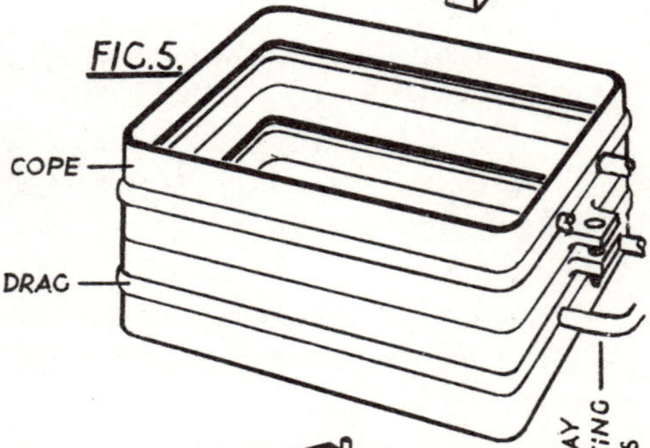

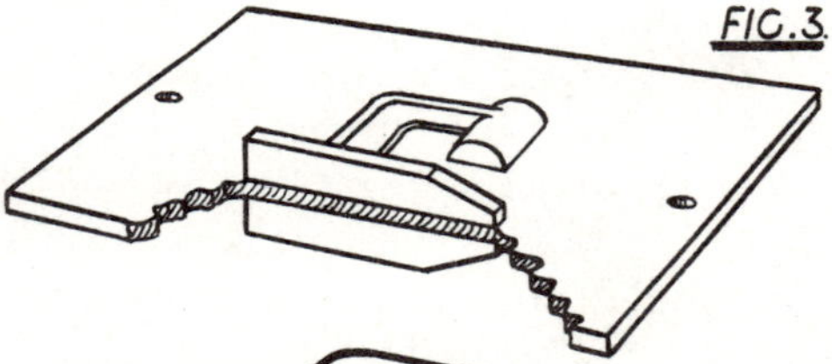

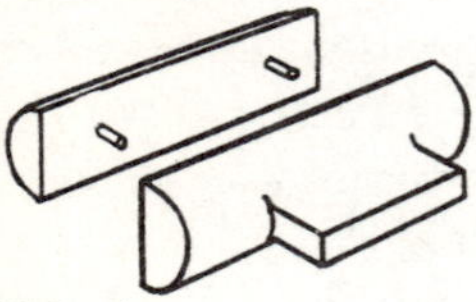

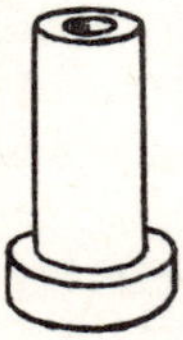

FIG.6.

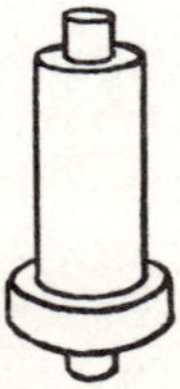

FIG.7.

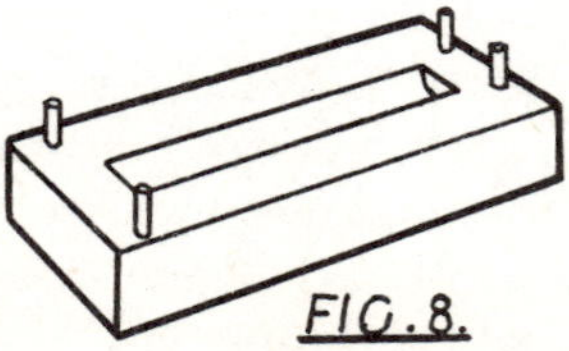

FIG.8.

cast; black for core prints; yellow where machining is to be done etc.

FLASKS OR MOULDING BOXES

These are usually made of steel, cast iron or aluminium alloy (fig. 5). The top half is called the cope, the pins of which locate into the sockets of the lower half known as the drag.

SAND

Oilbonded sand such as Petrobond is excellent for beginners because there is no need to worry about the correct moisture content; but it is more expensive than the popular Mansfield, Erith or Belfast sands which are natural sands and are made damp with water.

These natural sands are a mixture of sand grains and clay particles. They are refractory so that the hot metal does not bake or melt them, and they are more or less porous thus allowing the escape of steam and gases. The moisture content must be right. This can be judged by squeezing a handful, which should remain unbroken when the hand is opened and yet break when it is thrown down.

CORES

Cores are used where it is required that parts of the casting should be hollow. Figure 6 shows a hollow casting and figure 7, the pattern. The core prints are for making cavities in the sand in which to place the core. The core is made from sand bonded with oil to give cohesion. The core must be permeable to allow the gases to escape, and strong enough to stand handling, yet sufficiently brittle to crumble when the metal contracts. Cores can be made in a core box (fig. 8) or in metal piping.

For school work the core can be made of beach sand (sharp sand) bonded with linseed oil and baked in an oven until hard.

The linseed oil is mixed, a little at a time, into the sand until a handful squeezed does not exude oil and yet holds together. The core can be baked in an improvised biscuit-tin oven over a soldering stove, or in an old domestic oven, to a temperature of about 200°C. It will first go lighter in colour as the oil dries and then start turning brown. When it is a little darker than when first put in the oven, the baking is finished. Figure 9 shows the core in place in the mould resting in the cavities made by the core prints.

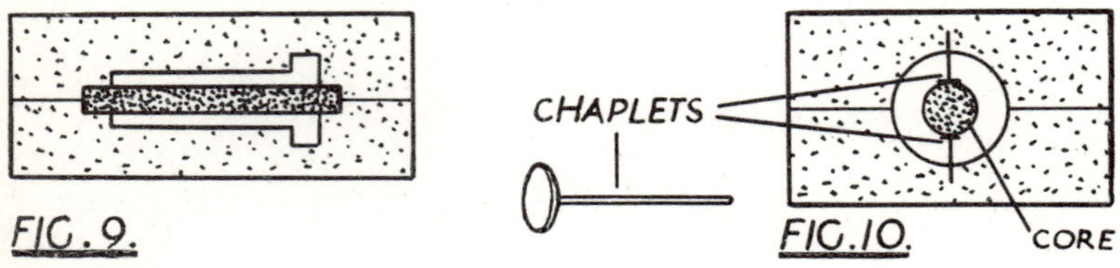

FIG. 9. FIG. 10.

Chaplets

Chaplets are small supports for the core (fig. 10) made of the same metal as the casting. When the metal is poured these fuse into the casting. Although seldom used in school work, they are found necessary in industry where intricate cores are used.

MOULDERS' TOOLS

A few of these are shown in figure 11. The large rammer is made of wood and the small one of metal. These are used for ramming the sand all round the pattern. The water brush is soft and comes to a point. It is used for damping the mould where small repairs are made (usually to the edges). The taper trowel is one of the many shaped trowels moulders use to make the sand flat where desired. The spoon tool is often used to make gates. The gimlet is screwed into the pattern and tapped in all directions just above the thread with a metal rod while the handle is held. This is known as rapping. It loosens the pattern in the sand so that it can be withdrawn easily. Bellows are used for blowing out particles of sand from the mould. The

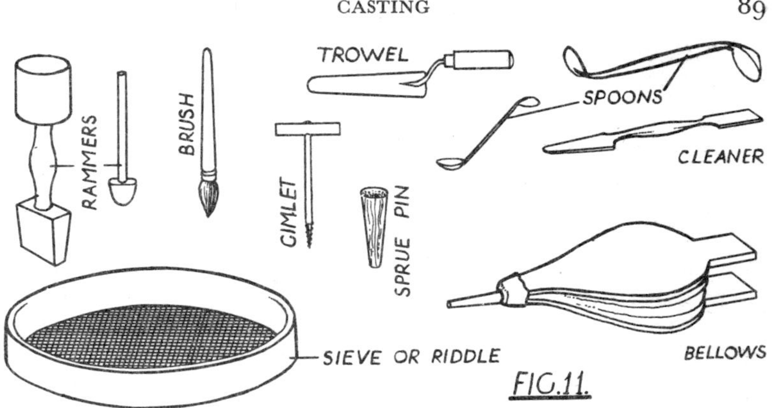

FIG.11.

sieve or riddle is used for sifting the facing sand over the pattern. Sprue pins are round tapered pieces of wood used for making the runners and risers.

THE MOULDING PROCESS

For simplicity let us consider preparing the mould from the pattern for a small vice shown in figure 2 (p. 86).

(*a*) Choose a flask which allows at least 50 mm spare round the pattern. Open the flask and turn over the drag on to a flat surface, preferably a flat board (turn-over board) and place the pattern as shown in figure 12. The parting powder, which can be French chalk or a proprietary make, is held in a cotton bag and dusted over the pattern. This prevents the pattern from sticking in the sand.

(*b*) Riddle sand over the pattern (Petrobond does not need riddling) until it is covered, then add unsifted sand and ram down using the peen end of the rammer. Fill to the top with sand and ram with the butt end of the ram and make level (strickle) by drawing a firm straight edge across the top of the drag.

(*c*) Turn over the drag and fit the cope. Sprinkle with parting powder. Press the sprue pins into the sand. Their position is determined by experience—this takes into account the flow of the metal and the removal of excess metal afterwards (fettling). Riddle first layer of sand then add more sand, ram and strickle as before.

(*d*) Make the pouring basin, rap and remove the sprue pins. With a finger smooth off the edges of the holes. Separate the cope from the drag taking care not to jar the cope.

(*e*) Make the runners from the pattern to the sprue hole as shown. Insert the gimlet and rap in all directions with rod sideways, and remove the pattern carefully. Blow out any loose sand with the bellows and make repairs as required. Remove any sharp edges in the channels by running a finger round.

(*f*) Take care not to jar the cope when replacing it on the drag. The mould is now ready, but if it is to be left for a time it should be covered (not necessary if Petrobond is used) to prevent loss of moisture.

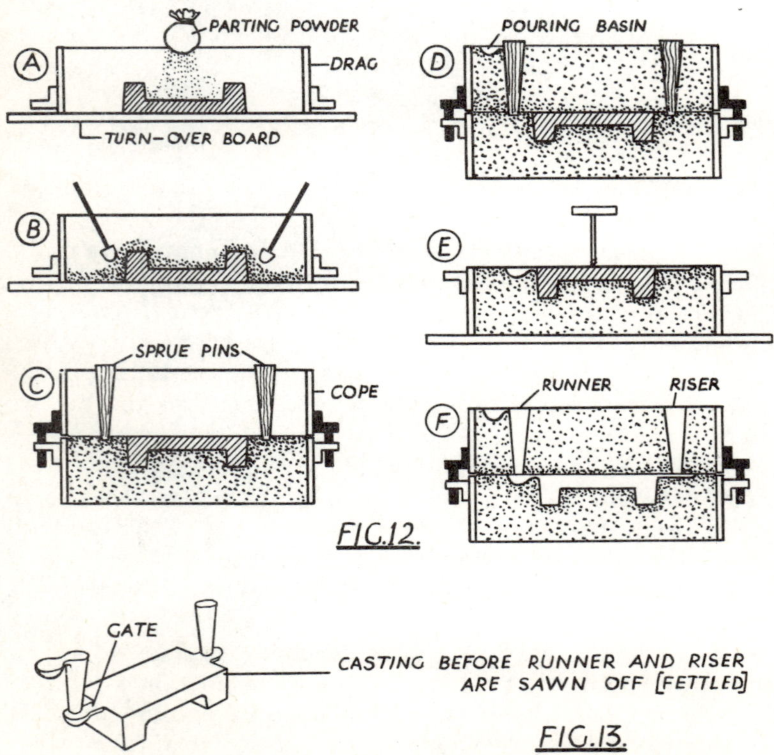

FIG.12.

FIG.13.

Odd-side Boxes

If the pattern does not have a flat back an odd-side box has to be made by placing the cope on the turn-over board with its locating pins upwards. Ram the cope with sand and then cut out the sand to take the pattern to half its depth. Then ram the sand round the pattern and strickle. Dust with parting powder and fit the drag, fill with sand, ram and strickle flat. Lift the drag with care and turn over. Knock out the sand in the cope (odd-side). With the pattern in the drag, place the empty cope in position, dust with parting powder, position sprue pins, fill with sand, ram and strickle. Rap and remove spruce pins and continue as for previous mould.

Pouring the Metal

Directly before the metal is poured the dross must be removed with a skimmer (fig. 14). Keep the crucible close to the pouring basin and pour in a continuous unbroken stream, as fast as the mould will take it, until the metal appears at the riser. When the metal has cooled and the casting been removed, it will be as in figure 13. This shows the relative size of the gate. The process of melting the metal prior to pouring must be properly done otherwise faulty castings result.

Melting the Metal

In school aluminium alloys and zinc alloys are widely used.

Aluminium alloys melt at about 600°C
Zinc alloys melt at about 390°C

These metals can be melted either in a plumbago crucible or a cast iron pot.

Furnaces for schools usually use gas and air. There are various types available, but whichever kind is used the makers' instructions must be followed regarding the lighting.

Small pieces of metal charged into the crucible will melt more quickly than large pieces. However, once the first charge is molten larger pieces can be added. The metal should never be heated much above its melting point and it should be poured promptly after skimming. Overheated metal results in the

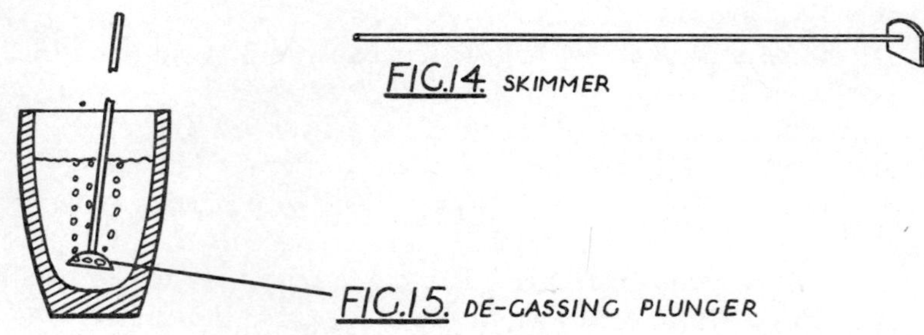

following typical faults: poor quality casting; excessive shrinkage and tearing of the metal.

When melting aluminium, fluxing and degassing are sometimes necessary.

Fluxing

A small amount of powdered flux (proprietary make) is applied to the charge as it becomes pasty. This melts on the surface and protects the metal from the atmosphere.

Degassing

If porous castings are being constantly obtained, degassing should be carried out before pouring. For school work it is convenient to use tablets which are plunged to the bottom of the melt with a domed tool (fig. 15).

6

Blacksmithing

THE HEARTH

There are various types of hearth available for school use but the two most popular ones have back blasts, i.e. the air blast comes from the back. One has a water cooled tuyère and the other a dry tuyère. The type with the water cooled tuyère is the better one because those with dry tuyères tend to burn away at the blast hole and require frequent replacement of the tuyère or tue iron. Figure 2, shows a part-section through the hearth. The hearth tools are shown above figure 1.

FUEL

Some smiths use coal and others coke breeze. The choice depends upon local custom. However, good blacksmith's coal is hard to obtain. The beginner is well advised to use coke breeze. This must be good smithy breeze, free from dust; a suitable size is known as "beans". Crushed or broken-up boiler coke or furnace coke is not suitable for forging.

The following points shouid be remembered:

1. Keep the fire in a small area. This is achieved by keeping the blast to a workable minimum.
2. Prevent the fire from burning hollow. The heat of the fire must be in the middle, just below the piece of metal being heated (see fig. 1). A hollow fire allows the blast air to oxidise the metal or may even burn it.
3. Remove clinker periodically. When clinker is cold it looks like crude black glass and makes a characteristic "clink

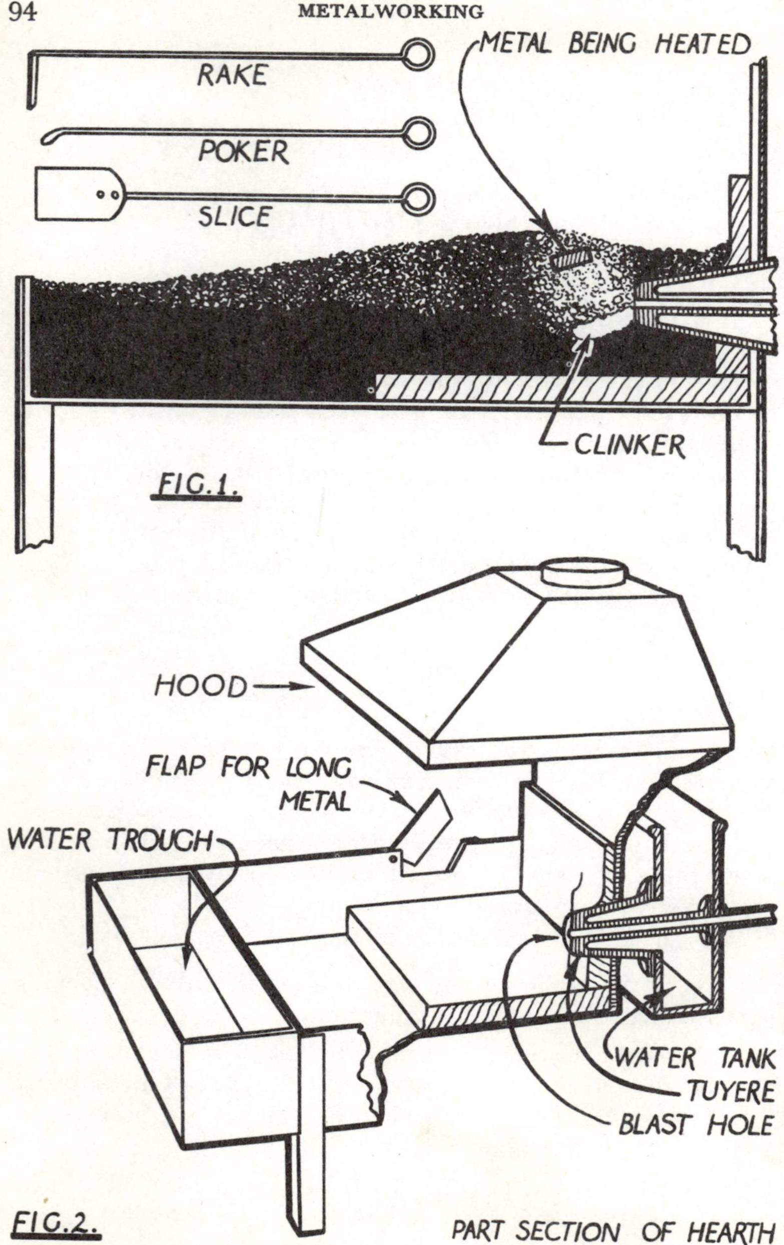
METAL BEING HEATED
RAKE
POKER
SLICE
CLINKER
FIG.1.
HOOD
FLAP FOR LONG METAL
WATER TROUGH
WATER TANK
TUYERE
BLAST HOLE
FIG.2.
PART SECTION OF HEARTH

clink" sound when touched with the fire tools. It is formed by the combination of oxygen and the impurities in the fuel.

The clinker forms just below the blast hole. The blast blows it on to the metal being heated to which it sticks, thus making forging difficult and dangerous because the clinker spurts out under the hammer blows. To remove the clinker turn off the blast for a few minutes to allow the clinker to solidify. It can then be hooked out in one piece with the poker which should be flattened and curved for the purpose (fig. 1). Knowing just where to find clinker and how to remove it without disturbing the fire too much is an art.

THE ANVIL

The London pattern anvil is the one most used and is shown in figure 3. Anvils for school work should not weigh under 50 kgms nor over 125 kgms. (They are sold by weight.) The body of the anvil is usually made from wrought iron or mild steel with a top facing of hardened carbon steel. Smiths often like to stand the anvil on an elm trunk. This reduces the noise a little and gives it a certain amount of resilience. In school they are nearly always on stands. Some resilience can be obtained by using the plywood pad shown in figure 3.

TOOLS

Hammers

A 0·5 kg ball pein hammer is a good size for most boys. The bigger boys can manage a 1 kg hammer providing the haft is shortened. A 3 kg sledge hammer for heavy striking is needed occasionally.

Swage Block

This is a useful tool although good work can be done if one is not available. A useful size is about 300 mm × 300 mm × 150 mm. These are used on a stand (fig. 3). It can be used in the vertical position or horizontally as shown by the dotted lines for shaping and swaging.

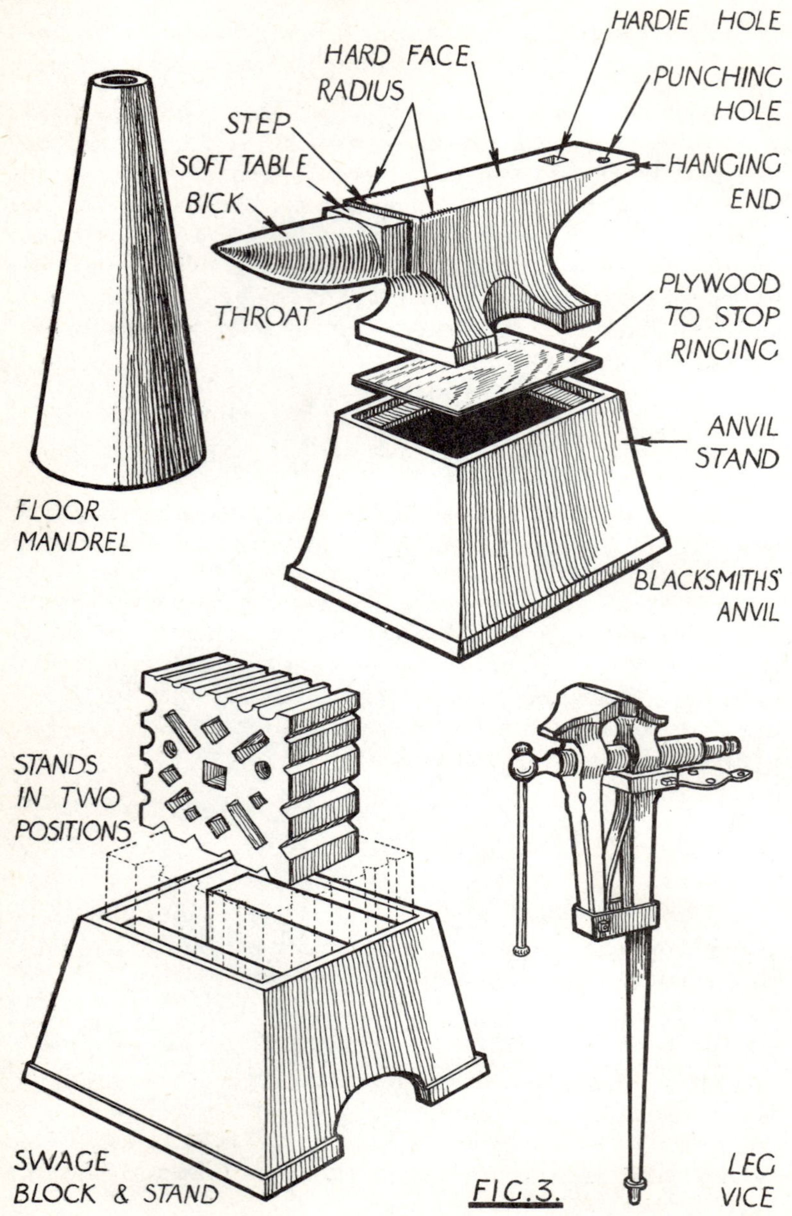
HARDIE HOLE
HARD FACE
RADIUS
PUNCHING HOLE
STEP
SOFT TABLE
HANGING END
BICK
THROAT
PLYWOOD TO STOP RINGING
ANVIL STAND
FLOOR MANDREL
BLACKSMITHS' ANVIL
STANDS IN TWO POSITIONS
SWAGE BLOCK & STAND
LEG VICE

FIG. 3.

Floor Mandrel

These are available in a number of sizes and are made from cast iron. They are useful for round work like rings and hoops (fig. 3).

Leg Vice

Although inferior in its gripping action to the engineer's parallel jaw vice, it is useful for heavy bending and withstands hammering (fig. 3).

Tongs

These are selected to suit the work. Traditionally a blacksmith makes his own tongs, but for school use they are bought ready made. A useful selection is shown in figure 4. Closed mouth tongs are used for thin metal. Usually these have a vee groove along the inside of the jaws for holding small section, round or square, metal.

Open mouth tongs are used for holding flat strip metal.

A tong ring can be slipped over the end of the tongs to keep the work gripped. This is useful when forging the end of metal

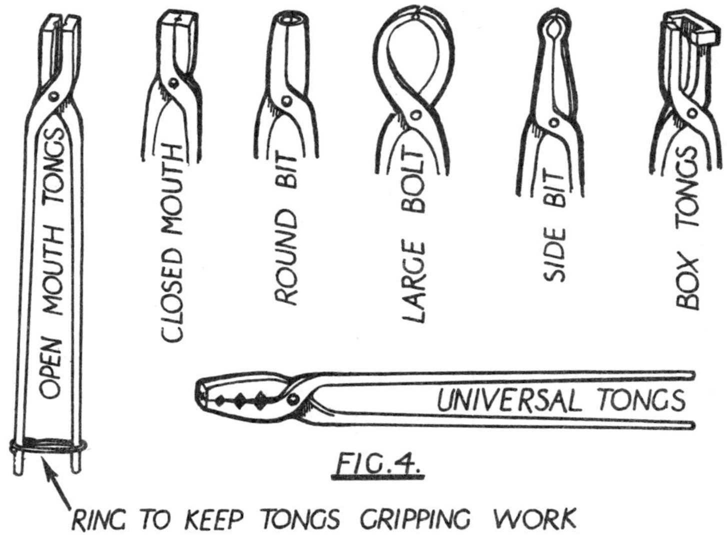

FIG. 4.

about 200 mm long, as time is wasted retrieving it from the hearth.

Hollow bit tongs (also known as round bits) are used for round or square metal.

Large bolt tongs often used in school for lifting small crucibles of molten metal from the forge when small castings are being made.

Rivet, sidebit or ring tongs are used to hold round work at right angles to the tongs.

Box tongs are used for holding flat strips securely.

The universal tongs are probably the most useful in school. They have a vee groove along the inside of the jaws as well as the openings at the side.

PROCESSES—BEGINNINGS

Most learners try to forge metal when it is not hot enough or continue hammering it long after it has lost its proper heat. This often results in splitting.

Overheating resulting in burnt metal (particularly on thin section material) is another hazard for the beginner.

A beginner should see a piece of metal, say 10 mm square mild steel about 1 metre long, heated up and withdrawn from the fire from time to time to observe the temperatures. Finally it should be heated until the end starts to burn and becomes completely spoilt. It is far better to see this happen and to learn to judge the temperatures on a waste piece of metal than to spoil part of a job.

A good heat for most simple forging operations on mild steel is a bright red heat. This is considerably hotter than the heat at which we harden carbon steel and slightly higher than the average temperature used in brazing.

Another important point is that the fire should be disturbed as little as possible when the work is taken out and inserted.

Holding the hammer properly is another consideration. Do not hold the hammer too near to the head.

Drawing Down and Flaring

Drawing down is a process of thinning the metal at the end either by increasing its width or reducing it on all sides and

making it longer. A round taper is a variation of this (fig. 5). The beginner must beware of splitting and piping. Splitting can be caused by hammering the metal when it is too cold or by faulty hammering. Piping is the forming of a hollow centre on the end of the bar or rod (fig. 6). This can be avoided if a blunt taper is first made on the end of the rod (figs. 5 and 7).

An example of flaring is shown in figure 8.

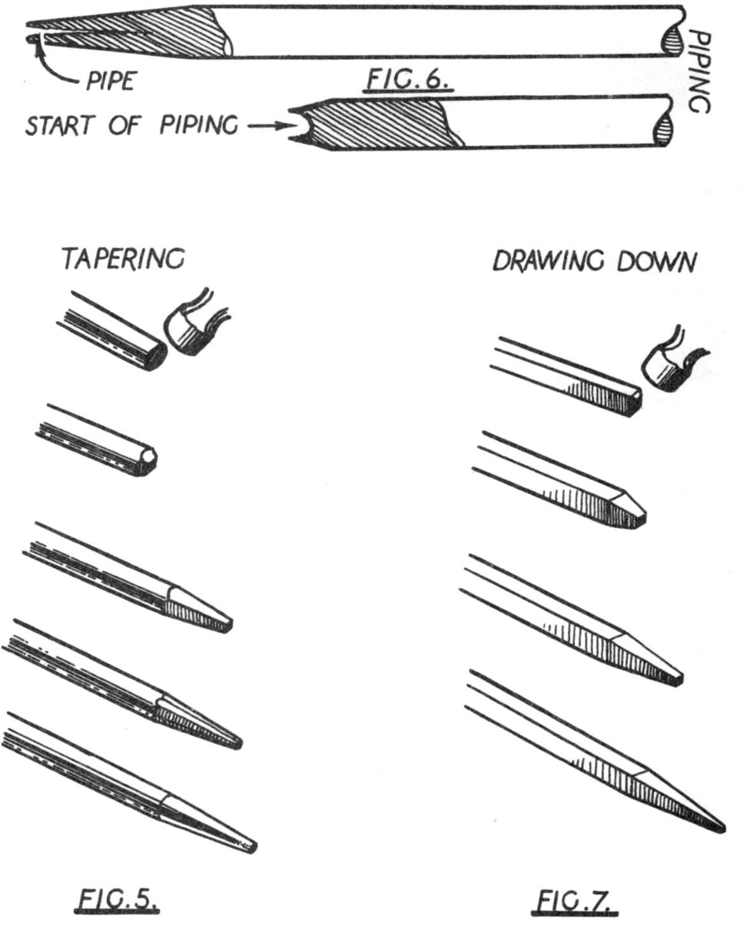

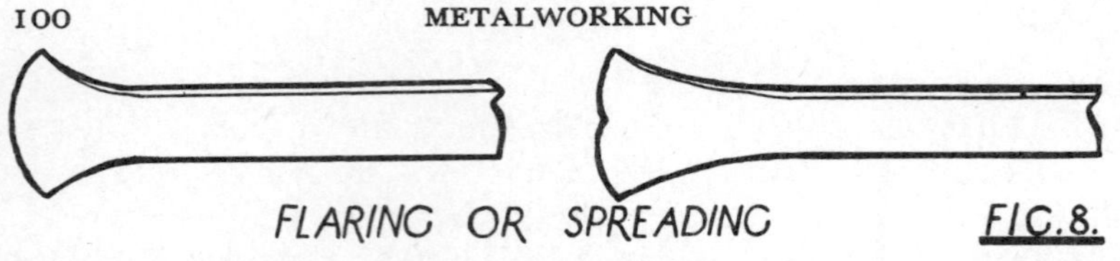

FLARING OR SPREADING FIG. 8.

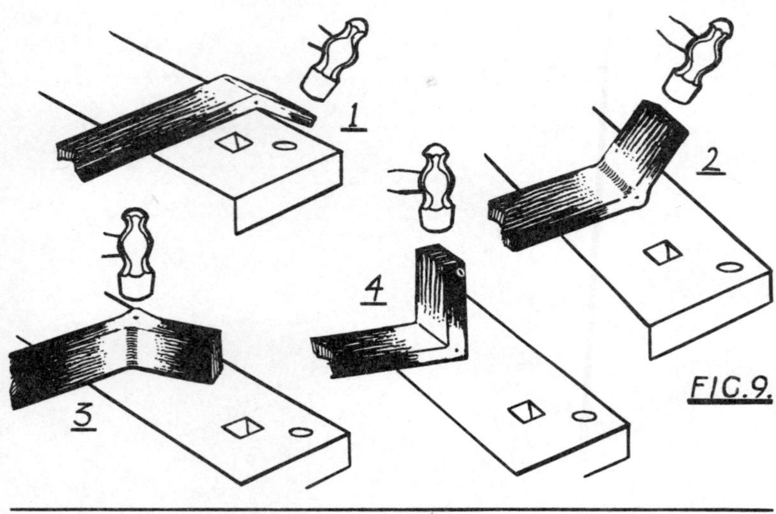

FIG. 9.

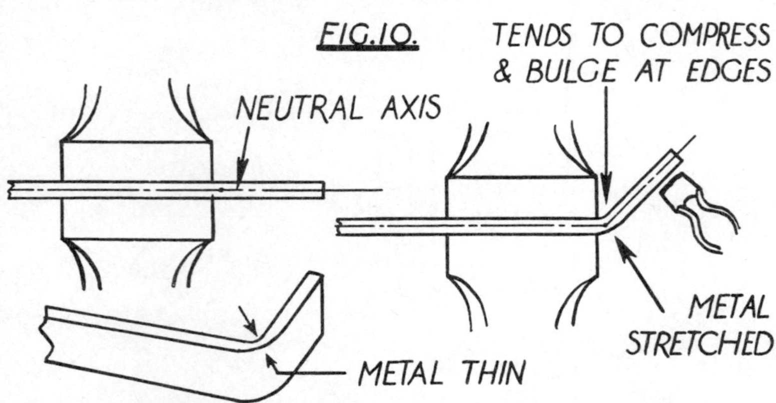

FIG. 10.

OUTSIDE OF BEND STRETCHES. THE INSIDE TENDS TO COMPRESS. THE AXIS REMAINS CONSTANT.

Bending

This can be done in the leg vice or on the anvil, or with bending horns and a wrench.

Small section metal can be bent in the leg vice but it is essential to work quickly, before the jaws have taken too much heat from the metal.

A centre punch mark on the metal will show where to hold it in the vice (fig. 10). Blacksmiths make up their own bending jigs and tools for more complicated work, particularly where a number of units are required.

These methods cause the metal to stretch on the outside of the curve and so become thin (fig. 10).

Bending without thinning can be done as shown in figure 9 on the anvil.

First a centre punch mark must be made. Then heat and bend to 45°, as shown. Next upset. Then complete the right angle as shown.

The bending of an eye as on the handle of a poker needs a little consideration. The length of metal needed to form the eye must be estimated. One method is shown in figure 11 (1). The dotted line shows the length of metal required.

The metal is then heated and bent at right angles as shown in figure 11 (2). Now reheat the metal and withdraw from the fire and quench the metal at the bend by dipping in the trough or with water poured from a can (fig. 11 (3)). Now bend on the bick as shown in figure 11 (4). Next reverse the work and continue shaping as shown in figure 11 (5). Close up the eye by tapping lightly round the outside of the eye (fig. 11 (6)). A good eye should be circular and should have its centre over the centre of the shaft.

Horns and Wrench

These are used for scrolls or other gentle curves. The metal is heated and the work is bent as shown in figures 12 and 13.

Twisting

This is a form of decoration often used on square metal, but metal of other sections can be twisted. The type of twist is

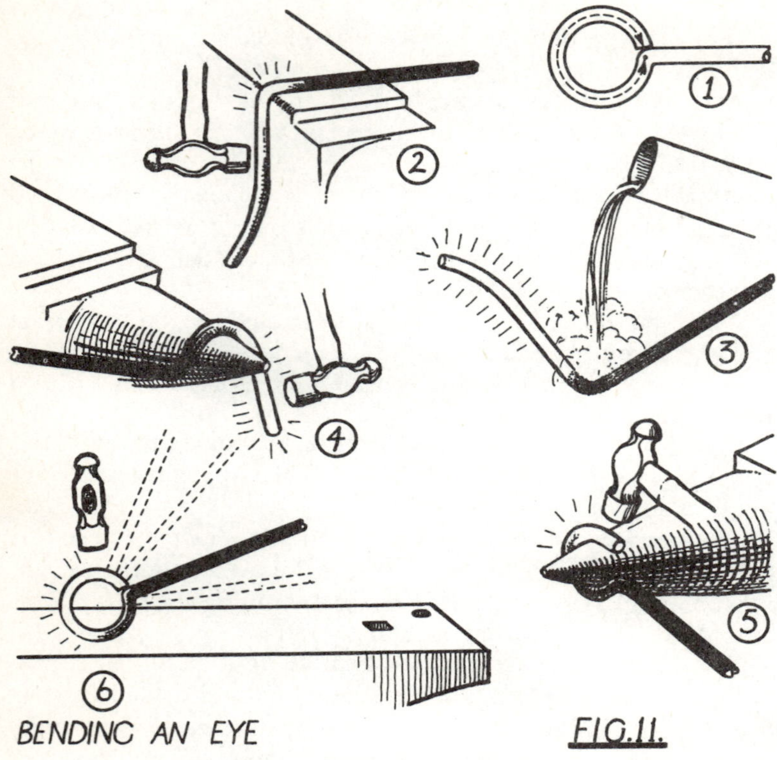

FIG. 11.

influenced by the heating. A good red heat over a long length will give a long gradual twist, but if the bar is heated more intensely over a short length a short sharp twist is produced.

Twisting should be done at one heat because it is difficult to obtain an even twist if the metal has to be returned to the fire. Care must be taken to keep the metal straight. For long bends or double twists a tube can be put over the metal as a sleeve. This must be an easy fit otherwise when the metal is twisted it is difficult to remove. This method is used by beginners. It is not wholly satisfactory because the actual twisting cannot be observed. Another method of obtaining a long even twist is to have an assistant who pours a little water on to those parts that are twisting too quickly. Long twists can also be kept in alignment by using a rest as shown in figure 12A.

Scrolls

These are usually in the form of a "C" or an "S". It is usual to make these by using a scroll tool which should be made after having gained experience in making a scroll by hand. The method of making a scroll by hand is shown in figure 12. First draw the metal down, keeping the width the same over the entire length. Next start the bend as shown.

When the metal needs reheating remember to heat the part which needs bending. Continue to bend the scroll using the close spaced horns as shown. A small scroll often needs a number of heats when being made by a boy.

Scroll Tool

These can be made in the same way as the scroll just mentioned except that they are made from stouter metal—18 mm × 10 mm is a good size. The end is flared on one side only. This is so that the centre of the scroll tool is higher than the rest of the tool to allow the first part of the bend to be made in the scroll as shown in figure 13.

Scrolls made on the scroll tool are started off as in figure 12. Then they are put on the centre of the scroll tool and held with

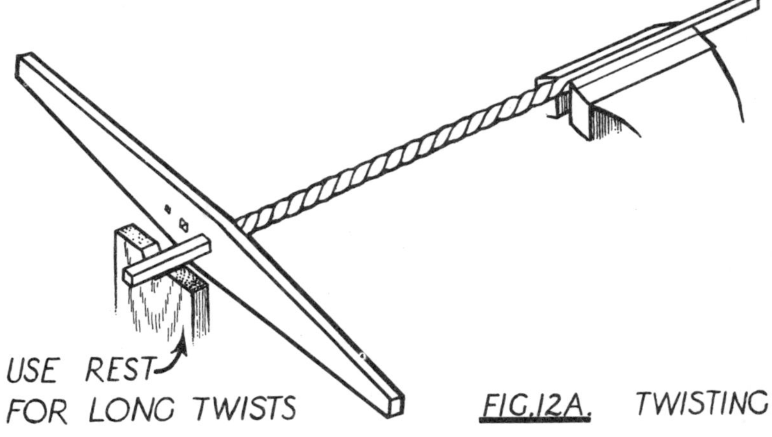

FIG.12A. TWISTING

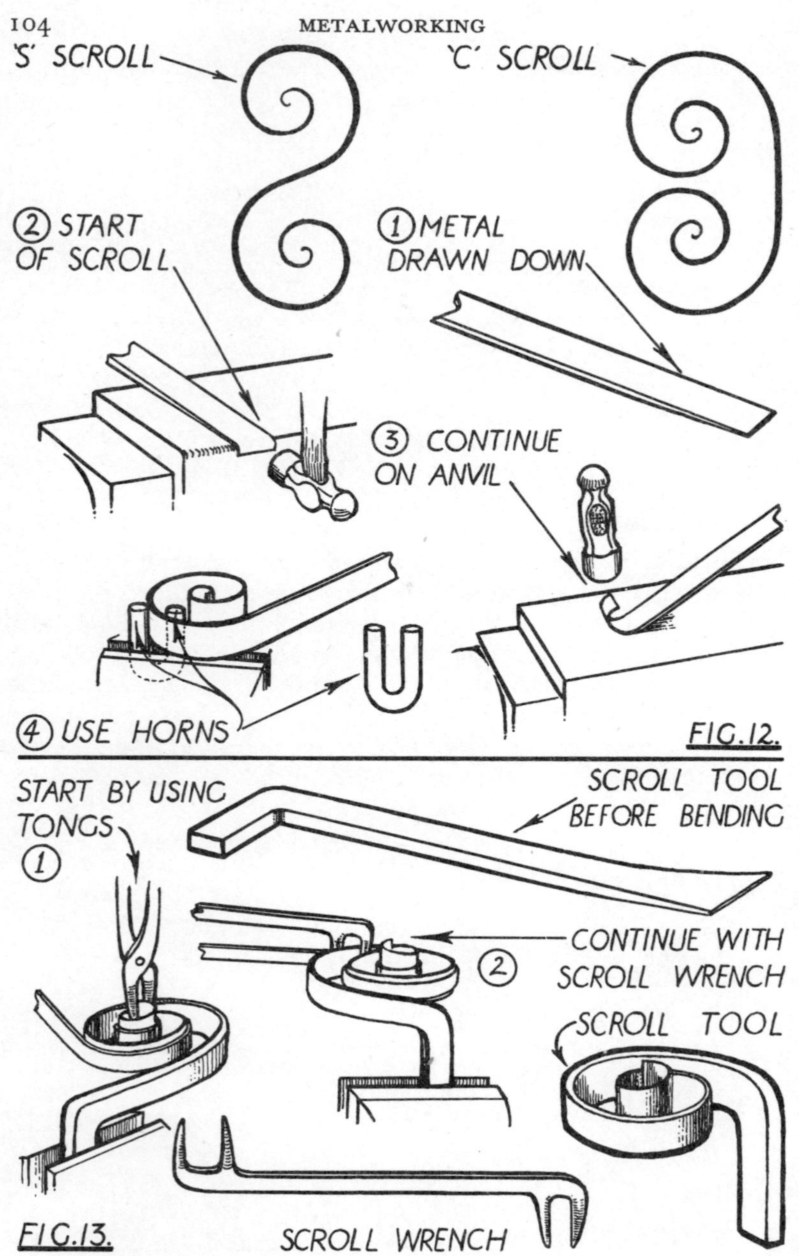
'S' SCROLL
'C' SCROLL
② START OF SCROLL
① METAL DRAWN DOWN
③ CONTINUE ON ANVIL
④ USE HORNS
FIG.12.
START BY USING TONGS ①
SCROLL TOOL BEFORE BENDING
CONTINUE WITH SCROLL WRENCH ②
SCROLL TOOL
FIG.13.
SCROLL WRENCH

round nose pliers and bent round. They are finished by using a wrench (fig. 13). Finally the scroll should be placed on the flat face of the anvil and lightly tapped to make it level.

Upsetting or Jumping Up

This is the reverse of drawing down. A good heat is needed; a slightly higher temperature than that used for simple forging operations. The process is made easier for boys if the end of the metal is prepared as shown in figure 14 before upsetting, particularly on small section metal, as this allows the thrust of the blow to be central. (This applies only to metal to be upset at the end.)

The upsetting can be done by striking the end of the metal on the face of the anvil as at A, or on the side (B), or on a chipping block on the floor (C), or with a hammer on the anvil if the work is short enough (D).

Any bend that occurs must be straightened out at once. The metal must then be reheated and the process continued. It helps if the tip of the bar is quenched before continuing with the upsetting. This allows the thickening to take place away from the very end. If the thickening is required in the middle of the bar then that part must be heated. The metal on either side of the area to be upset can be cooled by water poured from a can.

Swaging

This is usually a process of finishing the cross section of the work to size and shape. Top and bottom swages are usually used as shown in figure 15. For larger work the swage block can be used (fig. 3, p. 96).

Fullering

This process can be used for thinning down the metal by making grooves or hollows across it. This is usually done by using top and bottom fullers as shown in figure 15. If the thinning is required on one side only the top fuller can be used on its own with the work resting on the anvil.

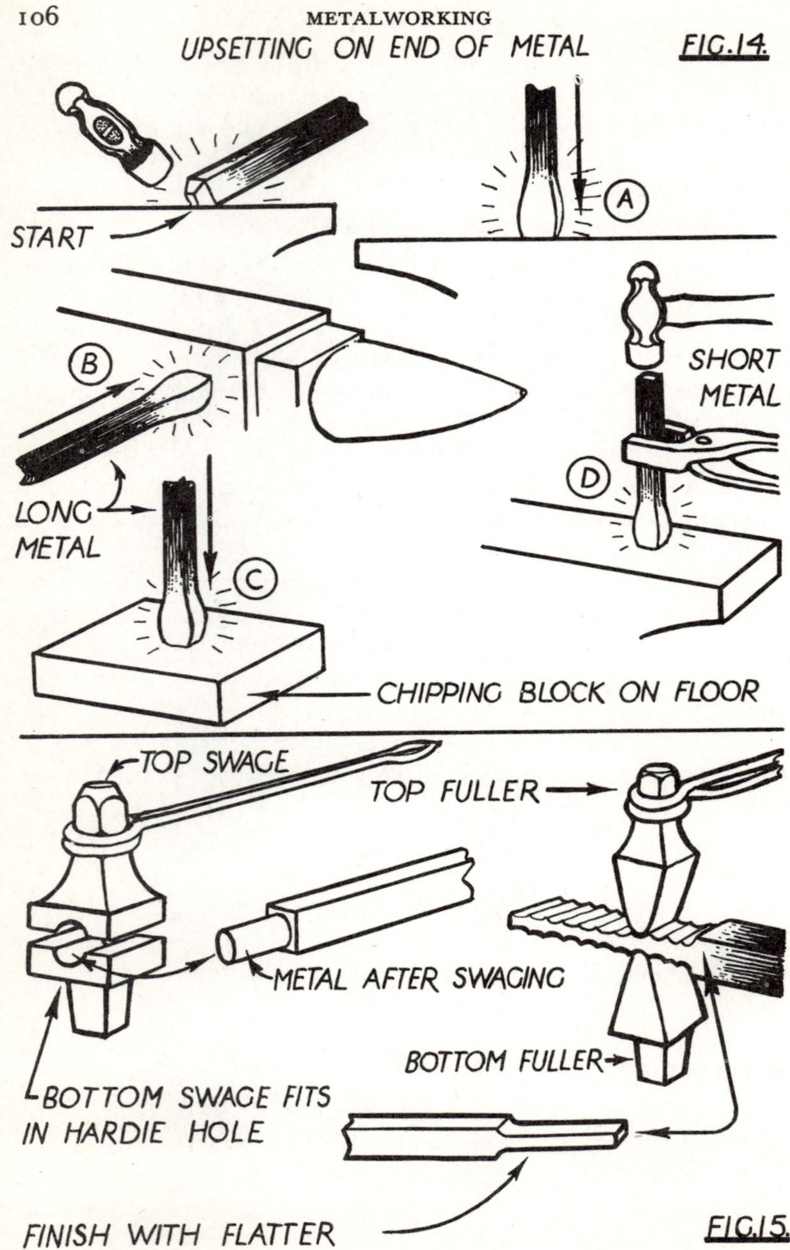
UPSETTING ON END OF METAL
FIG.14.
START
A
B
SHORT
METAL
D
LONG
METAL
C
CHIPPING BLOCK ON FLOOR
TOP SWAGE
TOP FULLER
METAL AFTER SWAGING
BOTTOM FULLER
BOTTOM SWAGE FITS
IN HARDIE HOLE
FINISH WITH FLATTER
FIG.15.

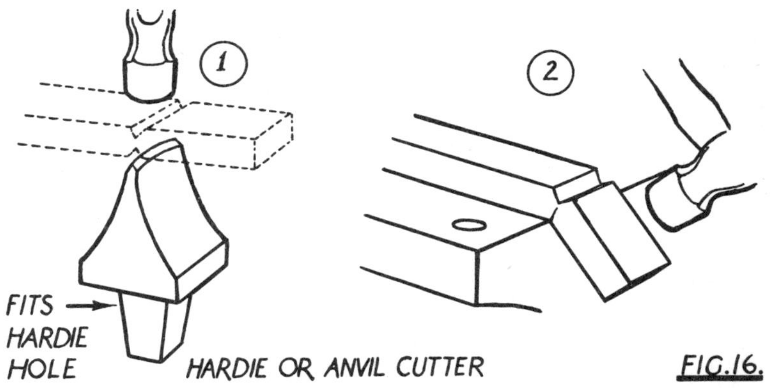
1
2
FITS HARDIE HOLE
HARDIE OR ANVIL CUTTER

FIG.16.

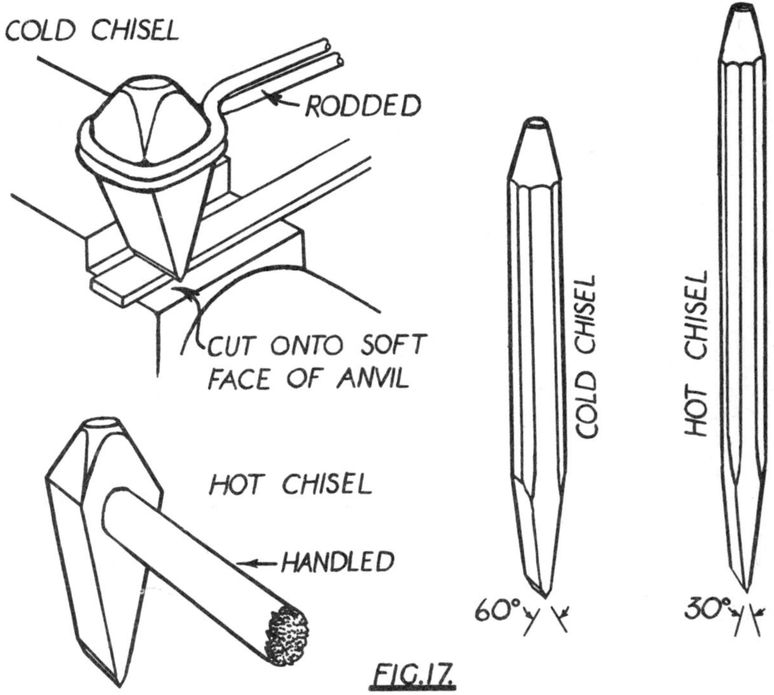
COLD CHISEL
RODDED
CUT ONTO SOFT FACE OF ANVIL
HOT CHISEL
HANDLED
COLD CHISEL
HOT CHISEL
60°
30°

FIG.17.

The Hardie or Anvil Cutter

This is used in the hardie hole. The metal is cut partly through from either side then tapped with the hammer over the edge of the anvil to break it (fig. 16).

Hot Chisel and Cold Chisel

These are known as hot or cold depending on whether they are used to cut hot or cold metal. Hot chisels are not hardened and tempered because the heat from the metal being cut would soften them. They are ground to a cutting edge of 30° and are long enough to keep the hand well away from the hot metal as shown in figure 17. Cold chisels are hardened and tempered and ground to 60°.

For large work the chisels are fitted with either wooden handles or metal rods as shown, and are often known as sets (fig. 17).

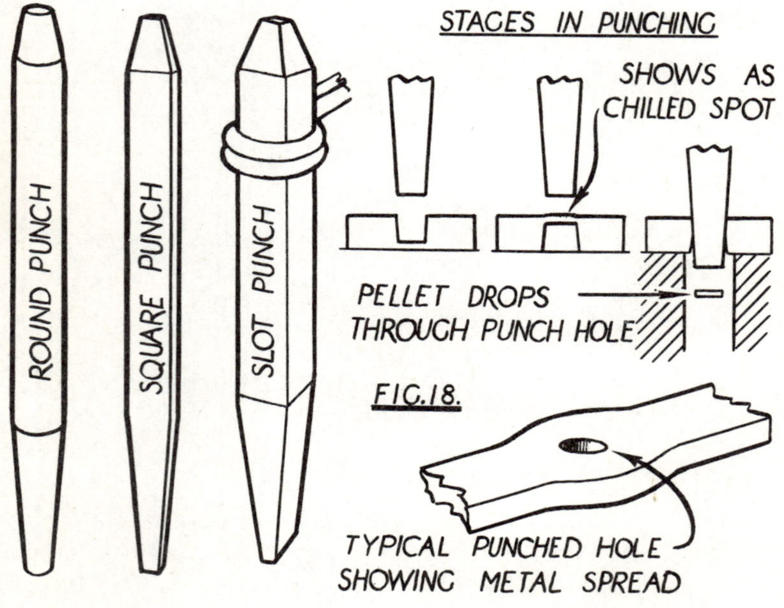

FIG.18.

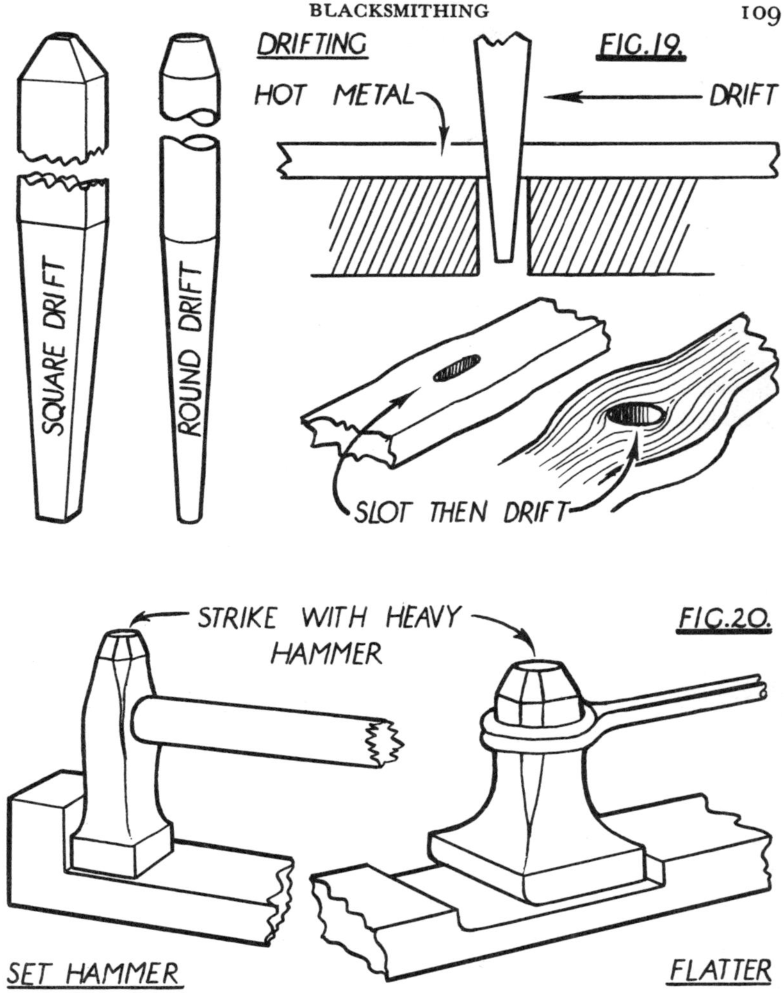

Punches for Hot Work

These can be round or square or any shape. They should be long enough to keep the hand away from the hot metal. Large ones can be rodded. Figure 18 shows a punch being used. The punch is first driven into the metal then removed and quenched. The metal is then turned over and punched from the other side on the chilled spot where the metal has been under pressure against the cold anvil. The billet shown should drop out. Greater strength of the forged metal can be obtained by using first a slot punch then a drift as shown (fig. 19). This is because less metal is removed with a slot punch.

Drifts

These are similar to punches and are used to open up punched holes, smoothing and shaping them at the same time (fig. 19).

Flatters and Set Hammers

These are used to smooth out the work after hammering and to get into sharp or radiused corners (fig. 20).

7

Heat Treatment of Steel

PART ONE

Hardening

We are here dealing with the kind of heat treatment normally done in the school workshop for which we need only use the brazing hearth and torch.

More information regarding the structure of steel is given in Part II. Although this is kept in simple terms it is probably best understood as a subject if done in conjunction with the science laboratory where there are suitable microscopes and possibly some testing equipment.

For hundreds of years such small tools as chisels, punches, knives, shears etc, have been hardened and tempered by metalworkers using similar methods to those mentioned here.

Many special alloy steels are available but these have to be treated as advised by the manufacturers. We are considering only plain carbon steel.

Steels may be roughly classified as follows:
Mild Steels 0·1—0·33% carbon. Medium carbon steels 0·34—0·60% carbon. High carbon steels 0·60—0·90%C and tool steels 0·90%—1·3% carbon.

For small tools we use steel with a carbon content of between 0·8—1·3% carbon. Files fall into this category and for this reason small tools are often made from old files.

If we heat a piece of carbon steel with the brazing torch until it is red hot and then plunge it quickly into cold water we find that it has become "dead" hard. This can be tested with the heel of a file, i.e. the part of the teeth nearest the handle, so as not to spoil the working part of the file.

The primary problem in hardening is judging the correct temperature at which to plunge the steel into water. This temperature is commonly known as "cherry red" and it is best judged in a shady corner away from direct sunlight or bright electric light.

If the steel to be hardened is heated with the torch the temperature will rise slowly until it reaches "cherry red" but then although the torch is kept on the steel it will cease to rise in temperature for a few seconds. This is known as the change point; the heat from the torch on the steel is now latent, that is "hidden", because it is used to bring about changes in the structure of the steel. This taking in of heat is called decalescence (see fig. 1), and it occurs between 700°C and 900°C approximately, depending on the carbon content.

It is at this temperature that we plunge the steel into the water and in so doing we arrest it in its changed state.

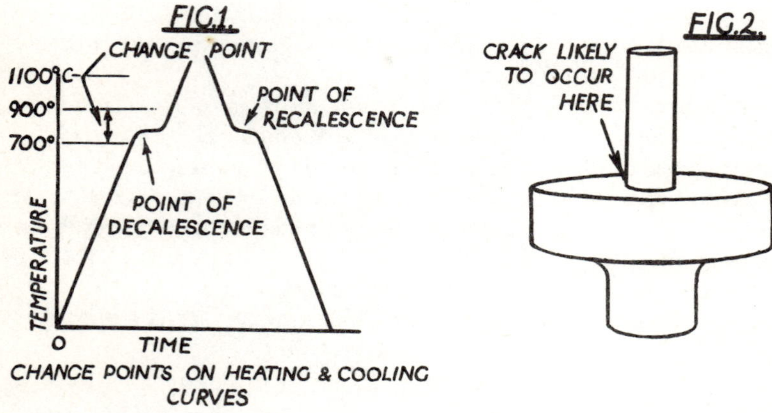

A way of showing this change at red heat is to heat the metal well above "cherry red" and then allow it to cool slowly in a darkened corner of a room. As the temperature slowly drops to the change point it will be seen to glow suddenly. This is caused by the latent heat being given out. This is called recalescence (fig. 1). However, this is only for demonstration purposes and it must not be used as a method for arriving at the temperature at which to quench the steel. The best results are obtained if the steel is slowly brought up to the change point and then plunged; that is, it is best plunged on a rising temperature.

The hot metal is usually plunged into clean water which is at room temperature. It is essential that the quenchant (the liquid in which the hot metal is quenched) takes the heat away quickly in order to arrest the steel in its changed state. If the cooling needs to be more drastic, cooking salt can be added to the water to make it into a saturated solution. This is best judged by adding the salt to the water until a slice of potato will float in it. This, however, increases the possibility of cracking. Cracks might occur even when using clean water. If this is happening it is often because the steel is being overheated, but it might be because the quenchant is taking the heat from the steel too rapidly.

If soap is added to clean water it will make it less severe as a quenchant. An even less drastic quenching medium is high flash paraffin and a slower one still is mineral oil.

It will also be noticed that cracks occur on steel where there are deep scratches or small grooves such as those left by a turning tool. To avoid this it is best to remove the rough surface and polish the steel before hardening.

Be careful when quenching long thin tools such as chisels, gravers or knife blades, that they are plunged into the liquid vertically and that they are moved up and down, not from side to side, otherwise distortion might take place. If they are plunged horizontally the side entering the water first will contract first, thus causing the steel to be badly distorted. It is good practice to stir the liquid vigorously just before plunging any piece of steel as this helps the liquid to conduct the heat quickly and evenly.

As previously mentioned cracks occur in steel, particularly large pieces, if they have been taken to a temperature too far above the change point and then quenched. This is owing to the fact that when steel reaches the change point it is also at its state of least density. In other words, when it is at this temperature of change it has expanded to its maximum.* If it is quenched

* To be precise, further expansion does actually take place at higher temperatures.

above this temperature it undergoes cooling contraction, the skin becoming hard and rigid. The inner portion has not yet felt the quenching effect and is still red hot. An instant later the quenching effect is transferred to this portion, which as it passes through the change point must expand, thus causing cracks on the outside.

For this reason large tools or tools which have a drastic change of section (fig. 2) should be heated to a temperature just approaching "cherry red" and, depending on the carbon content, dipped in oil or high flash paraffin.

Completely hardened steel is usually too hard and brittle for normal use and so we have to reduce the hardness by a secondary process known as tempering.

Tempering

Tempering reduces the hardness of the steel and increases the toughness, i.e. the capacity to withstand shock. The degree of toughness required is determined by the kind of job the tool has to do. Tools for turning brass, scrapers and engraving tools have to be much harder than repousse punches and these in turn must be harder than a screw driver which is just soft enough to be filed and yet tough enough not to be deformed when a twisting force is applied.

To temper a piece of hardened steel, polish the hardened portion with clean dry emery cloth (avoid using oil as this leaves a thin film) and let a small flame play on the metal a short distance from the part to be tempered (fig. 3A). Soon you will see the bright metal near the flame turn light yellow and then straw to middle-straw and then light brown to dark red brown to purple and then to blue. As the heat is conducted along the metal these colours which are in fact oxides will move along in bands. The lightest colour will be the one furthest from the source of heat. When the right colour has reached the part to be tempered, the steel is quenched in clean water. The lighter the colour (best seen in daylight) at which the steel is quenched, the harder the metal will be.

TEMPERING CHART

	°C	
Light blue	315	Too soft for cutting edges.
Blue	300	Springs, saws for wood, screwdrivers.
	290	Carving knives, fine saws, saws for bone and ivory.
	285	Needles, gimlets, axes, adzes, augers.
Purple	270	Flat drills for brass, cold chisels for light work, wood borers.
Dark straw or red brown	260	Wood chisels, plane irons, stone cutting tools, axes.
	250	Flat drills, reamers, taps, screwing dies, shears, punches, chasers.
Middle straw	240	Pen-knives, circular cutters for metal, boring cutters.
	235	Milling cutters, lathe tools, wood engraving tools.
Pale straw	230	Surgical instruments, razors, hammer faces, ivory cutting tools.
Pale yellow	220	Steel engraving tools, scrapers, light turning tools.

If a uniform temper is required along the whole length of the steel it can be held in light tongs in a tube which is heated on the outside (fig. 3B) or held over a heated plate (fig. 3C).

Beginners often have failures with tempering because they misjudge the colour at which to quench. It must be remembered that if in tempering, the steel is heated beyond the proper colour the whole process of hardening and tempering must be repeated. If, however, after quenching the temper colour is not dark enough it will do no harm to re-polish the tool and re-temper until the darker colour is reached then quench.

One Heat Hardening and Tempering

This is the method often used by blacksmiths usually on the end or point of tools.

The steel is heated at one end to cherry red and the tip only is quenched. It is moved up and down slightly to reduce the possibility of cracking at the water line. Then it is taken from

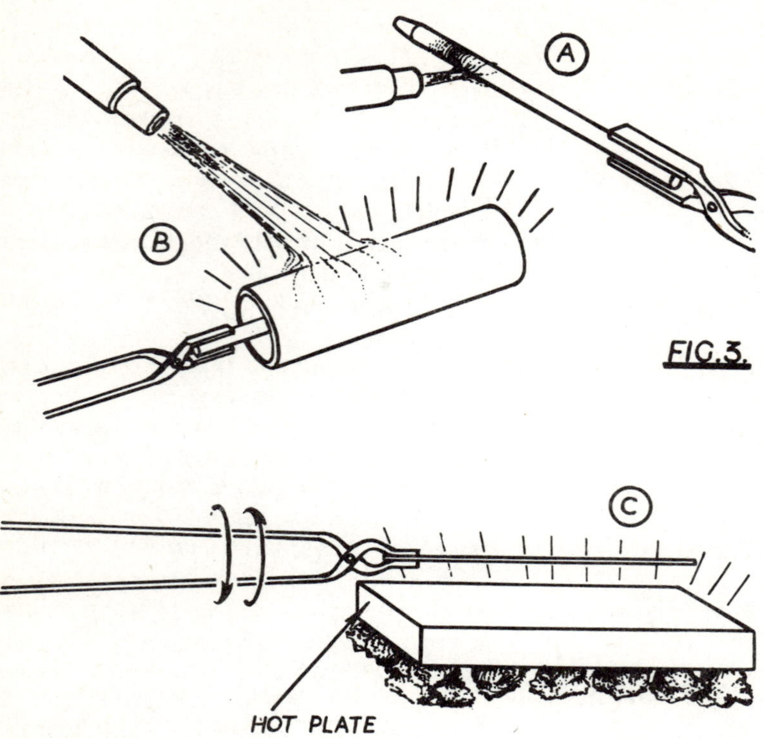

the water and the end is briskly rubbed with an old piece of carborundum stone or something similar so a portion of the tip is bright. After a few moments the heat from the unquenched part is conducted to the tip thus showing the usual bands of colour. When the correct colour reaches the tip it is completely quenched.

Case Hardening

This is a method of hardening mild steel by adding carbon to the "skin" or "case" of the steel and then quenching it as if it were a high carbon steel.

The work to be case hardened is put in a shallow steel tray or shallow open box and a powder rich in carbon (usually "kasenit", which is a proprietary brand) is sprinkled on top to cover the work. With a brazing torch the work is made red hot. This causes the carbon to be absorbed by the steel. The longer the work is kept at cherry red the deeper the carbon will go. It should be kept at cherry red in the kasenit for at least 15 minutes and then quickly removed and quenched in clean water. Beware of the loud "bang" it makes. If tested with the heel of a file it will be found to be hard. Usually, in school, because of the time factor it is not possible to make the hard case any more than about 0·2 mm deep.

Case hardening is excellent for such things as spanners where a hard surface and a tough core are essential.

Softening Steel

To make steel as soft as possible it must be heated to just above the change point and then quickly buried 150-200 mm deep in slaked lime or vermiculite which should first be heated. Slaked lime and vermiculite are very poor conductors of heat and they allow the steel to lose its heat very slowly, thus allowing the change to the soft state to be gradual. This process is known as annealing.

The easier workshop method which makes the steel soft though not quite as soft as by annealing is done without slaked lime or vermiculite. The steel is heated to the change point and it is left to cool on the edge of the hearth or on a fire brick. This is known as normalising.

The purpose of both of these processes is usually to make a hard piece of steel soft enough for it to be machined, filed, sawn, bent or twisted.

Softening relieves the internal stresses. Any tool which has to be re-hardened should first be softened to relieve the stresses set up by the first hardening. This helps to prevent cracking.

PART TWO

We have mentioned the workshop methods in Part 1. In this section we are looking a little deeper into the heat treatment processes and the structure of steel.

Steel is basically an alloy of carbon in iron, although other elements may be present either in residual amounts or as intentional additions to give specific properties.

Carbon in Steel

Carbon forms a chemical compound with iron of the formula Fe_3C (containing 6·68% C) which is known as cementite and may appear in steel either individually as the compound or intimately mixed with virtually pure iron to form pearlite. The latter contains 13% of cementite and 87% of the nearly pure iron called ferrite. Under a microscope pearlite is seen to consist of thin plates of ferrite interleaved with thin plates of cementite. Pearlite is so named because under certain conditions it has a pearl-like lustre.

Iron

Iron (Fe) may exist in different physical forms, even though its chemical properties do not alter. This characteristic is known as allotropy, and is common to other elements, such as sulphur.

Metallurgists name the different forms of iron after Greek letters, i.e. alpha α, beta β, gamma γ, and delta δ.

Iron in the cold state is known as α iron and it remains so up to 768°C when it changes to β iron, where only a magnet change takes place. At 910°C it transforms to γ and then at 1400°C to δ.

These are changes in the arrangement of the atoms, but the important change so far as the hardening of steel is concerned, is the change from γ, known as austenite, on cooling below 723°C.

The change from α to β occurs at 768°C and above this temperature the iron is non-magnetic.

The change to γ iron at 910°C on heating is accompanied by a marked contraction.

The austenitic (γ) form of iron *can* hold carbon in solid solution up to approximately 2%, whilst ferrite (α) can retain only about 0·002%.

In steel the existence of carbon up to a maximum content of 0·87%* dissolved in γ iron is able to depress the temperature at which the change from γ to α occurs and the resulting precipitation of cementite commences. Beyond this critical content however, the change temperature rises again. This can be seen more clearly if we plot the level of change-point temperatures against

* This figure varies with the purity of the iron.

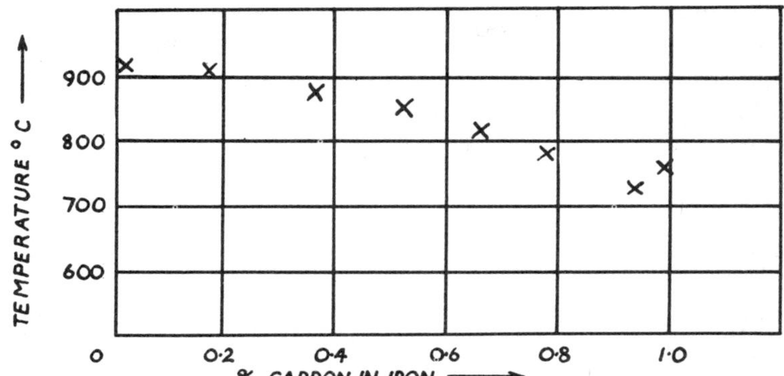

HOW THE START OF THE γ–α CHANGE TEMPERATURE IS DEPRESSED BY INCREASING CARBON CONTENT FIG.4.

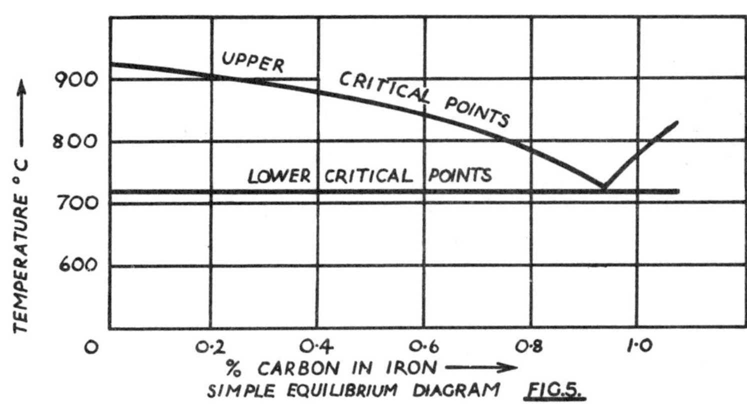

SIMPLE EQUILIBRIUM DIAGRAM FIG.5.

carbon content in steel as shown in figure 4. This diagram shows that as the carbon content increases to 0·87% so the temperature of change drops from 910°C to 723°C. Above the 0·87% carbon content, however, the temperature at which the change begins starts to rise again.

Figure 5 is a similar diagram to figure 4, but the individual points have been joined and the line so formed is labelled the "upper critical line". A horizontal line is also drawn through the minimum transition temperature reached and this is called the "lower critical line". Thus we have a simple version of what is known as an "equilibrium diagram".

From figure 5 we can see:

1. At all temperatures and carbon contents above the upper critical points the carbon is held in γ iron in solid solution, a form of alloy known to metallurgists as austenite.

2. The minimum possible transformation temperature occurs with 0·87%C, the change from γ to α iron throws all the carbon out of solution at once to form pearlite.

3. The change from γ to α iron takes place over a wider range of temperature as the carbon content is reduced below 0·87%. This range is indicated as the difference between the upper and lower critical points. The first constituent to appear is ferrite and this goes on appearing until the carbon content of the remaining γ iron has been enriched to 0·87%C, then this changes at once to pearlite.

4. At carbon contents above 0·87%C the change also takes place over a range of temperature, but this time the first constituent to appear is cementite, the compound of iron and carbon of the formula Fe_3C. This goes on forming until the carbon content of the remaining austenite is reduced to 0·87% at which time the remainder changes to pearlite.

Now we can complete our simple equilibrium diagram as shown in figure 6.

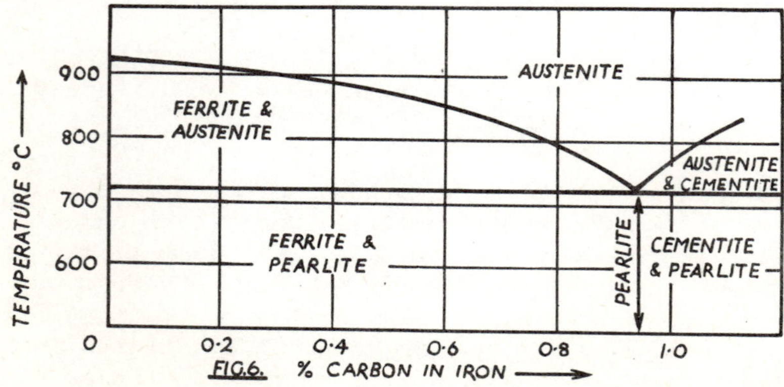

FIG.6.

Carbon Content and its Effect on Hardness, Toughness and Ductility

Ferrite is almost pure iron. It is soft and ductile. Steel containing a lot of ferrite will have a low tensile strength and will be tough and ductile.

Pearlite is a hard material mainly because of its intricate laminated structure of thin plates of ferrite and the extremely hard plates of cementite. As the carbon content increases up to 0·87% so does the hardness of the metal as a whole, but the toughness and ductility decrease.

Cementite. It is very hard and brittle. Steels containing more than 0·87% carbon have free cementite at the crystal boundaries. This causes extreme hardness in the metal as a whole and care must be taken with the heat treatment. It is used where great hardness is required, such as in ball-bearings, ball races and tools.

The Crystalline Structure of Steel

The crystal structure of steel can be seen under a microscope but the metal must first be prepared. The piece to be examined is first ground flat. Then it is polished with successively finer grades of emery paper and finished on soft cloth impregnated with alumina powder or diamond paste. The polished surface is then etched with dilute acid which attacks the different constituent parts differentially, thus revealing the crystalline structure. The four diagrams shown give an idea of the appearance of steels when seen through a microscope, but of course, no two pieces ever look exactly alike.

1. Ferrite or pure iron is as shown in figure 7.
2. Steel containing less than 0·87% carbon, figure 8.
3. Steel containing 0·87% carbon (eutectoid steel), figure 9.
4. Steel containing more than 0·87% carbon, figure 10.

Rate of Cooling and its Influence on Structure

Annealing. Annealing as previously mentioned is done to produce the maximum softness in metal. A piece of say 0·5% carbon steel is heated to just above the upper critical tempera-

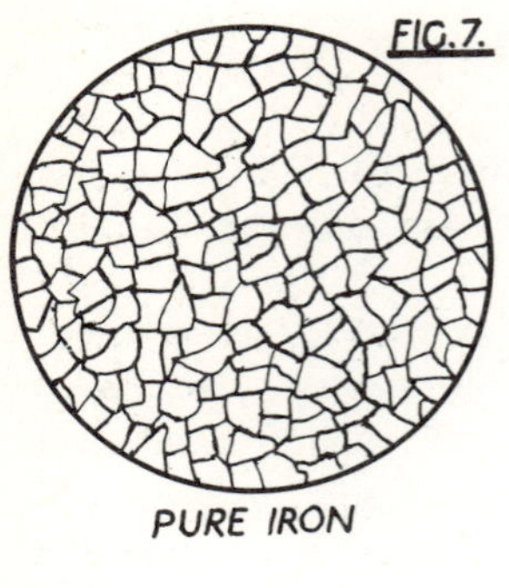

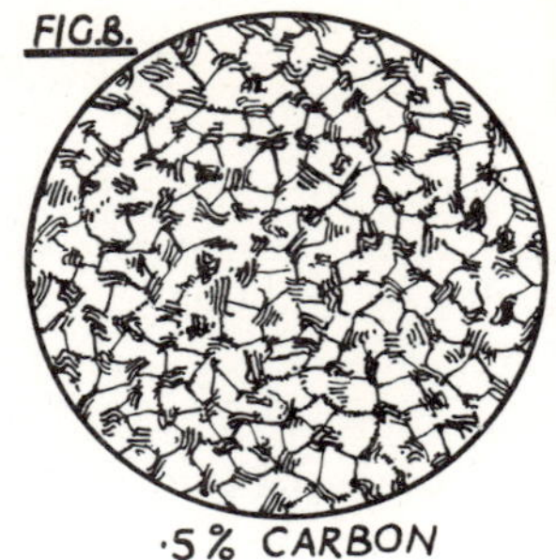

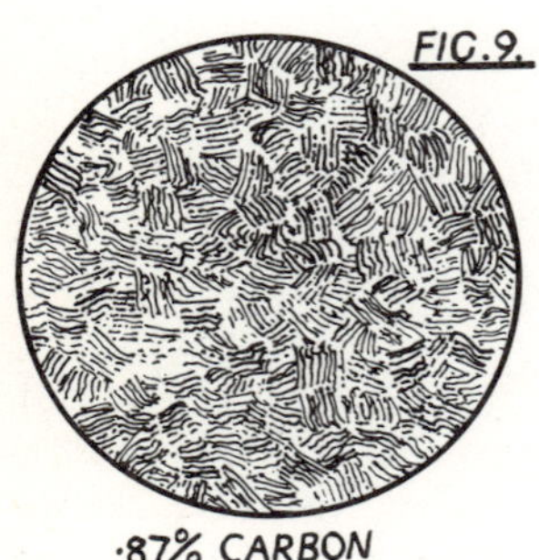

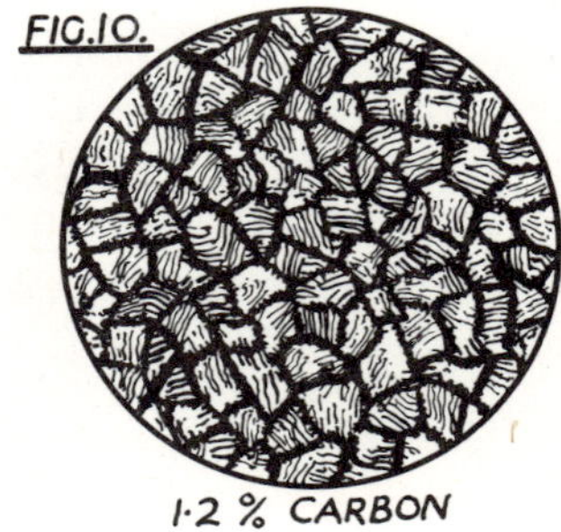

ture and then allowed to cool very slowly in the furnace, i.e. the furnace is switched off and the metal cools at the same slow rate as the furnace.

As the temperature falls ferrite is precipitated first forming new crystals of this nearly carbon-free constituent around the original austenite crystal boundaries. As more ferrite comes out it will form a series of large new crystals. At the same time the remaining austenite will be enriched in carbon until it contains 0·87% carbon. When the temperature drops through the lower critical point the remaining austenite will change at once to pearlite (fig. 11).

In annealing the slow cooling ensures that the carbon is allowed time to diffuse into the austenite as the ferrite appears along the crystal boundaries. This gives annealed steel a comparatively coarse crystal structure.

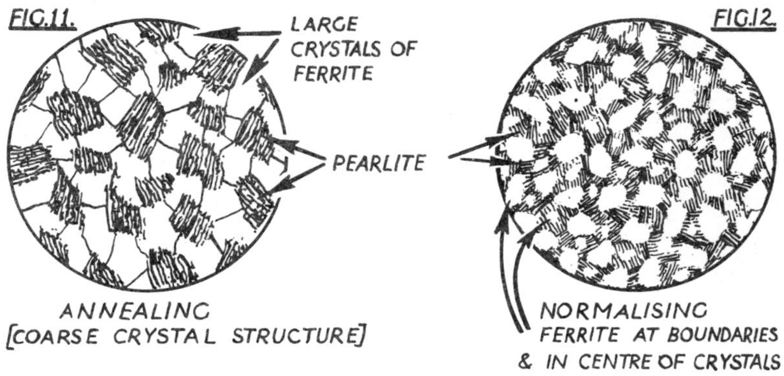

Normalising. Normalising is similar to annealing except that the rate of cooling is faster, the metal being allowed to cool in still air. Draughts may cause it to cool too quickly.

The metal is heated in the same way as for annealing, but because the cooling is quicker the carbon does not have time to diffuse so easily through the metal and small crystals of ferrite appear both round the crystal boundaries *and* in the centres of the original crystals as in figure 12. Normalised steel has a finer crystal structure than annealed steel and is slightly harder.

Low carbon steels from which boiler plate and some girders are made are usually normalised.

Quenching. When steel is quenched the cooling is so rapid that carbon does not have time to diffuse through the mass. Instead the metal is "frozen" and the carbon is prevented from precipitating as iron carbide (cementite) below 723°C and will remain in super-saturation until the temperature drops to a value where an instantaneous transformation will take place to form a product known to metallurgists as martensite. This product has a characteristic needle-like structure (fig. 13) which is extremely hard and brittle due to distortion of the ferrite crystal lattice by carbon. This brittleness must be reduced before the steel can be successfully used in service and therefore it is usual to follow the quenching by a tempering treatment.

Tempering. Tempering allows some of the carbon to redistribute itself as iron carbide and this reduces the stresses in the steel.

Only a relatively low temperature is required (up to 650°C) to permit this redistribution to take place, producing a structure of iron carbide finely dispersed in ferrite, in the past known as sorbite, but now more correctly known as tempered martensite. This tempered steel is less hard but much tougher (fig. 14).

Case Hardening. In Part 1 we mentioned case hardening mild steel using "kasenit". A piece of mild steel after being heated to just above the critical range for about one hour in "kasenit" and allowed to cool slowly would appear as in figure 15.

MARTENSITE [QUENCHED]

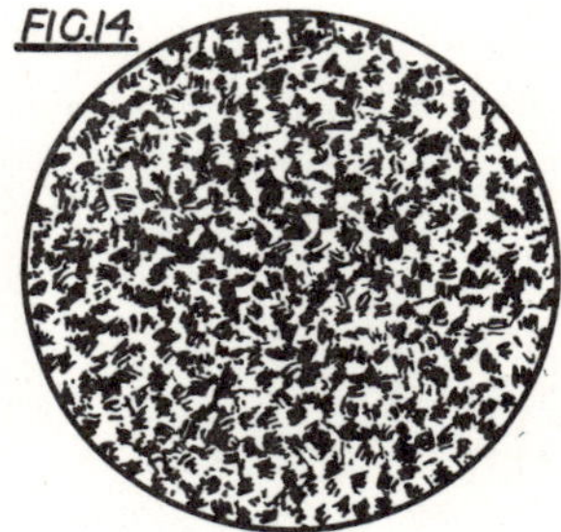

SORBITE [TEMPERED STEEL]

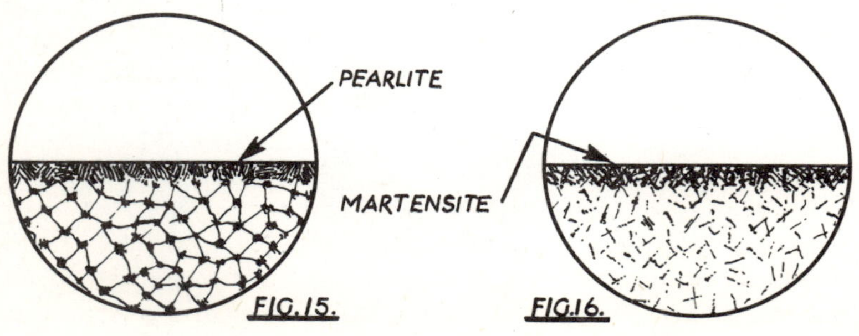

Notice that the body of the mild steel contains a very small amount of carbon, but not enough to affect the hardness.

If the same steel is rapidly cooled from just above the critical temperature by plunging it in water, the outside or case would become martensitic but the core, not containing enough carbon, would be soft. It would appear as in figure 16.

Low carbon steels can be case hardened to great advantage. Because the case contains more carbon than, the core the upper critical point of the case is lower than that of the core. The steel is quenched from the high carburising temperature thus making both the core and the case martensitic. Next it is re-heated to a temperature which will just turn the case (higher carbon content) austenitic but only hot enough to temper the core (lower carbon content). When quenched from this temperature the case will be martensitic and therefore hard and the core sorbitic and therefore tough.

There are various other methods of case hardening such as: sorbitising. This is not unlike the blacksmith's "one heat" hardening and tempering mentioned in Part 1. The red hot steel is taken from the rolling mill and the surface sprayed with water thus making it martensitic. The heat from the interior of the steel as it slowly cools then turns the martensite into sorbite thus giving a tough outside and a less hard centre.

For further reading see list of books at back.

HEAT TREATMENT OF NON-FERROUS METALS

In the school workshop we use copper, brass, gilding metal, aluminium, aluminium alloys and, less often, zinc and nickel silver.

All the above mentioned metals work harden, i.e. the crystal structure becomes distorted with bending and hammering. They can be softened in the brazing hearth using the torch for heating.

Copper. To soften heat to dull red and either allow to cool in air or quench in water. Quenching in dilute sulphuric acid will soften and clean the surface (see Chapter 9).

Brass. Soften by heating to dull red and allowing to cool in air. Quenching can cause some brass to crack.

Gilding Metal. Soften as copper.

Aluminium. Soften by heating and quenching in water, but take care not to overheat. The temperature can be judged by rubbing a piece of wood on the surface of the metal. When the wood leaves a black charred streak the aluminium is hot enough to plunge into cold water. This will make it quite soft. The correct heat can also be judged by rubbing streaks of soap on the cold metal. Heat until the soap turns brown and then quench. Another method is to put oil on the surface. Heat until the oil burns, then quench. In schools the first method has been found to be the most reliable.

Aluminium Alloys. Soften as aluminium.

Zinc. This can be made workable by placing in boiling water.

Nickel Silver. Soften as brass. Never quench.

8

Sheet Metalwork

This work includes, apart from tinplate, the use of sheet aluminium, brass, copper and galvanised iron, also sheet steel and terne plate. Industrially these metals are formed into useful articles by machines which can stamp, bend and form the sheet metal as required. In school we use hand processes usually on tinplate. Sometimes terne plate is used and more rarely galvanised iron.

Galvanised iron is in fact galvanised steel and is mostly used out of doors because of its rust-resisting property. It is mild steel coated with zinc. Terne plate is sheet mild steel coated with an alloy of lead and tin. Tin plate is sheet mild steel coated with tin. It varies in thickness between 0·254 mm and 0·52 mm. We often refer to the thickness of tin plate in decimals, but tin plate manufacturers have their own method of indicating the thickness (see metricated version of B.S. 2920).

SETTING OUT

Before a tinplate article is bent or formed into shape, the tinplate must be cut to the correct size and shape. This shape, before it is formed, is known as the development.

Simple developments can be drawn directly on to the tin plate with a hard pencil or copper scriber. The lines to be cut, or parts to be hidden by a joint, can be scribed. It is important not to mark with a scriber any part of the job which will be exposed, because this allows rust to form where the mild steel has been exposed. Care should also be taken to prevent the surface of the tin from being scratched: for this reason it is

JOINTS

LAP JOINT

FLUSH LAP

GROOVED SEAM JOINT

CORNER LAP JOINT

FIG. 1.

EDGES

WIRED EDGE

BETWEEN 3 & 6 M/M

$2\frac{1}{2}$ TO 3 TIMES DIAM. OF WIRE

BEADED EDGE

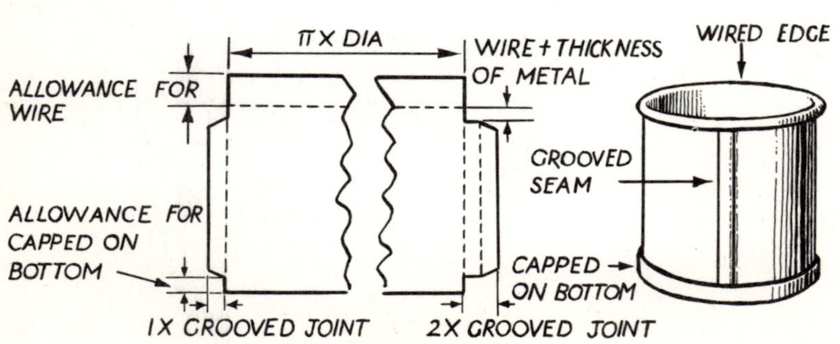

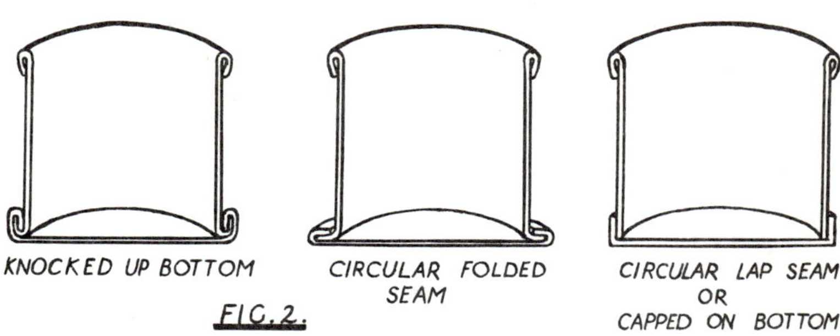

FIG. 2.

advisable to put newspaper on the bench on which to lay the tin plate.

Complicated developments are often drawn on paper and carefully cut out. By this means it is possible to see how the finished article will look and also to check the dimensions. With care this paper development can be used as a template, i.e. it can be laid on to the tinplate and drawn round with a sharp pencil or copper scriber. The parts to be cut must be carefully checked with a rule and then scribed. Another method is to stick the pattern on to the tinplate.

Allowances must be made for joints and seams. Figure 1 shows the allowances for joints and seams, also for the beaded edge and wired edge. Figure 2 shows the allowances for a circular lap seam, a circular folded seam and a knocked up bottom.

TOOLS (FIG. 3)

Bench Shears. There is usually one bench shearing machine bolted to a bench in each metalworkshop. The blade is curved so that it presents the same cutting angle in all positions. Any size sheet can be cut and there is a hole at the side of the blade into which a rod can be inserted for shearing. The fixed blade can be adjusted and locked in position by the screws provided.

Snips. Two kinds are shown: the universal snips can cut inside and outside curves and straight lines. The straight snips are to cut straight lines or outside curves. Curved snips are also available. These are for cutting inside curves.

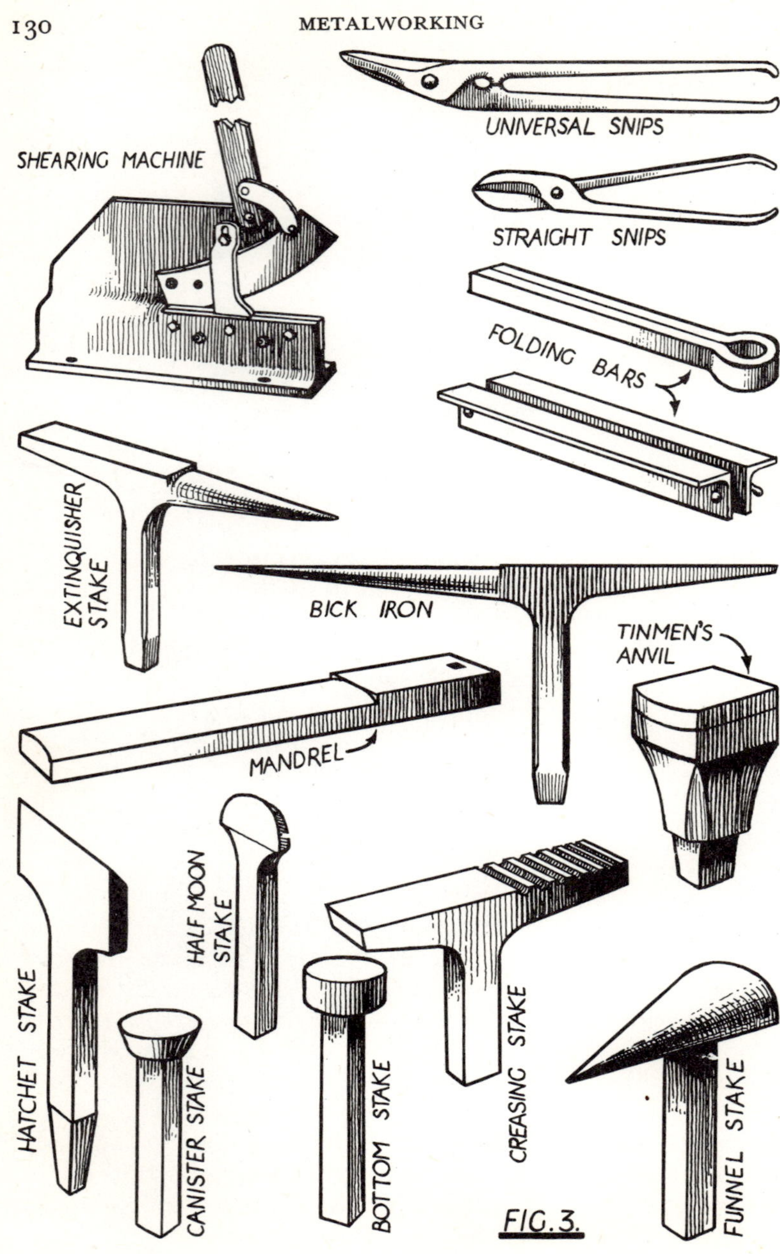
UNIVERSAL SNIPS
SHEARING MACHINE
STRAIGHT SNIPS
FOLDING BARS
EXTINQUISHER STAKE
BICK IRON
TINMEN'S ANVIL
MANDREL
HALF MOON STAKE
HATCHET STAKE
CANISTER STAKE
BOTTOM STAKE
CREASING STAKE
FUNNEL STAKE

FIG. 3.

Folding Bars. These are for bending and folding. The sheet metal is inserted up to the line where the bend is required and then the folding bar is gripped in the vice. The work is now firmly held and can be bent over using a mallet, or a piece of wood can be held against the sheet and this tapped with a hammer.

Extinguisher Stake and Bick Iron. These are useful for making conical work. The flat top and the square end are often used for box making.

The Mandrel. This is about four feet long. It is made of cast iron and has a rounded top at one end and a flat top at the other. There is a square hole at the flat end in which small stakes can be held. Sheet metal workers often use the mandrel on large work.

Tinmen's Anvil. The top surface is flat and one edge is curved. It can be held in a special socket or in the hardie hole of a large anvil.

Hatchet Stake. Used for bending straight edges beyond a right angle.

Half Moon Stake. Used for bending curved edges.

Canister Stake. Used on the bottom of a canister for "getting in" to the corners as in making a knocked up bottom.

Bottom Stake. Similar in use to the canister stake but the sides can be used for truing up the side of a canister.

Creasing Stake. The grooves are used for finishing off wired edges and other similar operations. The square end is usually cut back slightly so that it can get into the corner of a box.

Funnel Stake. Used for large conical work such as funnels which were once made by hand by tin-smiths.

Mallets (fig. 4). These are used on tinplate to avoid damaging the surface. The tinman's mallet has a head of boxwood or lignum vitae and a handle of cane. The bossing mallet, used for hollowing, also has a boxwood or lignum vitae head and a cane handle. The rawhide mallet has a hickory handle.

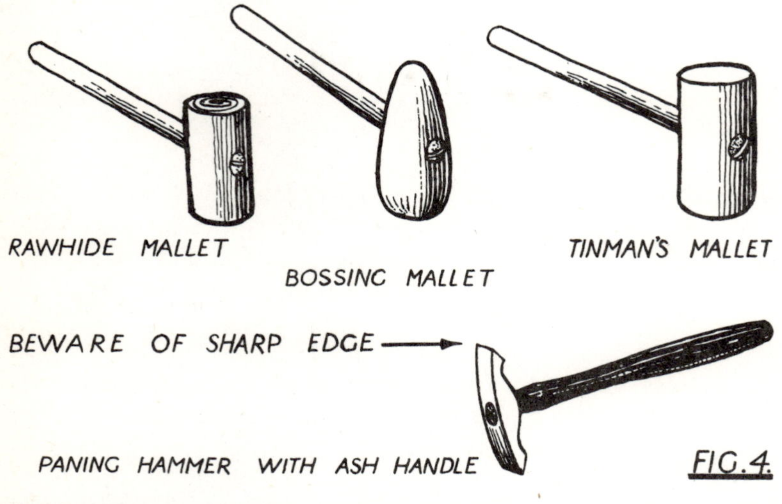

FIG.4.

Paning Hammer. Sometimes used for tucking in joints and wired edges. Care must be exercised in its use because it can easily damage the surface of the metal.

METHOD OF MAKING JOINTS

Flush Lap Joint. First make a lap joint then solder the joint. Now set the joint down on to a flat surface using a piece of hardwood and hammer as shown in figure 5.

Corner Lap Joint. Bend lap using folding bars and mallet as shown in figure 6 then solder.

Grooved Seam Joint. The size for this is usually stated on the drawing. For school work it is normally between 3 mm and 7 mm inclusive. The allowance for this joint is twice the joint size

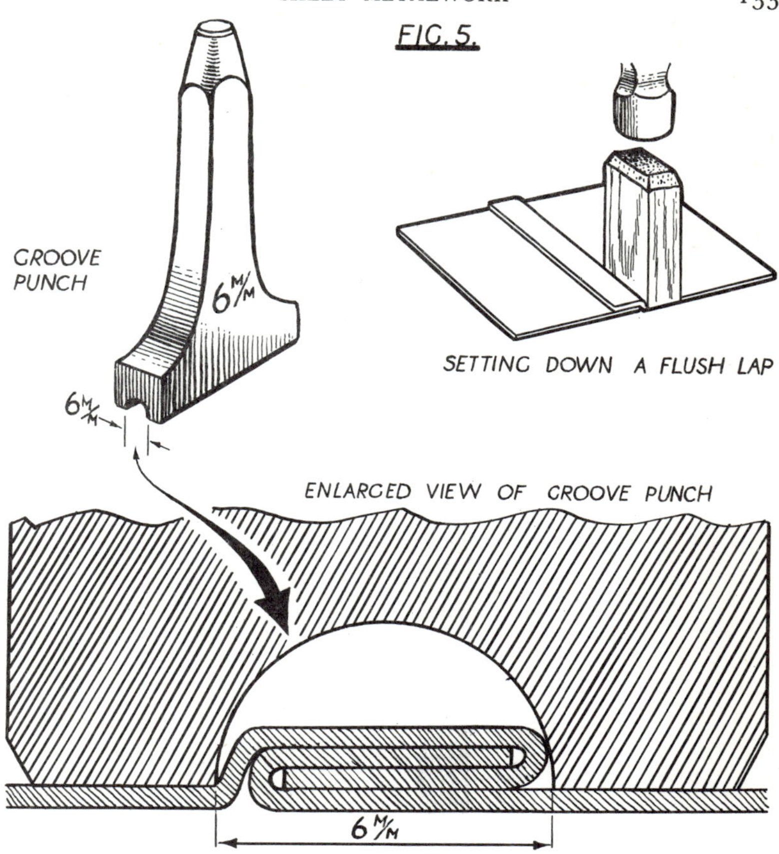

on one side and only once on the other (fig. 1). However, to allow the grooving tool (fig. 5) to fit over the joint, slightly less than the width of the joint must be bent over. Figure 5 shows this clearly. A reliable way to find out exactly how much to bend over for a particular thickness of metal is to make a trial joint using two small pieces of the same metal (see fig. 7 (1), (2), (3), (4), (5)). The grooving tool is offered up as shown in figure 8 and then set down using a hammer on the grooving tool. Finish off the joint by tapping down with a mallet along the top of the joint as in figure 9. For a good joint it is important that the bend in both pieces is parallel.

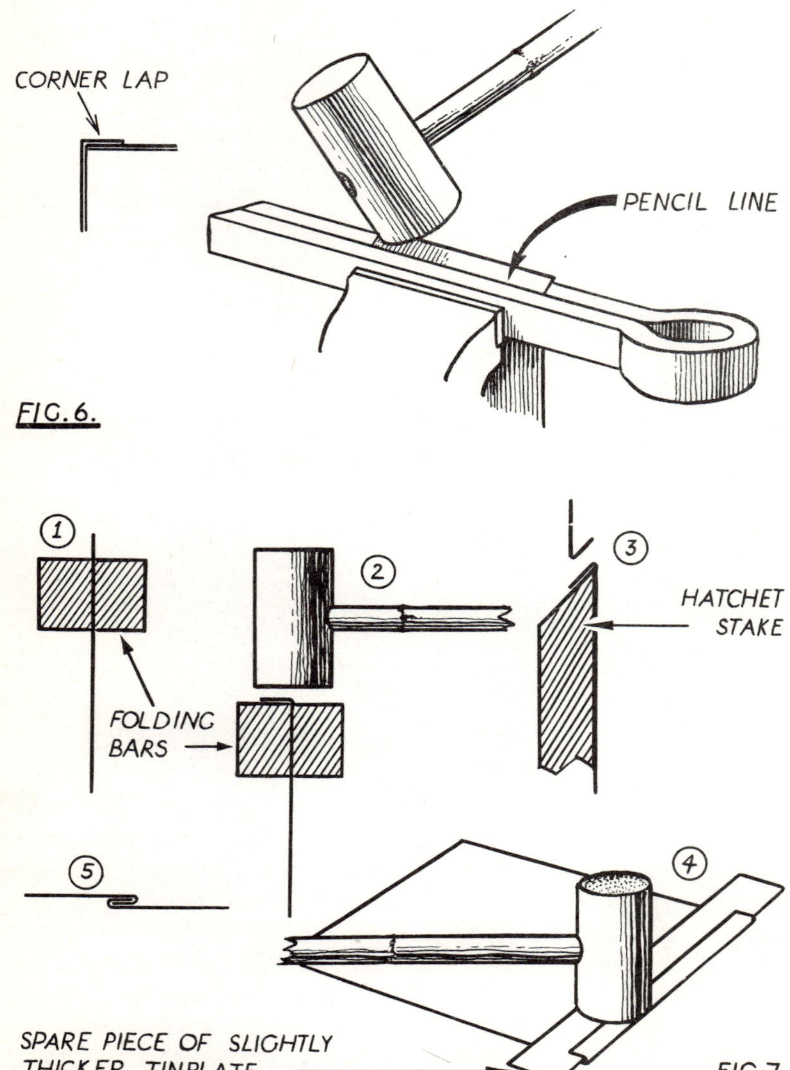
CORNER LAP
PENCIL LINE
FIG. 6.
1
2
3
HATCHET STAKE
FOLDING BARS
5
4
SPARE PIECE OF SLIGHTLY THICKER TINPLATE
FIG. 7.

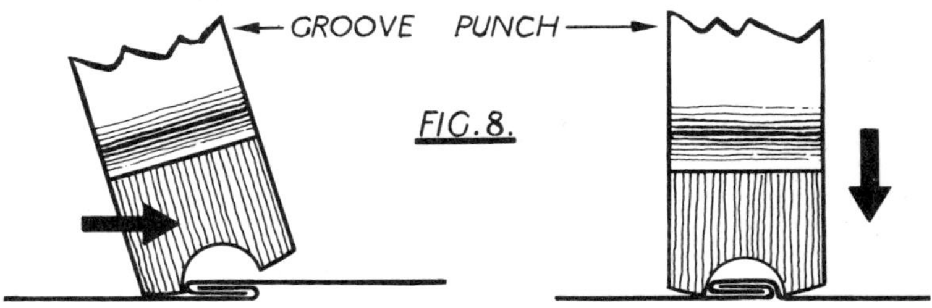

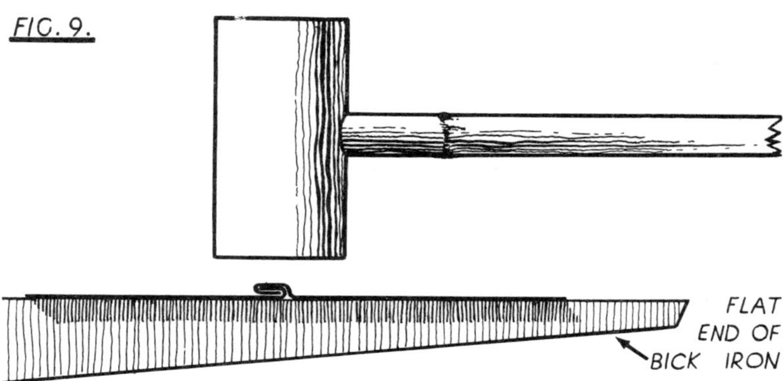

Capped On or Circular Lap Seam. Cut the disc for the bottom making allowance for the "turn up". Carefully set down on a canister stake with a mallet. Do not try to set down too much at each blow. The disc must be continually rotated using only light blows making sure all the time that the bend is occuring on the pencilled circle (fig. 10). An alternative way is to have a disc or former of metal of the right diameter and a backing disc. (This is not always possible in school owing to the large number of discs of different sizes that would be needed.) The tinplate circle is positioned centrally between these whilst they are held in a vice (fig. 10). Care must be taken not to lose the position of the tinplate when it is rotated in the vice. Any small wrinkles can finally be removed by tapping with a mallet on a bottom stake. When the bottom is finished it is soldered on to the container.

Circular Folded Seam. The cylindrical body is first made then the flange is made as in figure 11 (1), (2), (3), rotating the work anti-clockwise. Usually the body distorts at the joint as shown at A. Tap this true with a mallet as shown. The bottom is made as in figure 10 and set down as shown in figure 12. Care must be taken to avoid hammer contact with the sides of the vessel particularly when using the paning hammer.

Knocked Up Bottom. This is similar to the previous joint but it is taken a stage further as shown in figure 13.

The edges of tinplate articles are usually finished either with a wired edge or a beaded edge because tinplate is seldom thick enough to withstand damage. Safety is another consideration: bare edges are often sharp.

Beaded Edge. Between 3 mm and 6 mm is usually allowed for this. Start by bending on a hatchet stake (fig. 14 (1)) and proceed, as shown in figure 14 (2), to bend the edge over a piece of

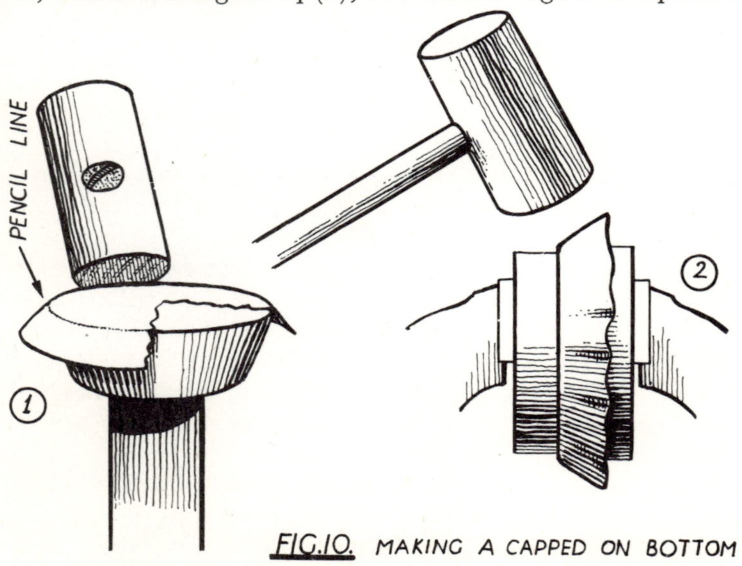

FIG.10. MAKING A CAPPED ON BOTTOM

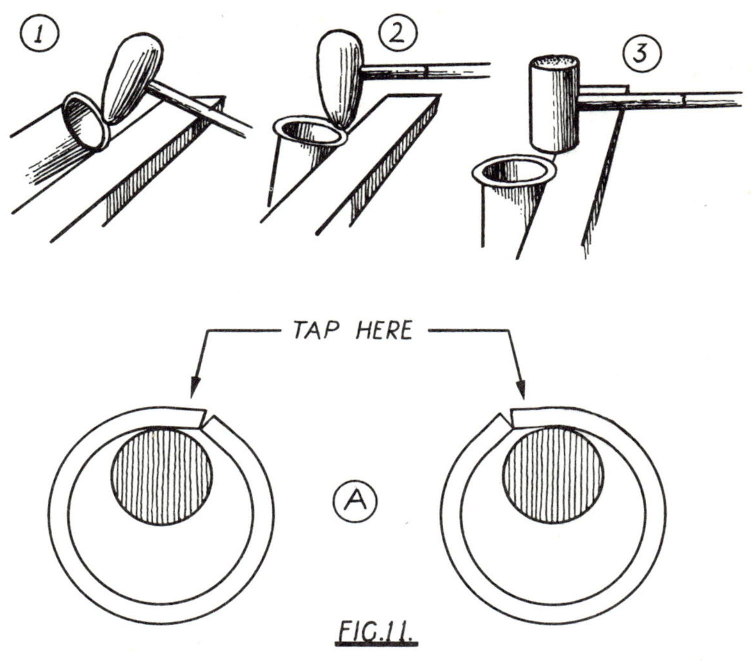

FIG.11.

FIG.12. CIRCULAR FOLDED SEAM

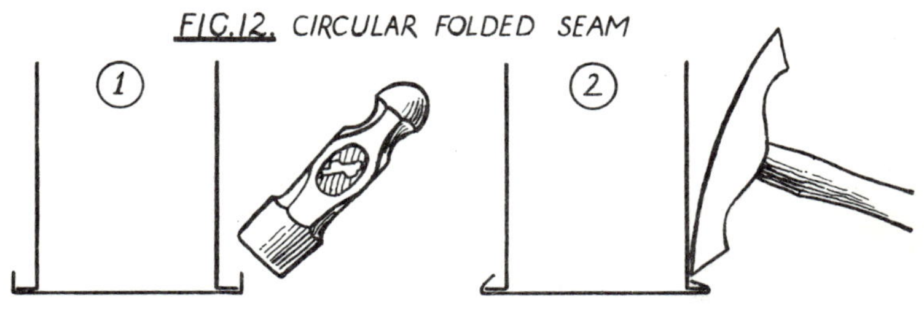

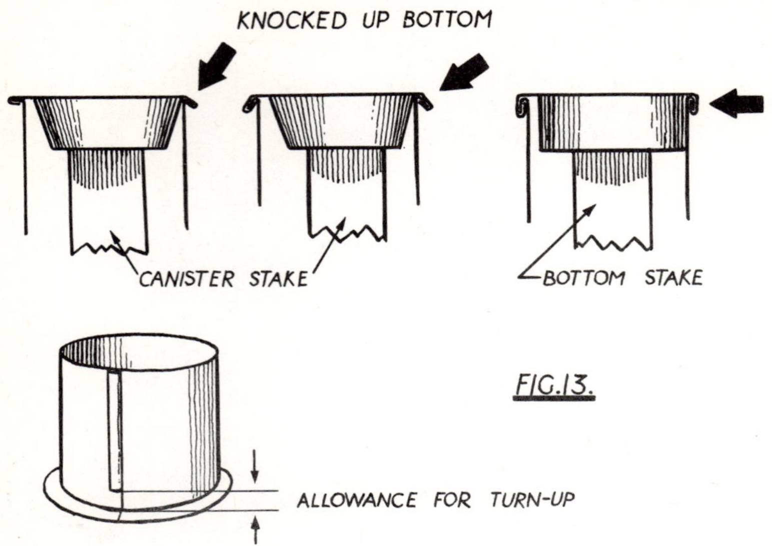
KNOCKED UP BOTTOM
CANISTER STAKE
BOTTOM STAKE
ALLOWANCE FOR TURN-UP

FIG. 13.

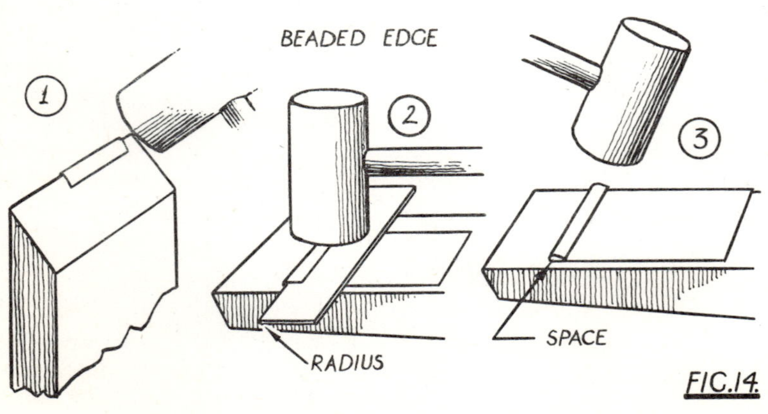
BEADED EDGE
1
2
3
RADIUS
SPACE

FIG. 14.

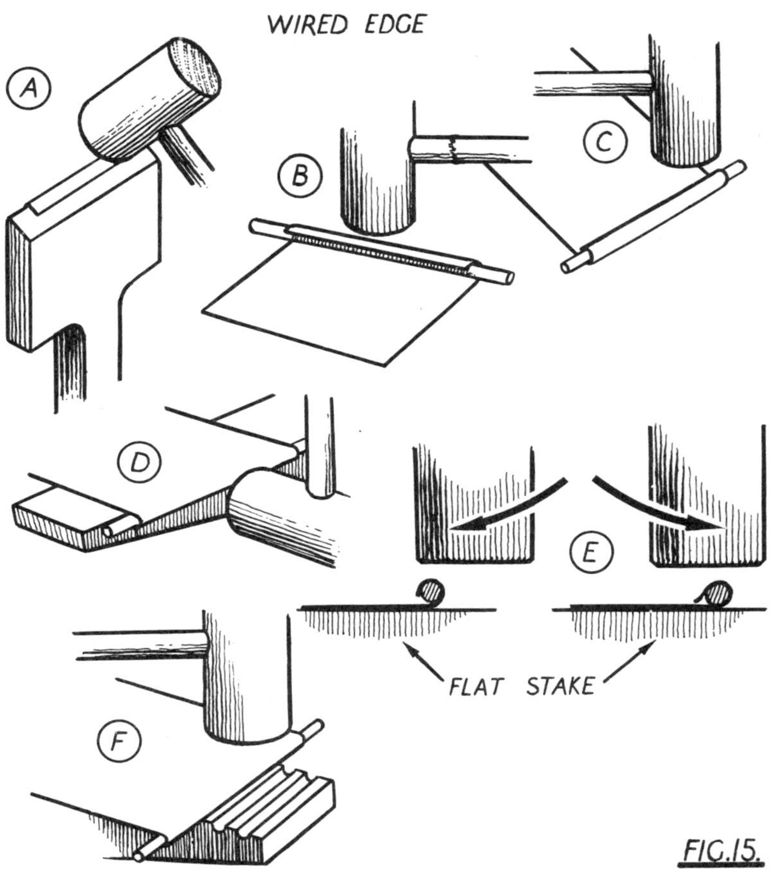

metal which has a radiused edge. Finish with a mallet as in figure 14 (3). Never flatten the edge completely otherwise it will lose its rigidity.

Wired Edge. Allow between two and a half to three times the diameter of the wire for this. Start by bending to the pencil line on a hatchet stake, figure 15A, then lay the wire in and tap down until the wire is trapped (B). Next, true the edge on a bick iron or similar stake as shown at C and D. If the tin plate does not enclose the wire, "dress" with a mallet using a sweeping action to one side as shown at E. If too much metal has been bent over, "dress" in the other direction. The edge can then be finished on a creasing iron as shown at F.

Soldering. This is almost invariably done with a soldering iron as explained in Chapter 4. On good tinplate work no edge is left with the mild steel exposed as this will rust. To finish these "raw" edges they are tinned with the edge of the soldering iron. Excess solder must be "lifted" off with the soldering iron. The surface of tin plate must never be filed or emery-clothed.

9

Silversmithing

The silversmithing operations are usually carried out in the school workshop in copper and gilding metal owing to the high price of silver.

The operations are the same and when sufficient skill has been gained using base metals the student can at a later date try working in silver. It is customary to have silver articles hall marked, but it is not compulsory if they are not to be sold. Hallmarking is carried out at the Goldsmith's Hall in London or in Sheffield, Birmingham, Edinburgh or Glasgow. The address of the Goldsmiths' Hall, from which full particulars are available, is given at the back of this book.

MATERIALS

Copper

This is a little easier to work than silver, but unless it can be finally workhardened by planishing it remains soft after the heat required for silver soldering.

Gilding Metal

Gilding metal is really a kind of brass having a composition of between 95% copper and 5% zinc, and 80% copper and 20% zinc. It is known as gilding metal because of its golden colour. Its working properties are very much like those of silver. It does not become too soft after soldering, and for this reason gilding metal is most used for the silversmithing operations in school.

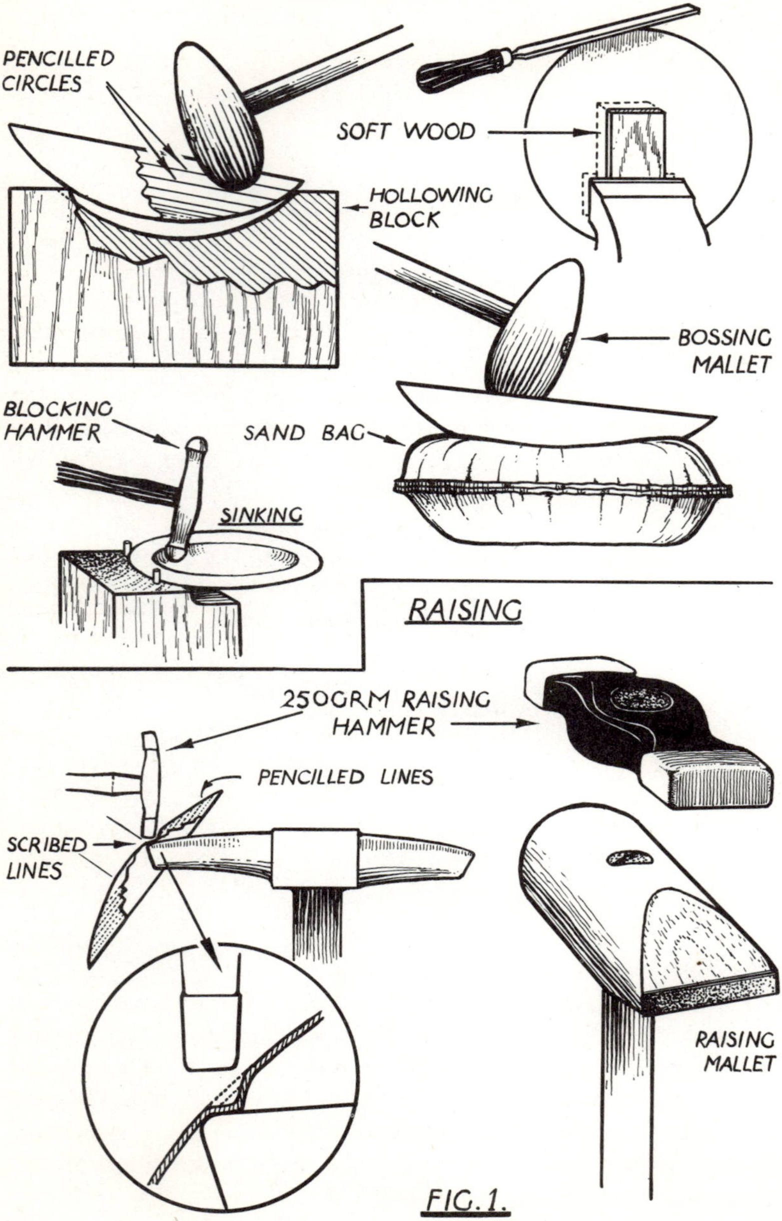

PENCILLED CIRCLES
SOFT WOOD
HOLLOWING BLOCK
BOSSING MALLET
BLOCKING HAMMER
SAND BAG
SINKING
RAISING
250GRM RAISING HAMMER
PENCILLED LINES
SCRIBED LINES
RAISING MALLET

FIG. 1.

NICKEL SILVER

This resembles silver in colour but it is harder to work. It can however be used on work which does not require a lot of forming.

CLEANLINESS

It is essential that all the tools and materials be spotlessly clean. Any speck of dirt, such as a metal filing, if left either on the tools or the sheet of metal will damage the surface of the metal if hammered. A slight burr on a hammer or a stake will also make nasty marks on the work and these are difficult to remove. Therefore all stakes and hammers should be kept polished and lightly oiled when not in use.

STAKES AND HAMMERS

The silversmith's most important tools are his stakes and hammers. Often special stakes have to be made to suit a particular job. These are sometimes forged from mild steel or they can be cast in iron from a wooden pattern. The bought stakes are often made of cast iron but some are made of steel. The working surface of a stake should be true and well polished. The raising stake and raising hammer are shown in figure 1, also the bossing mallet. The cylindrical mallet which is so often used for truing and removing dents etc. is shown in figure 3. The head is made from boxwood or lignum vitae and the handle is of cane.

Figure 2 shows some of the more common stakes. The treblet is used for truing rings and large conical work. It stands on the bench and is often about two feet tall. Mushroom stakes are mostly used for planishing. The two arm stake can be used for raising or planishing. The bottoming stakes can be used for truing the bases of canisters and boxes. The horse and crank are very useful because they can hold a wide variety of stake heads. The three arm mandrel is used in much the same way as the treblet but for work on a smaller scale. The large tray hammer

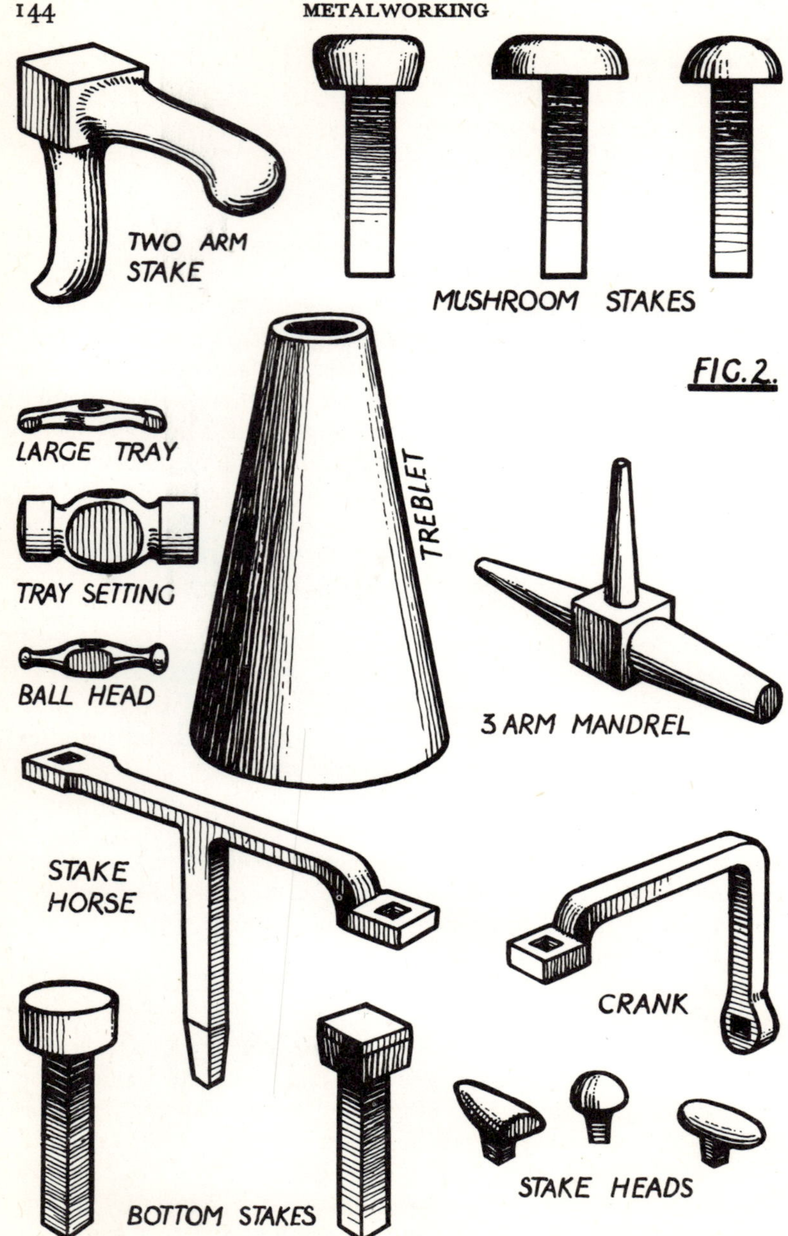
TWO ARM STAKE
MUSHROOM STAKES
FIG. 2.
LARGE TRAY
TREBLET
TRAY SETTING
BALL HEAD
3 ARM MANDREL
STAKE HORSE
CRANK
BOTTOM STAKES
STAKE HEADS

has oval faces of two different sizes for sinking and smoothing curves. The ball head hammer can be used for planishing inside curves of such things as ash trays. The tray setting hammer weighs about 1·1 kgm and is used for flattening large trays.

PROCESSES

Hollowing

This is the process used when making bowl shapes. It can be done with a bossing mallet using a hollowing block or a leather sandbag. Hollowing blocks can be made from beech or similar hard wood with the hollow on the end grain as shown in figure 1, or they can be made by gouging out hollows in the end grain of a tree stump which can stand on the floor.

To make a simple bowl shape first cut out a circle of metal with snips. Usually between 0·9 and 1·3 mm is used, but on larger diameters 1·6 mm is more suitable. The roughness is taken off the edges by filing (fig. 1) and the disc is softened by heating to dull red and quenching in water or dilute sulphuric acid, which is usually kept in an earthenware trough under a sink or near a water tap. This dilute sulphuric acid is known as "pickle". It is made by adding approximately 1 part acid to 9 parts water. Remember always add the acid to the water, not the water to the acid, otherwise it splutters and can be dangerous. If the disc has been plunged in water it will be soft but the oxides will still be on the surface and they must be removed by rubbing with pumice powder on a rag. If the disc has been plunged in the pickle it will be free of oxides but should be rinsed in water to remove any trace of acid and dried.

When starting to hollow keep the centre mark from which the circle is scribed on the convex side. The centre for the other side should be found with a pencil compass and concentric circles drawn at about 12 mm intervals. Now place the disc over the hollowing block or leather sandbag and with the pencilled lines uppermost gently tap with the bossing mallet slowly rotating the work and keeping the blows in concentric circles (fig. 1). It is usually better to start with the outside circle and slowly work inwards. If the work becomes too hard it should be softened from time to time as required.

The diameter of the disc will alter very little and the edge will remain at the same thickness; but where the metal has been stretched into the hollow it will have become thinner. If we wish to retain the thickness of the metal and make a deeper vessel we do it by raising.

Sinking

This is similar to hollowing except that a flat rim is left on the work as on a small tray. Often a blocking hammer is used instead of a mallet.

One method is shown in figure 1. The edge of the disc is kept against the pins (3 mm diameter steel is suitable for these) and the work is slowly rotated as it is being hammered. After each time round it should be inverted on a flatting plate and the rim trued using a block of wood and a hammer. The bottom can also be kept flat by this method.

Note. Flatting plates may be bought. Actually they are nothing more than a sturdy surface plate. For school work an old surface plate can be used, but it should be painted round the edge with a distinctive colour so that it will not be confused with the surface plates used for marking out.

Raising

This is the process of making a hollow vessel by hammering or malleting from the outside.

The disc is best prepared from 0·9 mm sheet. Only slight hollowing is required, about 25 mm deep on a 175 mm diameter disc.

Now a raising stake and raising hammer or mallet must be used. The raising hammer is the more suitable tool because a mallet, owing to its softness, needs continual re-shaping at the face. This means that a new mallet will be required from time to time.

The raising hammer is shown in figure 1. It is important that the shape is as shown. Most raising hammers when bought need filing or grinding to the proper shape.

The stake can be made from 50 mm diameter mild steel about 400 mm long and held in a sturdy vice or a bought cast iron stake can be used. Ideally the bought stake should be held in a heavy stake block, but it may be held in a heavy vice.

Before starting to raise you should have a sketch of the vessel you intend to make. The size of the blank can be estimated by adding the average diameter of the vessel to the height. This will give you the approximate diameter of the blank. Experience is needed to estimate the blank accurately, particularly since some people tend to stretch the metal more in hammering than others.

Start by making the base circle with a pair of dividers. It is better to have this circle scribed with dividers because a more precise base can be obtained in this way. Now make concentric circles with a pair of compasses on the outside of the work about 8mm apart starting from the scribed circle. These are guide lines for raising.

Place the disc over the stake as shown so that the scribed circle is just over the edge of the stake (fig. 1). Start hammering. Be sure that the face of the hammer makes a flat mark on the work. The hammer must bring the metal down to the stake but don't hit too hard otherwise stretching will result. Usually about three blows are necessary before the metal is properly down to the stake. The work is then turned about 12 mm and the next flat made. Continue until you have completed the first circle, then start on the next one 8 mm up. When this is done go on to the next and so on until you reach the last one. At this last circle the metal is usually wrinkled. It is better to tap these wrinkles hard down on to the stake using a cylindrical mallet. If a hammer is used stretching might occur at the edge. The diameter of the disc is now about 6 mm smaller than before. Now soften, rinse and dry the work. Draw the concentric circles with the pair of compasses. The scribed circle should still show. Continue as before. The work will need softening at the end of each raising.

From time to time check the work to see that the sides are going up evenly. For this a cardboard template may be used (fig. 3). The work can be trued with the raising hammer on the stake but, instead of working right round, the raising is kept in short rows on the side which is protruding. Figure 3 shows how

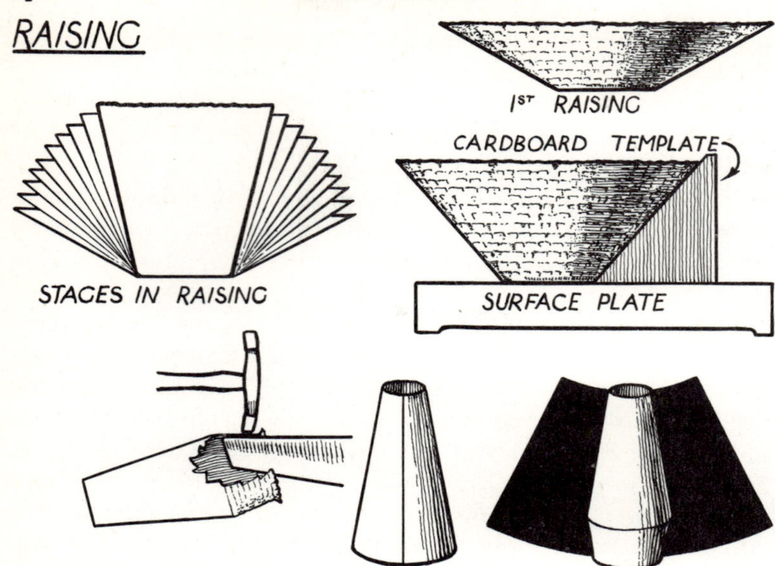
RAISING
1ST RAISING
CARDBOARD TEMPLATE
STAGES IN RAISING
SURFACE PLATE
SEAMED & RAISED VESSEL

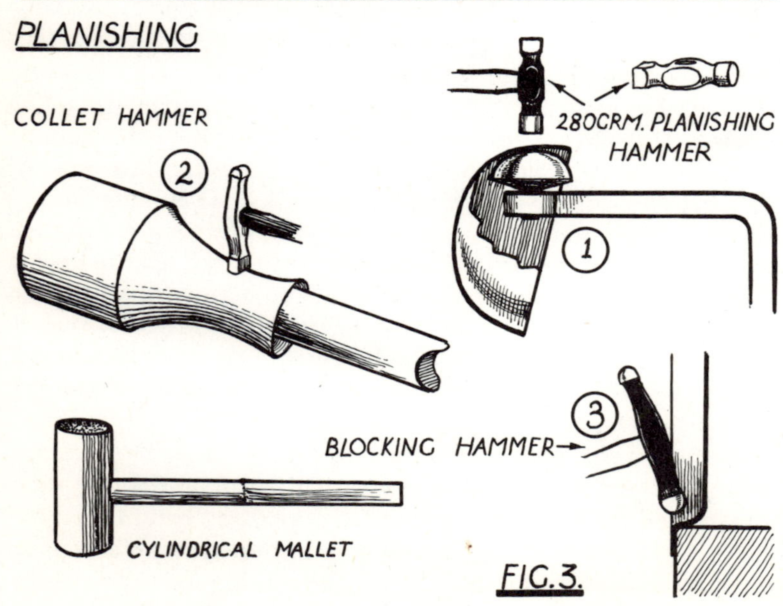
PLANISHING
COLLET HAMMER
280CRM. PLANISHING HAMMER
2
1
3
BLOCKING HAMMER
CYLINDRICAL MALLET

FIG. 3.

the shape alters with raising. Figure 4 shows a teapot which has been raised.

Often to save time tall vessels like coffee pots and vases are first developed and seamed using hard solder (the enamelling grade is too hard) and then finished by raising (fig. 3).

When raised work has reached the desired shape it can be planished to remove the raising hammer marks.

Planishing

This is the process of making the work "plain", but in fact the planishing hammer leaves small facets on the work which can be attractive if done regularly.

Before starting to planish, be sure the stake is highly polished, also the work and the hammer.

On hollow work the stake must have a slightly smaller radius than the work so that when the hammer strikes the work it is trapped between the stake and the hammer (fig. 3 (1)) and makes a clear ringing sound. Often a different stake and hammer are needed for different parts of the job. A simple bowl as shown in figure 3 (1) could be done using one stake.

Before starting to planish work similar to figure 3 (1) draw concentric circles about 3 mm apart and start planishing from the centre. If the work and the hammer are polished it is difficult to see the hammer marks, but this can be overcome by rubbing the hammer backwards and forwards on a piece of 3/0 blue back emery paper. This gives the hammer a very fine satin-like surface which shows as a fine matt surface on each of the facets. When the planishing is finished this slightly matt surface is easily polished using crocus or rouge block on a soft mop such as a "swansdown".

Each facet in planishing should overlap the previous facet and each row should overlap the previous row. After planishing the work is hard. Sometimes to remove the raising marks the job has to be planished two or three times.

Some planishing has to be done with a collet hammer (fig. 3 (2)) or a blocking hammer (fig. 3 (3)). A 280 gms planishing hammer is shown (fig. 3 (1)) but for small work a 140 gms hammer can be used.

FIG. 4—RAISED TEAPOT IN BRITANNIA SILVER
Designed and made by the author

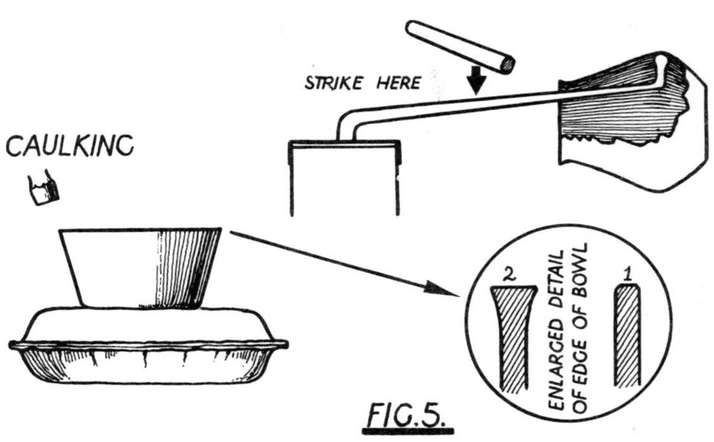

FIG.5.

Planishing does three things:
1. It makes the work hard.
2. It spreads the metal slightly.
3. It makes the metal a little thinner.

SNARLING

This is the process of striking a blow (usually on the inside of a container) by utilising the rebound of a long slender tool, one end of which is gripped in a vice (fig. 5). By this means it is possible to alter the shape or remove the dents from deep awkward shaped vessels.

CAULKING

Caulking is a method of thickening the edge of a piece of work by hammering as shown in figure 5. It is done for strength and appearance.

Start by slightly chamfering the edge as at figure 5 (1). Then hammer round and round three or four times, keeping the blows close together, until a thick edge is obtained as at figure 5 (2). The hammer marks and any burrs can be removed with a water of Ayr stone. Water of Ayr stones have a mild abrasive quality. They are available in sticks about 95 mm long ranging in size from 3 mm square section to 25 mm square section. They are used with water.

Built Up Work

Often a hallowed or raised bowl requires a base or foot. One of the simplest kinds is shown in figure 6A. The base ring is made first and the joint soldered with hard or enamelling solder. Notice the little spacing pieces of iron wire to prevent the solder from running on to the binding wire; also the extra loops for tightening the wire.

The ring is next soldered on to the body using easy or easy-flo solder. To be sure the base ring is properly positioned it is a good plan to make stitches with an engraving tool as shown at B. This ensures that the base will not move during soldering. Be sure to keep the graver sharp or it will tend to slip. Engraving tools are discussed in Chapter 10.

Wires can be applied on rims or on bases. These can be held in place with bent cotter pins as shown at C.

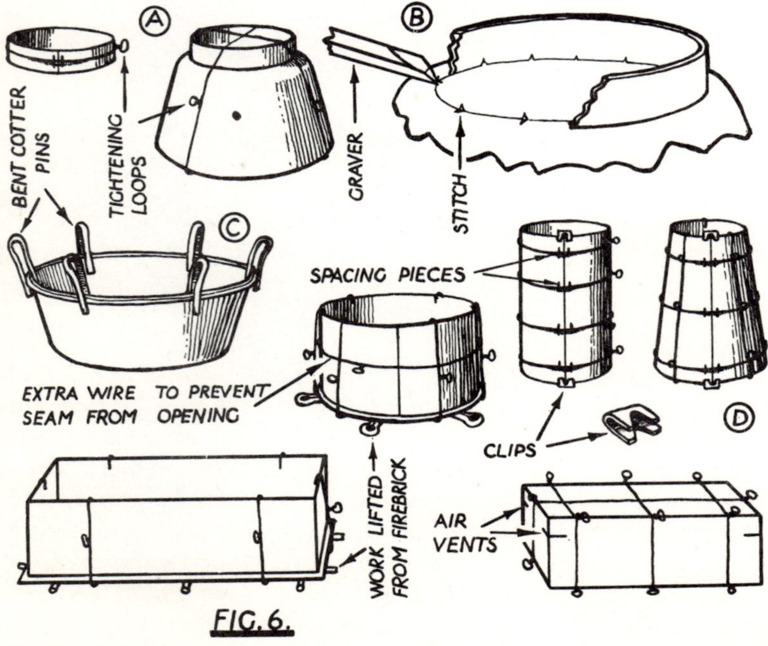

FIG. 6.

Boxes and Seamed Work

Figure 6D shows the method of using iron binding wire on several seamed jobs. The clips shown are made from 0·9 mm annealed mild steel. These are particularly useful for large work on which the edges tend to come out of alignment on heating.

When finally soldering the cover on a box, air vents must be made, as shown, usually by starting to saw at the joint line of the box and the cover.

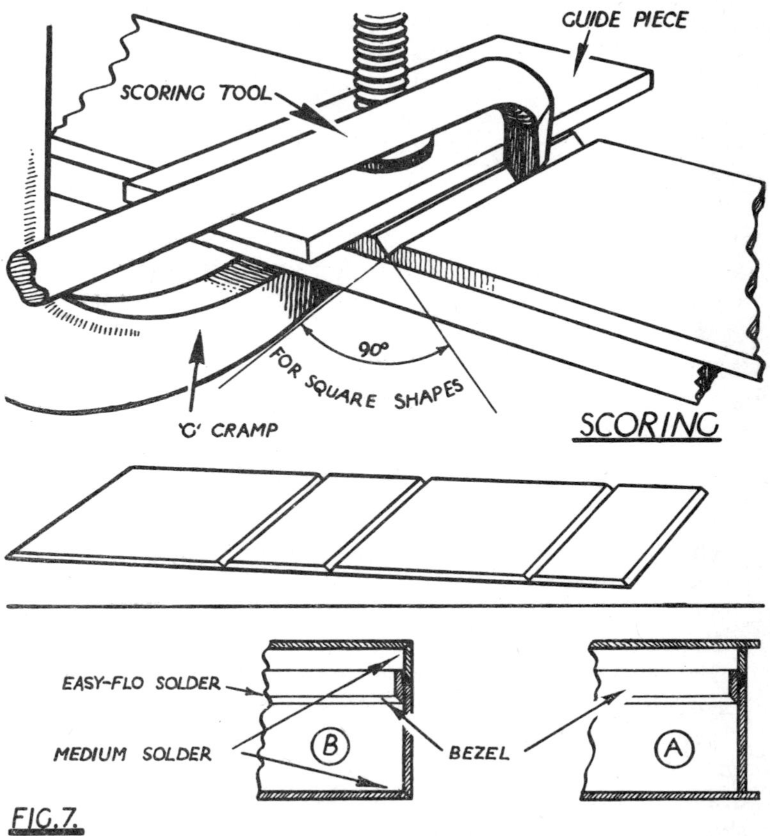

FIG. 7.

When soldering the bottom on to a box it must be lifted from the firebrick slightly to allow the flame to heat the bottom. The circular box is shown on cotter pins and the rectangular box on 3 mm diameter iron wire.

Rectangular boxes are developed from a flat sheet and "V" grooves are made where the sharp bends are required.

"V" grooves are usually made with a scoring tool (fig. 7). This can be made from silver steel which is then hardened and tempered to light straw. The edge should have an angle of 90° for rectangular boxes, 60° for hexagonal and 45° for octagonal shapes. A piece of metal is clamped beside the line to be scored to act as a guide. The score should be made so deep that when the metal is turned over it shows as a slightly raised line. If the scoring is not deep enough, the bend will not be sharp. Care must be taken, however, not to score right through the metal.

Scoring can be done with a properly ground cold chisel or a file, but the filing method is only to be recommended when the grooves are short.

After the box is folded it is usual to silver solder along all the folded joints. The base can be mitred as shown at B, or soldered flat on to the sides (A). When the top has been soldered on and the box finally sawn through with a piercing saw, the sawn edges must be filed flat and tested on a surface plate. The inside edges of the box are finished with a bezel. This helps to locate the cover and gives the box rigidity. The bezel is soldered to the box with a lower melting point solder than is used for the rest of the joints.

Wire Drawing

Often wires are required to strengthen the edges of bowls or for bezels in boxes.

Wire can be altered in section and reduced in diameter by being pulled through a drawplate.

Drawplates are available with round, square, oblong and triangular holes. They are made from hardened and tempered steel.

Figure 8 shows a drawplate. The holes progress in size from one end to the other. Each hole is tapered. The wire to be drawn is first softened and the end is tapered with a file as shown. The tapered end is inserted in the largest hole through

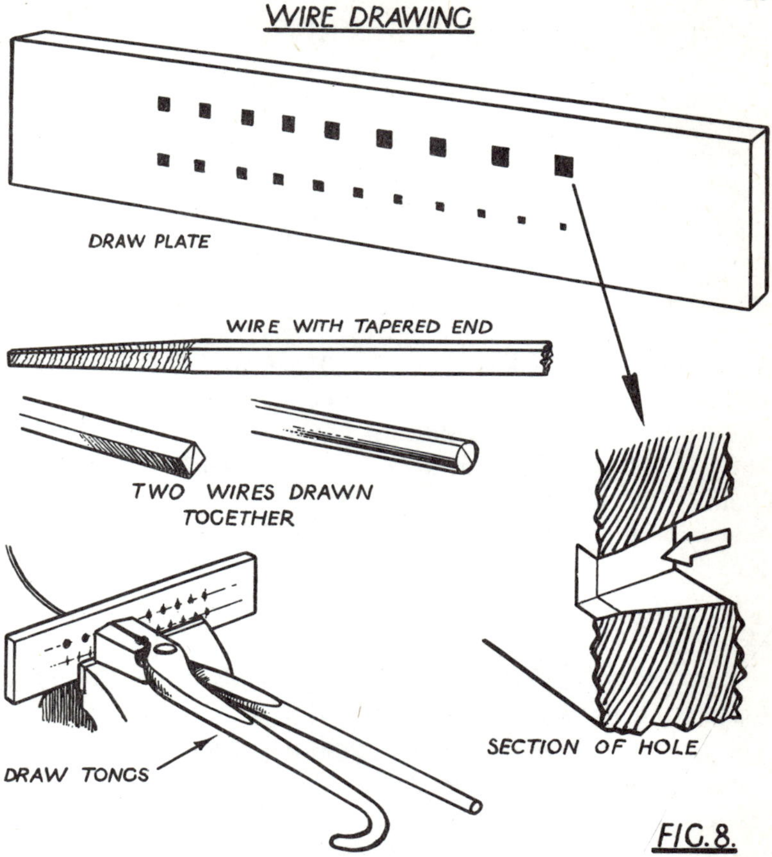

WIRE DRAWING

DRAW PLATE

WIRE WITH TAPERED END

TWO WIRES DRAWN TOGETHER

DRAW TONGS

SECTION OF HOLE

FIG. 8.

which the untapered part of the wire just cannot pass. The drawplate is held in a vice and the wire is oiled or rubbed with beeswax or soap and then the tapered end which is protruding through the hole is gripped with the tongs and pulled through. It is then drawn through the next hole. Drawing causes work hardening so the wire must be softened often. To do this, coil it up so all the coils are touching each other, otherwise stray coils will become burnt before the others have reached the annealing temperature. Clean and lubricate the wire before continuing with the drawing. With care two wires can be drawn through the plate together as shown.

10

Decorative Processes

ETCHING

Etching on metal is done with acid. The metals used are usually copper, gilding metal, brass and aluminium. Certain parts of the metal are covered with an acid resisting substance so that the bare parts only are attacked when the work is in the acid. The depth of the etching depends on the strength and the temperature of the acid, the type of metal being etched and the length of time it is exposed to the acid.

Acids

Four parts water to which 1 part nitric acid is added is often used. This can be dangerous if spilt, also fumes are given off which might cause discomfort. A much more reliable acid is a saturated solution of iron perchloride. (This and all the other materials here mentioned can be bought from the addresses shown at the back of this book.) The saturated solution is made from lumps. No fumes come from this and it is relatively harmless if splashed on to the skin. However, as a precaution against staining, always wash your hands after using it.

Cleaning the Metal

Before any acid resist is applied the metal should be degreased with fine pumice powder or whiting and water to which a few drops of ammonia have been added. This can be mixed in a saucer and vigorously rubbed on with cotton wool. A good detergent can be used instead of ammonia.

RESISTS

For convenience we can put these into three groups but there are of course other ways such as dusting with powdered resin etc.

Applied resists. These are applied in the form of cut out shapes of plastic material known by the trade names "Fablon" and "Contact", which have a strong adhesive on one surface.

Figure 1 shows a small dish on which a cut shape has been stuck. Be sure that the plastic shape is pressed well down at all the edges.

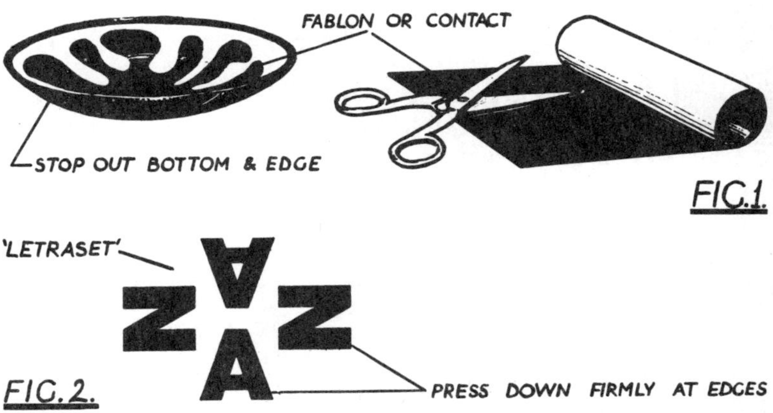

"Letraset," which is the proprietary name for sheets of transfer letters and motifs which are available in scores of different sizes and type faces, may be used as acid resists. The sheets may be purchased from most artists colourmen and the letters can be stuck on to the metal either in the form of a pattern or as lettering for wall plaques etc. Providing they are well stuck down very accurate lettering can be produced by this means (fig. 2).

Painted Resists. The best known of these is quick drying stopping-out varnish which can be bought or made in the following ways:

(*a*) 1 part benzine or benzol } by volume
1 part asphaltum powder }

This must be made in a screwtop jar. The asphaltum powder should soon dissolve. Always screw the lid on after use. If benzine or benzol are not available petrol may be used as a substitute.

(*b*) 114 gms asphaltum
0·25 litre turpentine

The asphaltum and turpentine is put in a jar which should be stood in a saucepan of water and heated until thoroughly dissolved.

Stopping-out varnish is painted on to the parts to be protected; this includes, of course, the back and edges of the work.

Dabbed Resist. This is also known as "dabbed ground" and it can be bought. It is in a small box and is sometimes known as etching ball. Do not buy the "soft ground" which looks the same and is often sold in the same size box. Soft grounds are used by etchers for obtaining the effect of pencil lines on a copper plate. This method does not concern us here. Solid etching ground can be made as follows:

28 gms beeswax
28 gms asphaltum
14 gms Swedish brown pitch

The wax and pitch are melted together in an enamel saucepan and the asphaltum powder gradually added while stirring with a glass rod. The whole is allowed to simmer for 20 minutes more or less (depending on the quality of the pitch) and then poured into lukewarm water and rolled into balls. This mixture is applied to the work with a dabber which is made in the following way. A disc of cardboard about 50 mm in diameter is cut; a bunch of rag is placed on this and a wad of cotton-wool over all. A piece of pure silk being placed over the wadding, the bunched ends are held firmly in the left hand and whipped with string beginning next to the fingers and working towards the card. This gradually strains the silk tighter and tighter over the cotton-wool (which must be worked into shape) so that no folds are left over the front surface of the pad (fig. 3).

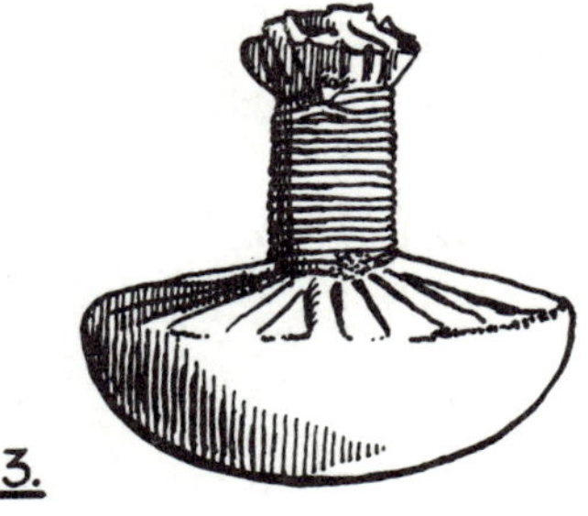

FIG.3.

The work is warmed on a hot plate to such a heat that the etching ball will start to smear on the article as it is stroked across. At this heat it can just be held in the fingers. With the dabber, carefully start dabbing the smears of ground evenly over the article. Do not overheat! Ideally it should feel tacky when being dabbed. The thickness of the ground should be such that it is slightly translucent. When the article is evenly covered it should be returned to the hot plate and moved about until the whole surface becomes glazed. It can then be stood against a vertical surface, face inwards, so that the dust will not settle on the surface while it is cooling.

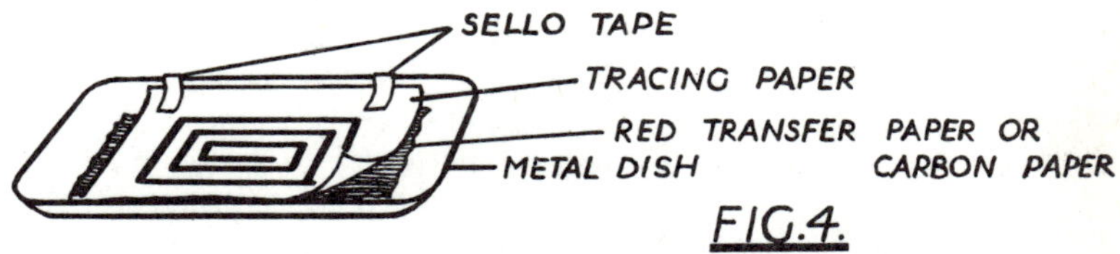

FIG.4.

The design is transferred from tracing paper on to the metal using red transfer paper or carbon paper (fig. 4). When the design is transferred on to the ground it can be scratched through with a needle or for broad areas a small knife blade. Remember that clean sharp edges will remain sharp during etching, but ragged lines will become more ragged.

Ideas for designs can often be developed from natural forms. Figure 4A shows six sketches taken from nature and from much

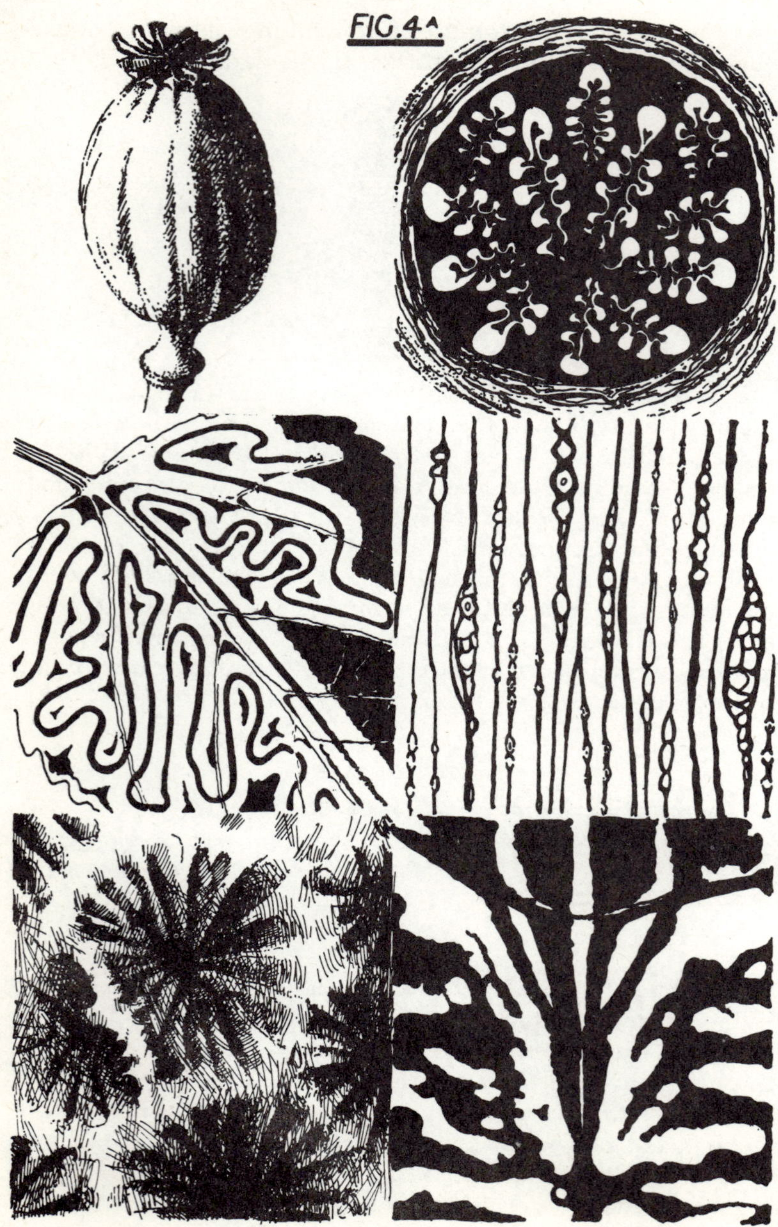
FIG.4A.

enlarged photographs of details of natural forms. However, natural forms should not be copied slavishly but used as a basis for designs.

Use of Acid

When using nitric acid the work is either immersed in the acid which can be in a porcelain, glass or plastic container, or if the work piece to be etched is deep enough, such as a bowl, the acid can be poured in. Nitric acid works vigorously forming bubbles which should be brushed off with a feather every few minutes whilst the work is being etched. If this is not done ragged lines can result.

Work done with iron perchloride should be bitten either face down or on edge in the acid because the sediment which forms tends to "choke" the effect of the acid if done face up. If the work is such that it must be done face up then the acid must be agitated with a feather every few minutes to remove the sediment.

To see how deep the acid is biting, remove the work from the acid (avoid putting your fingers either in the iron perchloride or the nitric acid) and wash under a tap. Dab with a soft cloth to dry. If it has to be returned to the acid check to see if the acid resist, front and back, needs "touching in" with stopping out varnish. This is sometimes necessary because small "pin holes" can develop in the ground.

Removal of the Resist

The plastic applied sheets can of course be peeled off. The other grounds can be removed with a soft cloth and turpentine.

Never buff etched work as this ruins the characteristic sharp edges of the etching. Use a soft hand brush with metal polish or whiting and methylated spirit. Finish with a soft polishing cloth.

ENAMELLING

Enamelling is the process of fusing glass on to a metallic base. The glass is usually crushed and it can be coloured or clear, opaque or translucent. The metallic base, for school work, is almost always copper, although gold, silver and steel can be enamelled.

The art of enamelling has been known for centuries. The earliest examples were found in Cyprus in the form of enamelled gold rings dating back to the thirteenth century B.C.

Enamelling is a fascinating art and there are many different techniques. The interested reader should refer to the bibliography at the back of this book. However, here is a simple enamelling technique which can be used readily in school with the minimum of equipment.

Requirements: small slightly hollowed copper dishes (to be enamelled)

pumice powder and ammonia
powdered enamels
fine mesh coffee strainer
gum tragacanth made up in liquid form (from any chemist)
a water colour brush
heavy gauge wire mesh
small cover bent from 0·8 mm stainless steel
blow torch
brazing hearth and fire bricks
carborundum slip 150 mm × 12 mm × 12mm.

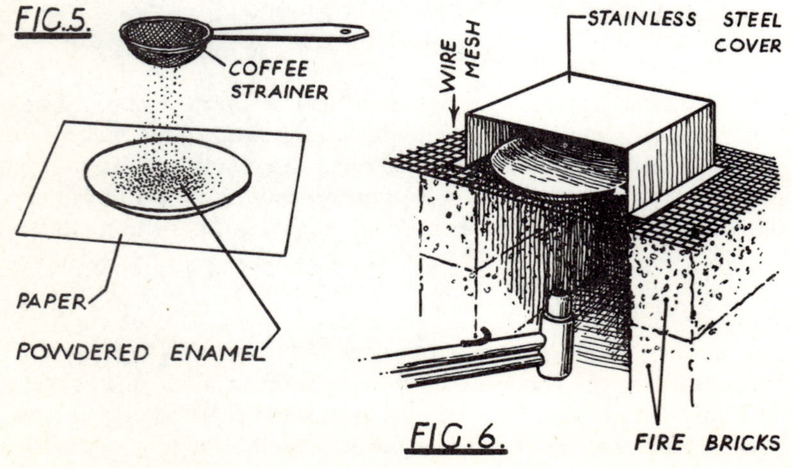

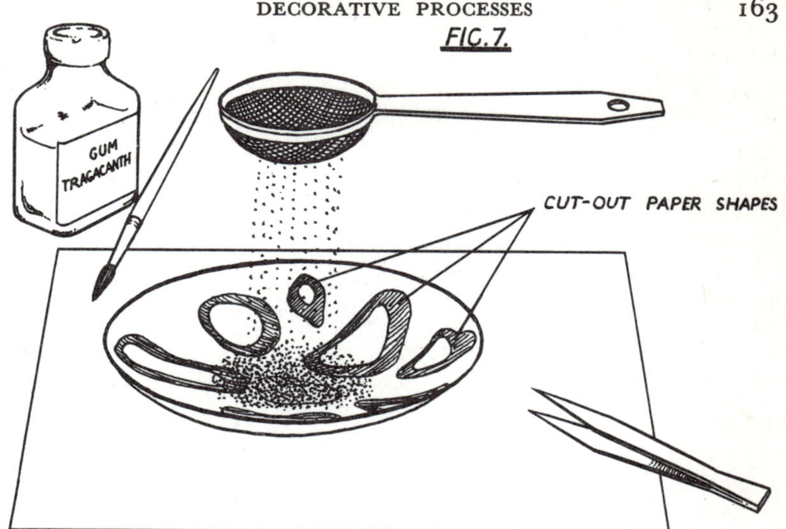

Method: Clean the copper dish as for etching. Rinse thoroughly and brush on gum tragacanth. Lay the dish on a piece of clean white paper and sieve your chosen enamel evenly over the surface (fig. 5). Do not leave any bare patches and be sure the enamel goes right to the edge of the dish. The layer of enamel should be about 0·75 mm thick. Carefully place the dish on the wire mesh for firing (fig. 6). Any enamel left on the paper after the dish is removed should be returned to the enamel container.

Start firing with a very small soft flame to dry off the enamel, then heat evenly to cherry red with a large intense flame. When the enamel has fused allow to cool slowly on the mesh.

The first coat is now on the dish. Paint with gum tragacanth as before and stick into place the cut-out paper shapes (fig. 7). The second layer of enamel is then dusted over the dish as before. With a pair of tweezers carefully remove the cut-out shape thus leaving the original fired surface free of powdered enamel. Fire as before. Now we have a dish in two colours. This could be quite satisfactory at this stage, but if further dustings, possibly with transparent colours, are required they can be done.

Finish the dish by carefully stoning the edge with the carborundum slip and water. Clean the back with fine emery cloth. Take care not to distort the work or the enamel will fracture.

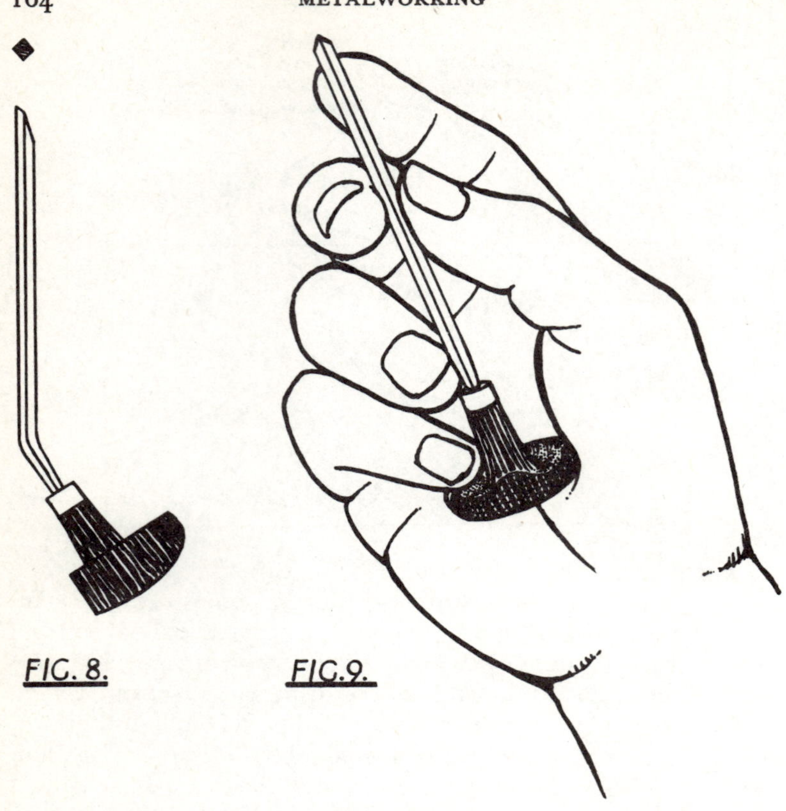

ENGRAVING

There are many different tools available for engraving, but the one most used is the square graver (fig. 8). It should fit the hand as in figure 9. This graver can be made from 3 mm square silver steel. The tang is filed and bent and the tip hardened and tempered to light straw—do not go beyond light straw. The point is stoned as in figure 10, first on a medium India stone and then finished with a circular motion on an Arkansas stone (fig. 11).

Professional engravers often test the sharpness of the graver by touching the point at an angle against the thumb nail. If the tip catches and does not slide, it is sharp.

TRANSFERRING THE DESIGN TO BE ENGRAVED

1. For highly polished surfaces. Trace the drawing. Rub Russian tallow or plasticine on the back of the tracing paper, then lay it on the article to be engraved and with a blunt scriber transfer the drawing. This will leave a copy of the design on the metal. The fine lines of Russian tallow or plasticine on the metal can then be gone over with a scriber to prevent them from being rubbed off. The metal is now ready to be engraved.

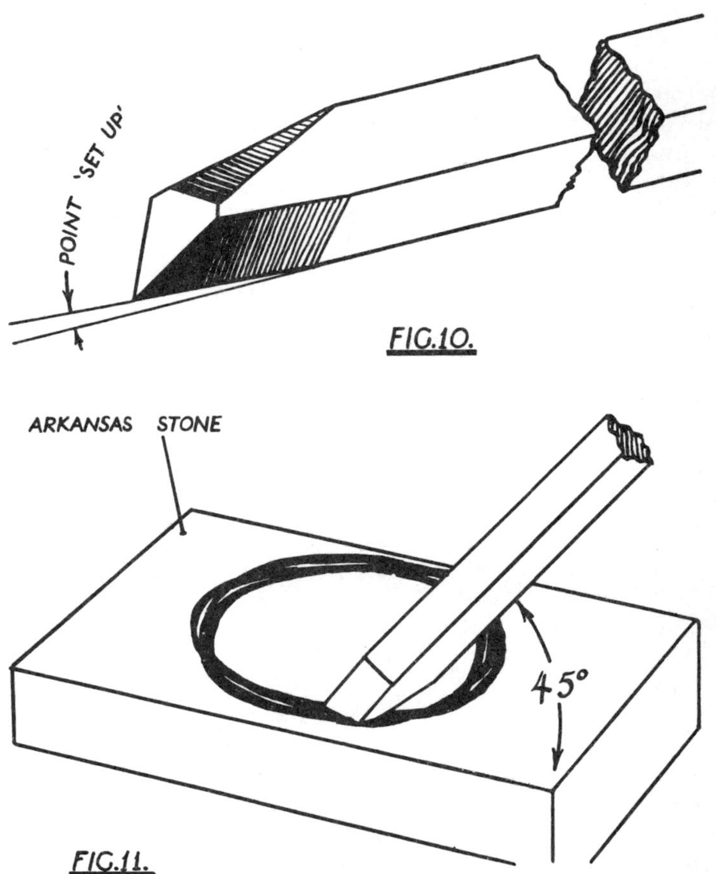

FIG.10.

FIG.11.

2. Rub plasticine or beeswax all over the area to be engraved and then dust with whiting. Now with a sharp pointed piece of hardwood draw the design. This can be corrected as many times as you wish. Finally, lightly scratch in with a scriber and engrave.

3. To reverse the design. Trace the design on transparent acetate sheet (0·25 mm thick works well) with a scriber. Rub pencil lead into the tracing. Now lay this (in reverse) on the metal which has been rubbed with beeswax. Rub the back of the acetate sheet with a burnisher or the back of a spoon. The design will now be transferred on the work in reverse. Go over this lightly with a scriber before engraving.

The work to be engraved is usually rested on a sand bag and the engraving tool point is pushed gently along the marked-out lines—lightly for the first cut—turning the work and not the tool at the curves. Make the lines deeper where required by re-entering with the engraving tool and taking more cuts. Figure 11A (*designed and engraved by the author*) shows an example of engraving.

REPOUSSÉ

This is a method of decorating a sheet metal article by means of raised or indented motifs, made with punches (these are blunt and never cut the metal) whilst set in pitch. The tools and materials used are:

Punches made from silver steel (fig. 12)

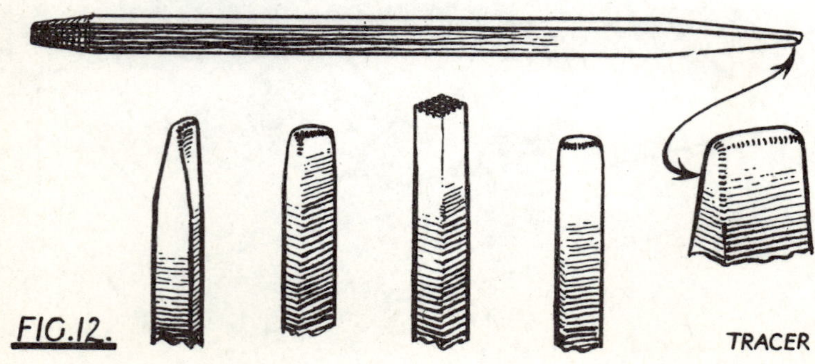

FIG.12.

Designed, made and engraved by the author

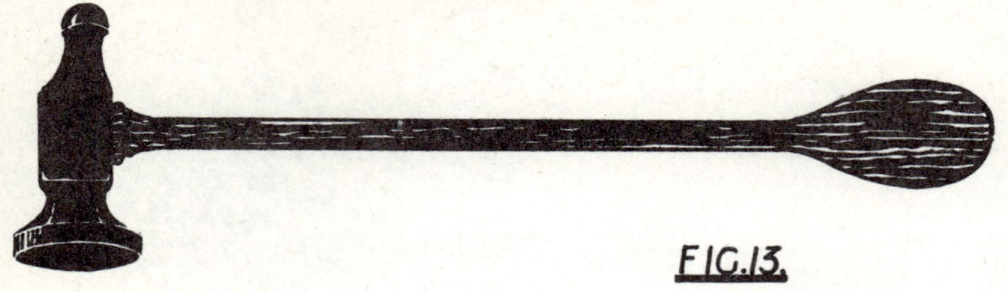

Repoussé or chasing hammer (fig. 13)
Pitch
Cast iron pitch bowl and leather ring stand (fig. 14)
(A shallow metal tray will suffice for most school work.)
Blow pipe

The Pitch

This must be tough enough to support the work and yet resilient enough to allow the metal to be driven in by the punches.

A good recipe for pitch is as follows:

3 kilos Swedish pitch
3 kilos Plaster of Paris
227 gms tallow

The pitch is melted, the tallow added and the plaster stirred in a little at a time. Before the work is set into this pitch it should be lightly greased to facilitate cleaning after removal from the pitch.

Method

Assume we are starting with a flat piece of 0·8 mm (this is probably the best gauge for repoussé work) soft copper. Have the pitch in a 25 mm deep metal tray about 25 mm larger all round than the workpiece. Warm the surface of the pitch with a soft flame and press the copper sheet on to the surface so that the pitch just comes over the edges. Be sure there are no air bubbles under the copper. Allow to cool. Trace the design on the copper using carbon paper. Remove the carbon paper and lightly scratch through the design with a scriber. Hold the tracing punch in the left hand at such an angle to the work that when it is struck repeatedly with the chasing hammer it moves towards you making a smooth indented line following the lines of your traced design. A little practice is necessary before this can be achieved. When you have finished with the tracing punch, warm the surface of the work with the blowpipe and remove. Clean with rag and paraffin. The design now shows in the form of raised lines on the back. Set the work in the pitch as before but face down this time. The parts to be embossed are now punched down with suitably shaped punches. The work may be reversed as many times as required until the desired effect is obtained. Figure 15 shows a part sectioned piece of repoussé work. Figure 14 shows the cover of a circular box set in pitch. Cast iron is used for the pitch bowl because it is heavy and withstands the effect of the punching.

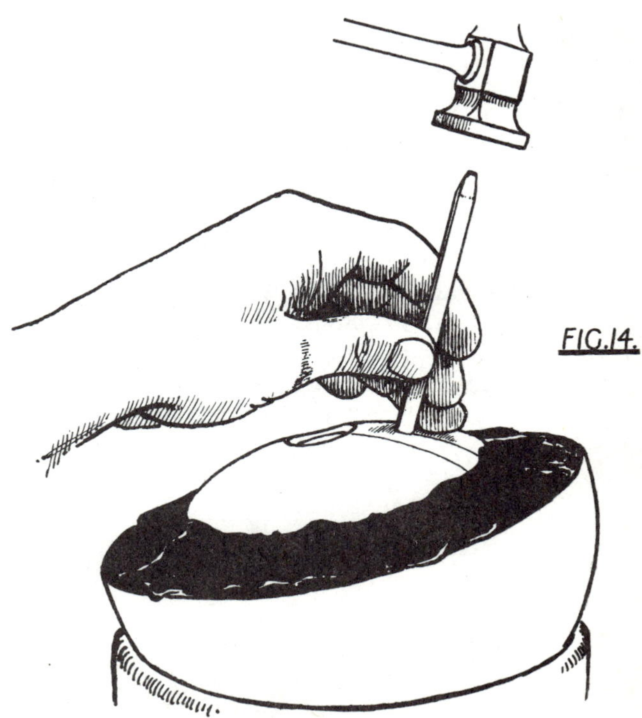

FIG.14.

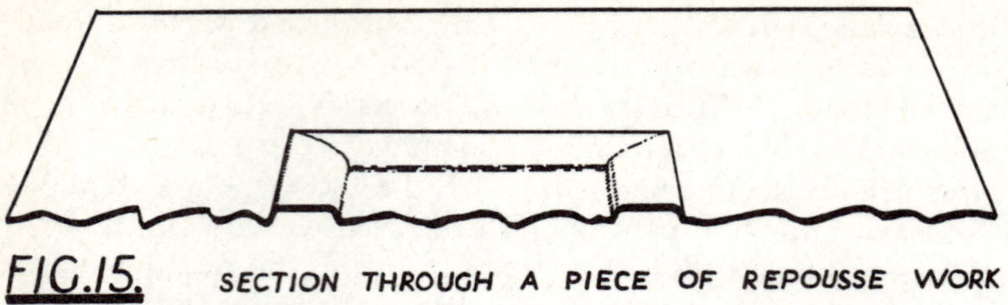

FIG.15. SECTION THROUGH A PIECE OF REPOUSSE WORK

CHASING

Chasing is often not unlike repoussé work in appearance and it is done with similar punches, but it is done from the outside of the work—not from both sides. Castings can be chased with fine corrugated punches which produce a matt surface and also close up any small blow holes.

EMBOSSING

This is the term given to work which is punched entirely from the back. Often a snarling iron (fig. 5, Chapter 9) is used for this purpose.

BENT WIRE DECORATION

The base of vessels can be decorated by the soldering on of wire bent to form a repeating pattern. Figure 16 shows soft brass wire being formed on a jig. The jig can be made from hardwood using sawn-off nails which have been carefully spaced and rounded at the top to allow the wire to be removed easily. For more precise work the jig can be made of brass with accurately spaced steel pins.

COLOURING AND FINISHING METAL

Anodising or Anodic Oxidation

This is the process whereby the oxide film on aluminium is thickened electrolytically. This thick film increases the resistance to corrosion and it can also be dyed.

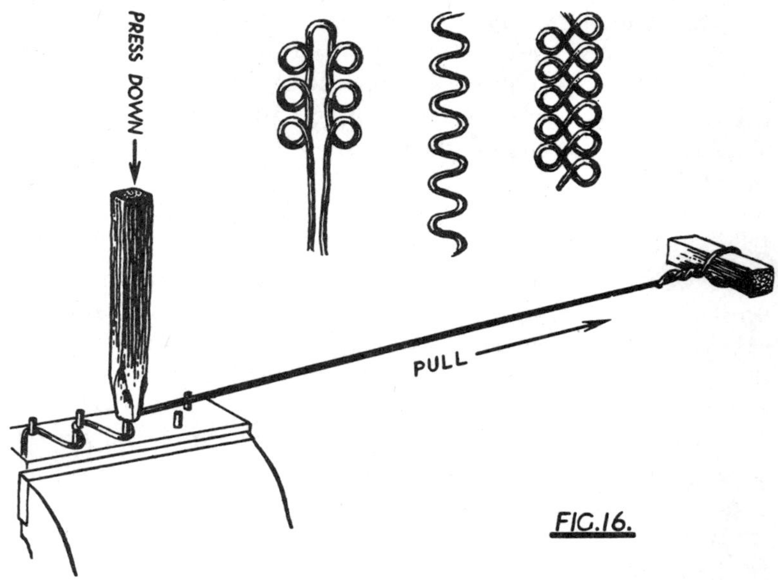

FIG. 16.

The aluminium is first de-greased. The most common electrolyte is dilute sulphuric acid which is in a lead lined bath (cathode). The aluminium article becomes the anode. After 30 to 60 minutes the article should be taken out, thoroughly rinsed and dyed if required.

The Aluminium Development Association publishes a booklet for schools on this subject in which full instructions are given.

Colouring of Copper, Brass and Gilding Metal

There are various colouring agents which can be bought and many recipes available, particularly in some of the older books. However, many of these recipes are not reliable. A good mixture which will colour these metals chemically can be made as follows:

photographer's (plain) hypo	10 parts by weight
sugar of lead (lead acetate)	1 part by weight
citric acid	1 part by weight
water	40 parts by weight

Clean and de-grease the work to be coloured. Dip in the

mixture. The metal will slowly change colour, first golden, then rose, blue, grey-green to grey. It will take 5 to 10 minutes to reach the final colour. If the mixture is kept moving the colour will be more uniform. When the desired colour is obtained the work should be lacquered after it has been washed and dried.

Blackening Steel

1. Small steel items can be blackened by heating gently until hot enough to scorch a piece of wool blanket which is rubbed on the surface. The blackened article should then be lightly oiled. This method is particularly good for small items but beware of the nasty smell!

2. Coat the steel with mineral oil and burn off on the brazing hearth until black.

3. Heat the steel and rub with saltpetre.

Blueing Steel

Polish the work with fine emery cloth avoiding oil and grease. Heat to blue as for tempering, quench in paraffin and polish with beeswax.

Burnishing

This is the process of polishing soft metals, such as gold, silver and copper, by rubbing with a hard smooth tool made from agate, bloodstone or hardened steel. Various shaped burnishing tools are used and soapy water is a popular lubricant. The polish obtained by an expert can be remarkable. The action is one of pressing down the minute surface irregularities so that the surface becomes consolidated.

Mottling

This is a finish obtained on small pieces of engineering work by means of carborundum paste and 6 mm diameter dowel rod held in a drilling machine chuck. As the rod spins the end is pressed against the work causing the carborundum to make polished circles on the surface. If the circles are kept in neat rows this type of finish can enhance the surface, but it should be used with restraint.

Electroplating

This is a process whereby a thin layer of metal is deposited on another by means of an electric current passing through a solution of metallic salts.

It is possible by this means to deposit gold, silver, nickel, chromium, cadmium and copper. There is a mistaken belief among some students that plating will hide blemishes in their work. It will not: plating emphasises blemishes.

Lacquering

Lacquering is done to protect metals from the atmosphere. It is a clear varnish (often with an amyl-acetate base) to which colouring matter is sometimes added. It is applied to thoroughly cleaned metal by brushing, dipping or spraying. In school, lacquer is usually applied with a brush; for best results a good quality camel hair brush should be used. Care must be taken to ensure that every part of the surface is covered, otherwise the uncovered parts will oxidise and show later as streaks. Badly applied lacquer must be removed using the solvent recommended by the manufacturer and then re-lacquered.

Painting

Iron and steel work which is to be exposed to the weather should be protected, unless it is stainless steel. Paint is the commonest protector. Before painting the work should be free of rust, oil or grease.

The paint may be brushed or sprayed. Several thin coats are better than one thick coat. Cracks often occur on a thick layer of paint because the outside of the paint dries first and contracts, whilst the layer of paint nearest the metal is still soft and cannot "anchor" the top layer to the metal.

If castings are to be painted any blow holes must be filled with a filler which suits the paint to be used and rubbed down between coats of paint with wet and dry emery paper.

Plastic Coating

This gives a durable and attractive finish to metal articles such as draining board racks or shoe racks which are never quite satisfactory when painted.

The article is heated in an oven to about 200°C then covered with a layer of a proprietary powder which is then fused on to the metal by reheating. Take care to follow the maker's instructions. (See information at the back of this book).

11

Safety

Strangers entering a school workshop are often amazed that there are so few accidents involving personal injury.

It would seem that in a busy school workshop the stage is set for a drama in which all sorts of dreadful accidents will occur from decapitation to being burnt alive!

The vigilance and good common sense of our handicraft masters, in no small measure, make the workshop a safe place in which to work.

However, here is some general information for the prevention of accidents.

Clothing. When starting to work take off your jacket; roll up your sleeves and tuck your tie into your shirt so that it does not hang loose. Wear either an overall or an apron which should not be loose fitting. In the forge area wear a leather apron if one is available. Wear shoes with stout soles. Do not wear gym shoes: a sharp piece of bent metal on the floor can easily pierce these, or a hot piece of coke from the forge can burn through them.

Hair. Beware of hair that is too long. This can easily be caught up on a drilling machine or on the end of the horizontal milling machine arbor.

Oil or Grease on the Floor. If any oil or grease gets on the floor see that it is cleaned away and if possible put sawdust down to prevent people from slipping.

Never Run in the Workshop. Walk wherever you go and if you are carrying a tool or a piece of metal, have proper regard for anyone who might accidentally step into your path.

Safety Stop Switches. School workshops are usually fitted with these to enable anyone to stop all the machinery in case of emergency. You should know where these are in your workshop and how and when to use them.

Fire Blanket. This is often kept in a red cylindrical container hung on a wall, usually by the brazing hearth or forge area. Should anyone's clothing catch fire this asbestos blanket is used for the purpose of smothering the flames.

Acids. When putting hot work into dilute sulphuric acid (pickle) do it at arm's length to avoid being splashed and don't drop the work in. Avoid inhaling the fumes as far as possible.

Acids are best kept near a water tap so that if anyone is splashed they can quickly wash away the acid.

Electrical Faults. If you suspect that any machine is electrically faulty report it at once to the master in charge of the workshop.

Blacksmithing. Do not leave hot work where anyone might stand on or touch it. Beware of hot scale when hammering white hot metal.

TOOLS

Hammers. Report loose hammer heads to your teacher. Never strike two hammer heads together because it might cause a splinter of steel to fly off one of them.

Files. Always use a file with a properly fitting handle.

Cold Chisels. Take care when cutting through metal on a chipping block because often this causes the small pieces you are cutting off to be shot away at great speed. To prevent this stand up another chipping block or something similar in the path of these flying pieces. Report to your teacher any undue mushrooming of the chisel top.

Bench Shears. If you are guiding the metal into the bench shear be sure that it is *your* hand that is operating the handle. Do not let someone pull the handle down while your fingers are near the blades. The handle itself is in fact as dangerous as the cutter, so keep clear when metal is being cut.

MACHINE TOOLS

Do not talk to, or otherwise distract, a person who is using a machine tool.

If you leave a machine, switch it off.

Drilling Machine. When using this machine be sure the work is properly held in a vice and also be sure that there is a bolt or something similar to prevent the work and the vice from spinning round should the drill get caught. Never hold small work in your fingers.

Lathe. Make sure the work is firmly held in the chuck before starting the machine. Never leave the chuck key in the lathe chuck. Do not open the guard which covers the gear trains at the end of the machine unless the isolating switch is off. Never try to remove swarf whilst the machine is in motion. Remember the swarf nearly always has razor-like edges and it is often hot. Do not try to use your hands as a brake on the chuck. Never try to clean or polish work with a rag whilst the machine is revolving. When brushing the lathe down after work beware of the sharp tool.

Shaper. Do not bring your eye down level with the work being cut and in line with the ram. The chips are flicked away at the end of the cut and can cause eye injury. If you want to see how near to the line you are cutting, stop the machine. When setting up work be sure the isolator switch is off.

Milling Machine. Keep your hands away from the cutter when it is in motion. Do not remove any guard which has been fitted to the machine for your safety. Switch off the isolator when setting up work. Never try to apply soluble oil to the work with a brush when the cutter is revolving. Do not sweep the table with your hand because milling chips are often like needles.

Grinding Machine. Always use the eye guard or goggles. Be sure the gap between the rest and the wheel is not more than about 2 mm. If this is not so, small work can be dragged down into the gap.

Power Hacksaw. Do not press down on the top weight in order to speed the cutting. This often causes the blade to break and the sharp fragments shoot in all directions. Be sure there is enough metal for the vice to hold, otherwise it might be wrenched out when the machine is set in motion, thus causing the blade to break.

Finally, always report any accident to the teacher in the workshop.

12

Drilling

The drilling machine, because of its simplicity and the early need for drilled holes, is usually the first machine to be used by boys in the metalwork room.

When starting to drill the following hints will be useful:

1. Check that you have the correct drill and be sure the chuck is properly tightened.

2. Secure the work either in a hand vice or a drilling vice.

3. Take precautions against drilling into the vice or drilling machine table when (a) using a hand vice by resting the work

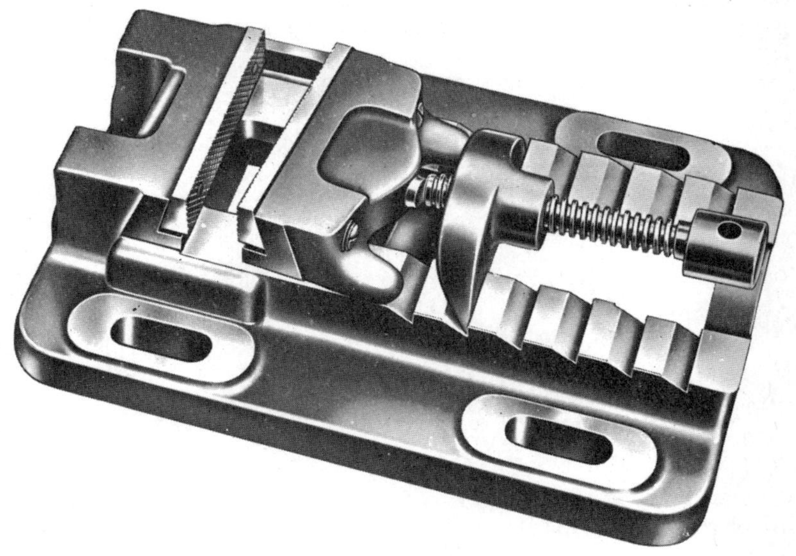

FIG. 1—MACHINE VICE
Courtesy of Jones and Shipman & Co.

on a piece of accurately planed hardwood or, (b) by using packing strips when using the machine vice. A typical machine vice is shown in figure 1. A hand vice is shown in Chapter 3, figure 21.

4. Check that the speed is correct for the drill and the material you are drilling.

5. Bring the drill down to the centre punch mark and press hard enough to start the drill cutting and keep it cutting—do not let it rub, as this overheats the drill tip and makes it blunt. Ease off the pressure when the drill is about to break through because at this stage it tends to "grab" the work.

6. Use a coolant if applicable to the material you are drilling.

CENTRE PUNCHING

This must be done accurately on the marked out cross lines. When a large hole is to be drilled the work should be marked out as shown in figure 2 with the outside circle to the finished diameter. Drilling is then started with a small "pilot" drill and then opened up with successively larger drills. If the small

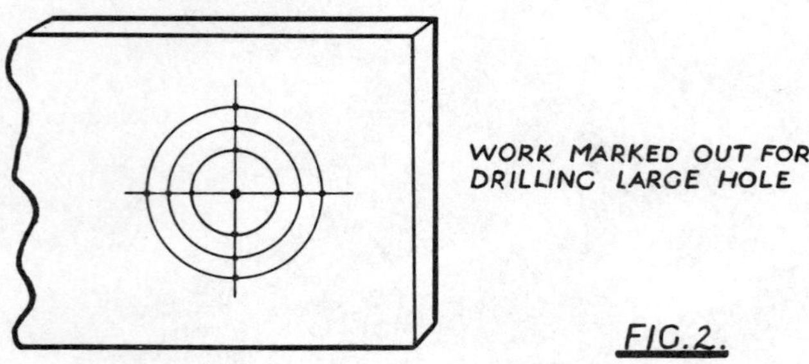

FIG. 2.

drills run out of true it can be seen against the smallest marked-out circles then corrected by filing out with a round file until finally the largest drill just splits the dot punches on the outside circle.

FIG. 3—HAND DRILL
Courtesy C. & J. Hampton Ltd. Record Tools

FIG. 4—ELECTRIC HAND DRILL
Courtesy of Stanley-Bridges Ltd.

HAND DRILLS

Hand drills (fig. 3) are used for making holes up to 8 mm diameter. They are useful for making holes in work which cannot be taken to the drilling machine.

FIG. 5—ELECTRIC HAND-DRILL STAND
Courtesy of Stanley-Bridges Ltd.

FIG. 6—PILLAR DRILLING MACHINE
Courtesy of B. Elliott (machinery) Ltd.

Electric Hand Drills

These do a similar job to the hand drill and have maximum capacities between 6-12 mm diameter. Figure 5 shows a stand on which an electric hand drill (fig. 4) can be held for use as a sensitive drilling machine.

DRILLING MACHINES

In the school workshop these are either bench drilling machines or pillar drilling machines. Bench drilling machines have a capacity up to 12 mm and should stand on a sturdy bench. The pillar drill (fig. 6) is bolted to the floor and has an intermediate table which can be raised or lowered and on some models tilted. Taper shank drills can be inserted into the taper socket spindles of these machines when the chucks are removed (fig. 7). If the taper shank drill is too small for the spindle socket the difference in size can be made up with a sleeve (fig. 7). These are made in single steps, e.g. 1 to 2, 2 to 3, and so on. Others are available which step up from 1 to 3 or 1 to 4. These sleeves should be tapped into place with a hide mallet and removed by lightly hammering a drift into the slot provided. The speed of the drill can be altered by adjusting the position of the vee belt on the pulleys.

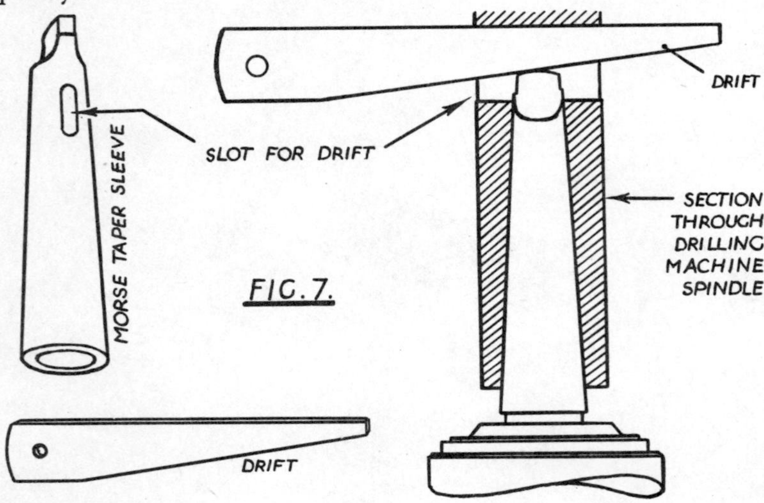

FIG. 7.

TWIST DRILLS

Twist drills are available in H.S.S. or carbon steel. Carbon steel drills are cheaper than H.S.S. but must be run at half the speed. However, the smaller sizes of these, with proper use, will last almost as long as the H.S.S. kind.

The speed of the drill should be calculated in the same way as for turning and the coolants recommended for turning also

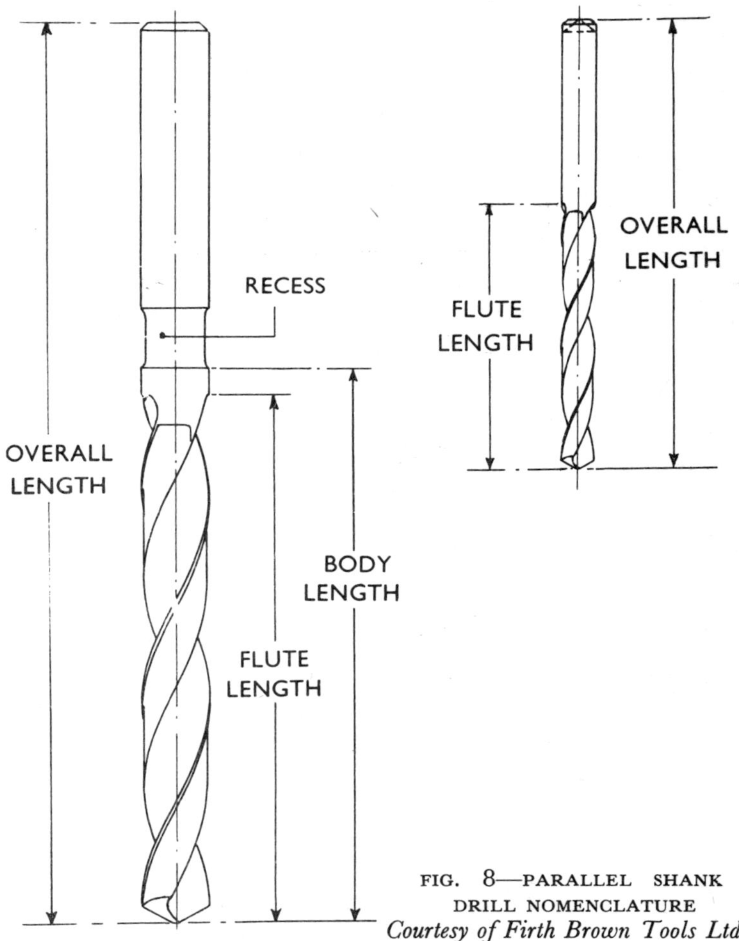

FIG. 8—PARALLEL SHANK DRILL NOMENCLATURE
Courtesy of Firth Brown Tools Ltd.

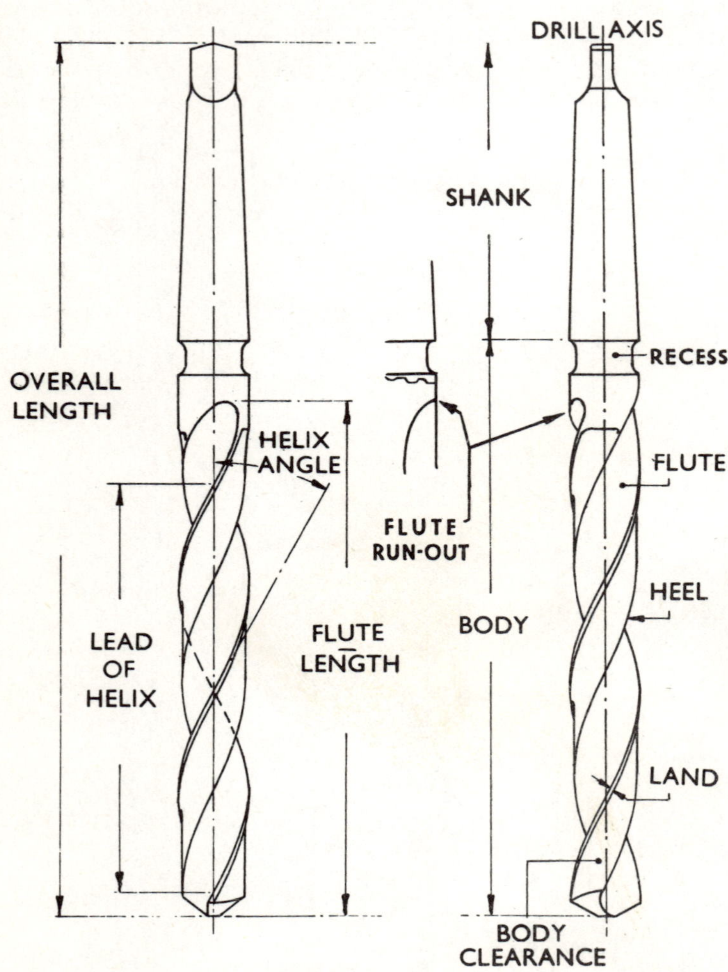

FIG. 9—MORSE TAPER SHANK DRILL NOMENCLATURE
Courtesy of Firth Brown Tools Ltd.

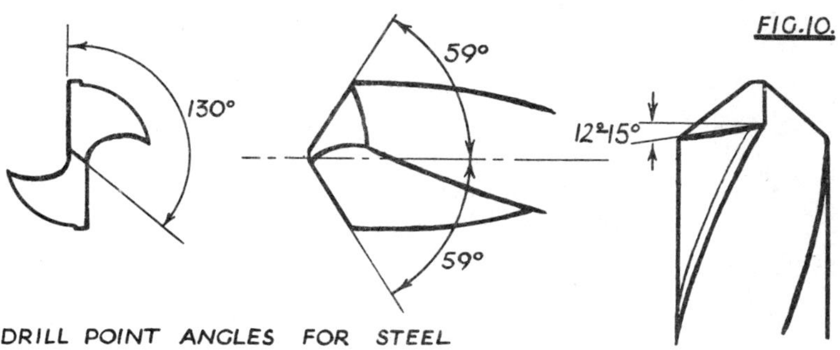

DRILL POINT ANGLES FOR STEEL

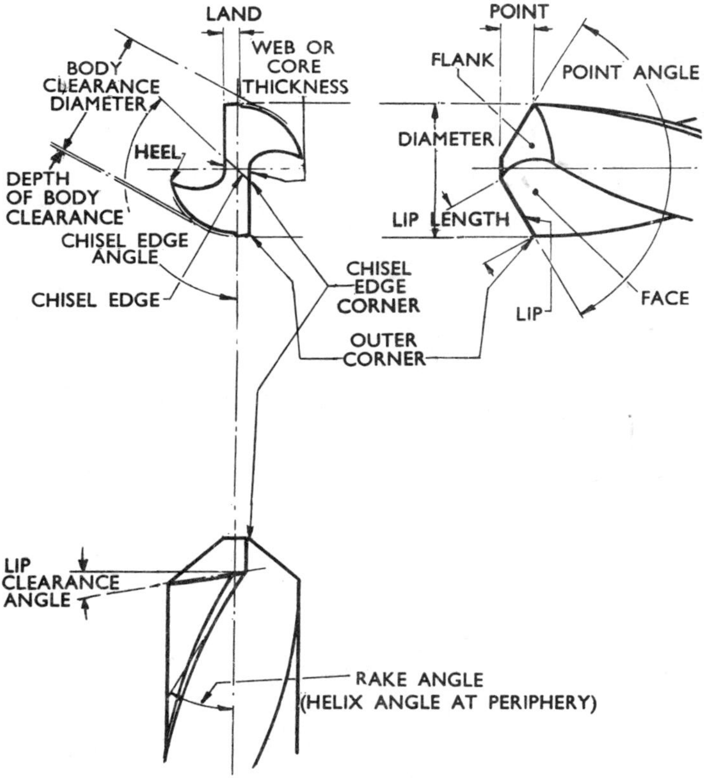

FIG. 11—DRILL NOMENCLATURE
Courtesy of Firth Brown Tools Ltd.

apply to drilling (see Chapter 13). It is important to know whether a drill is made from high speed steel or carbon steel if it is to be run at its proper speed. Often drills are marked either H.S. or C.S. but if no such marking is visible the sparks must be observed when it is being ground.

Twist drills are made with either parallel or taper shanks. Sizes up to about 12 mm have parallel shanks and above this morse taper shanks. Straight shank drills are usually called "jobbers drills". Figures 8 and 9 show the twist drill nomenclature in accordance with the British Standards Institution.

Drills are made in sizes from 0·5 mm to 65 mm. diameter.

The drill commonly used in the school workshop is ground to the angles shown in figure 10. The nomenclature is given in figure 11. The relationship between a lathe tool and a twist drill is shown in figure 12.

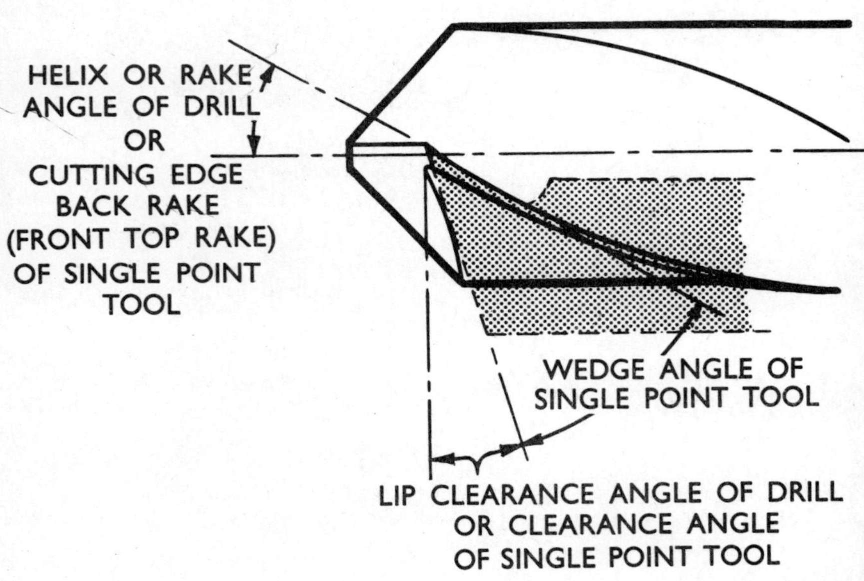

FIG. 12—RAKE AND LIP CLEARANCE ANGLES
Courtesy of Firth Brown Tools Ltd.

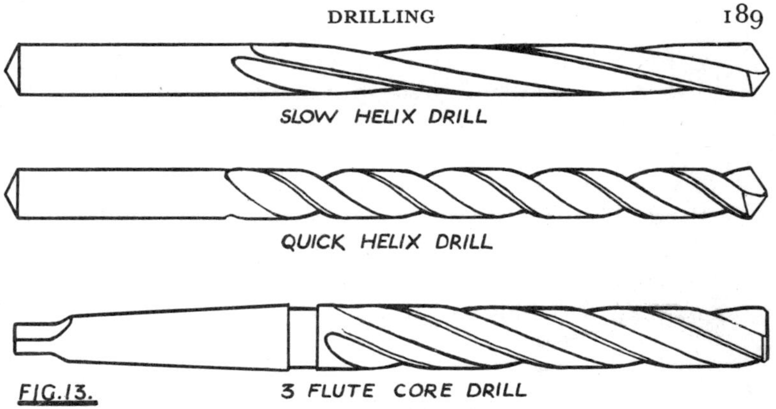

FIG. 13.

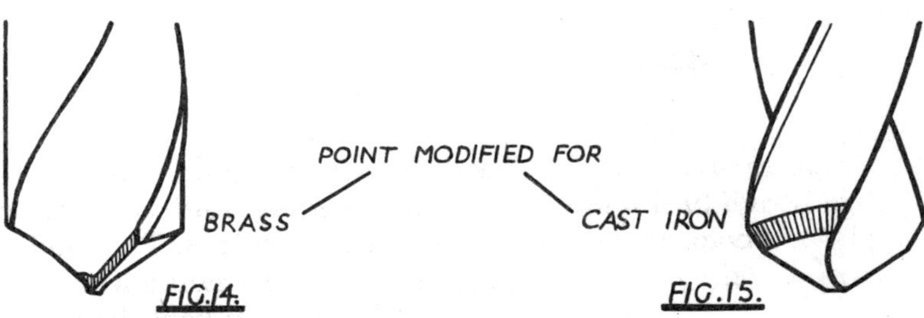

FIG. 14. FIG. 15.

Special drills are available (fig. 13):

Slow Helix drills used for brass, gunmetals and phosphor bronze (the rake angle is decreased).

Quick Helix drills used for soft metals such as aluminium and copper (the rake angle is increased).

Multi-flute Core drills may have 3 or 4 flutes and are used for enlarging existing holes, particularly cored holes in castings. These drills are strong because the flutes are not deep and therefore the web or core is relatively thick.

In the school workshop these special drills are seldom used, but the tip of an ordinary twist drill can be modified to a certain extent to suit the material being drilled. When drilling brass almost no rake is needed and the drill helix angle is ground at the tip as shown (fig. 14). Cast iron can best be drilled with a drill ground as shown in figure 15.

Sharpening Twist Drills

When accuracy is required in drill grinding it is done with a drill grinding attachment as shown in figure 16. This type of attachment is essential for large drills but drills below 12 mm can be ground with a reasonable degree of accuracy by the off-hand method. When doing this it is helpful to use a new drill as

FIG. 16—DRILL GRINDING ATTACHMENT
Courtesy of B. Elliott (machinery) Ltd.

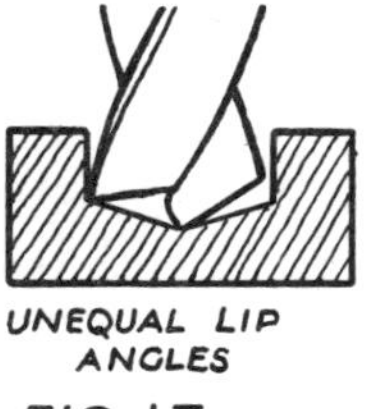

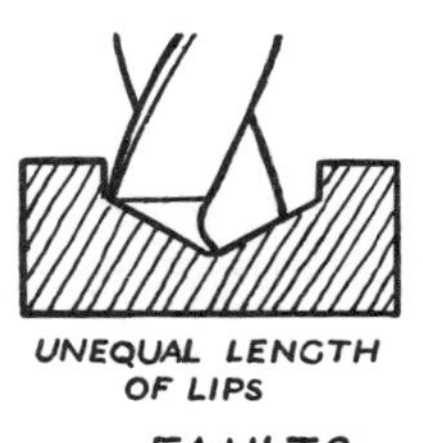

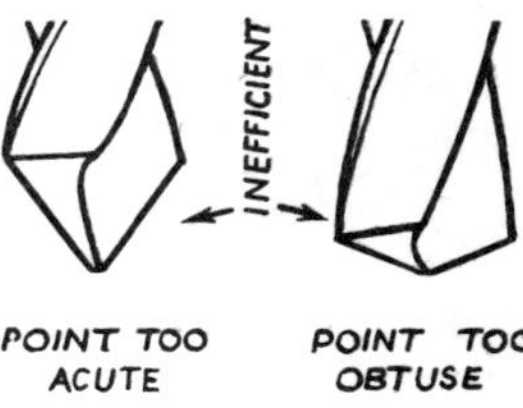

FIG.17. FAULTS

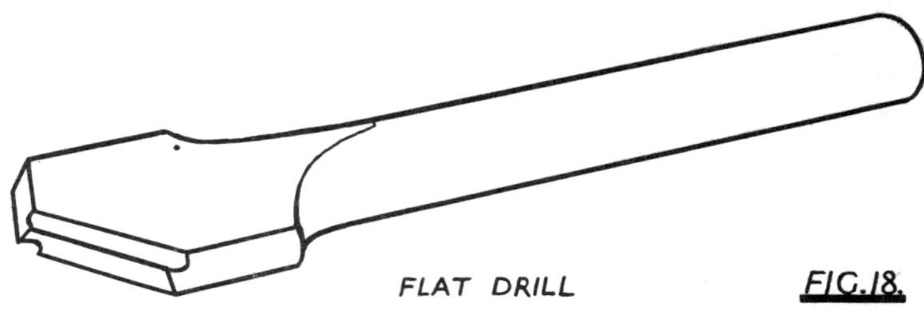

FLAT DRILL FIG.18.

a model in order to obtain the correct angles and clearances: but practice is necessary to achieve proficiency in this type of freehand grinding. Some faults in drill grinding are shown in figure 17.

FLAT DRILLS (figure 18)

These can be made from silver steel or carbon steel in the school workshop. They must be hardened and carefully tempered usually to a light straw.

PROCESSES

Countersinking

This is done with a countersinking cutter (fig. 19).

Counterboring

This is done with a counterboring cutter (fig. 19) to accommodate a cap screw or cheese head screw. Counterbores made from H.S.S. may be bought or they may be turned in the workshop from silver steel or plain carbon steel, and the flutes filled. Care must be taken with hardening as cracking may occur where there is a change of section. Temper to a mid-straw colour and sharpen with a slip stone.

Spot Facing

This is done with a counterboring cutter on rough or uneven surfaces, but only deep enough to provide a square seating for a bolt head (fig. 19).

Reaming

This is a secondary process which is done when smooth accurate holes are required. Reaming may be done using a hand reamer (fig. 20) which has a parallel shank and is turned with a tap wrench, or with a machine reamer which has a morse taper shank and is held either in the tailstock of the lathe or in the drilling machine. Adjustable reamers (fig. 21)

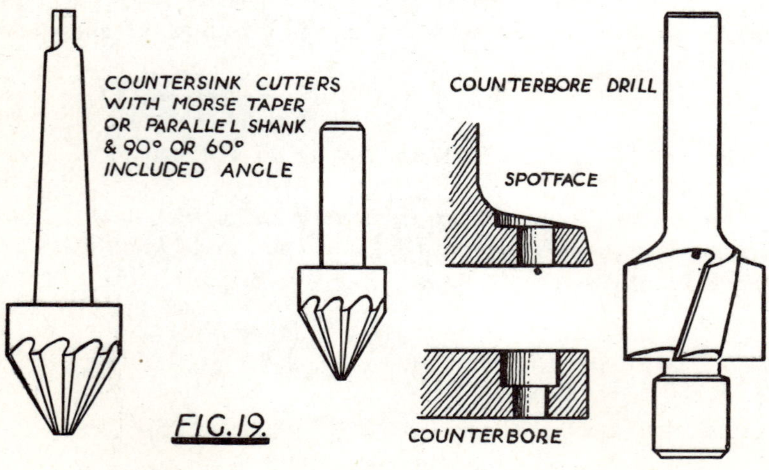

FIG. 19.

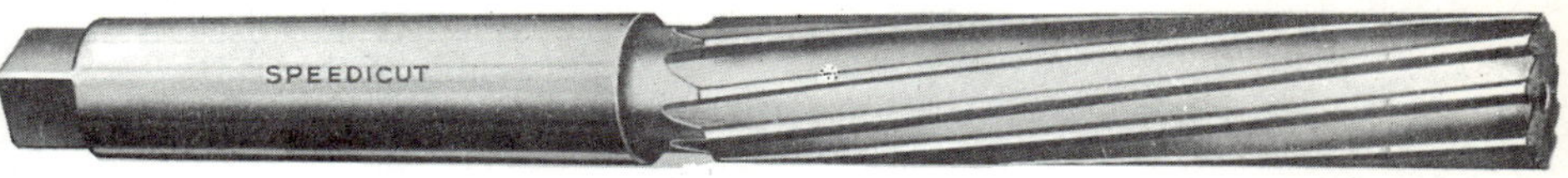

FIG. 20—HAND REAMER
Courtesy of Firth Brown Tools Ltd.

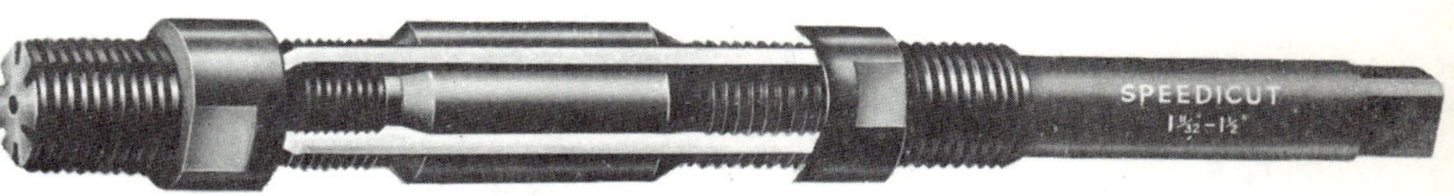

FIG. 21—ADJUSTABLE REAMER
Courtesy of Firth Brown Tools Ltd.

can be slightly enlarged after each pass through the hole until the correct size is obtained.

Whichever reamer is used care must be taken not to turn them backwards but keep them rotating in the cutting direction both in entering and withdrawing, otherwise the swarf tends to become wedged behind the cutting edges causing them to chip. Reaming should be done slowly and cutting fluid used when applicable. Holes to be reamed should be drilled out to about 0·125 mm to 0·25 mm below size for holes up to 12 mm and between 0·3 mm and 0·6 mm below size for larger holes.

13

The Lathe

The lathe is probably the most used machine tool in engineering workshops and, with the exception of the drilling machine, the oldest.

In principle the lathe is the same today as it was hundreds of years ago. There is evidence, in the form of turned bowls found at Glastonbury Lake Dwellings, that the early Iron Age people had learnt the art of turning.*

The simplest form of lathe still used today is the pole lathe as used by the chair leg turners in the Chilterns (fig. 1). We believe because of its simplicity, this could have been the kind of lathe used by the Iron Age turners. This lathe is operated by a treadle which pulls on a thong wound round the work and attached at the other end to a springy branch of a tree. The work revolves in one direction under foot pressure and in the other direction when the branch pulls the thong. The operator cuts as the work turns towards him and withdraws his chisel as it returns.

The modern engineers' lathe differs only slightly in principle from the pole lathe in that the tool is held in a tool post and is moved mechanically.

Henry Maudslay, an English engineer, is reputed to have made the first lathe of this kind in 1800.

A good modern lathe suitable for school use is shown in figure 2. Figure 3 shows many of the hidden details.

In England the size of a lathe is given as the height from the centre of the headstock spindle to the bed and the maximum distance between the centres. In America it is stated as the maximum diameter of the work that can be turned, i.e. the swing and the overall length of the bed.

* *Everyday Life in Prehistoric Times* by C. H. B. and M. Quennell (Batsford)

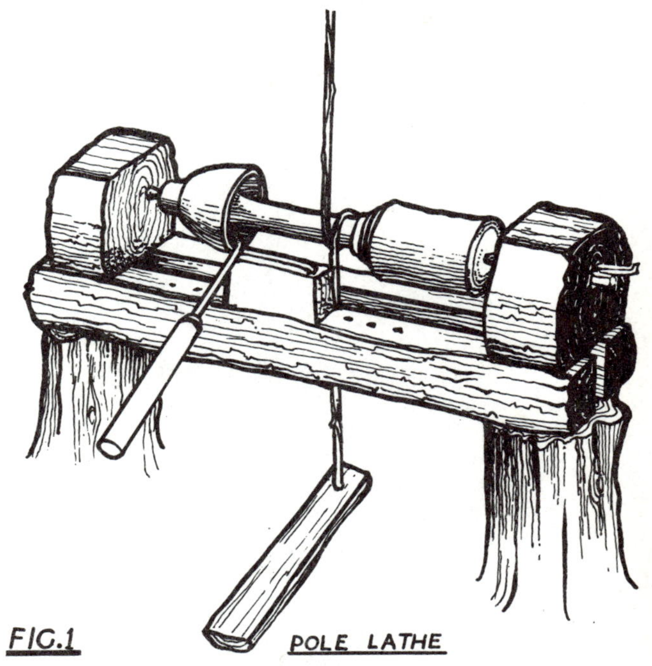

HINTS ON USING THE LATHE

The beginner usually starts by doing a piece of simple turning rather than by first learning the names of all the parts. Let us then start by assuming he is given a piece of 25 mm diameter mild steel 150 mm long.

Start by putting the workpiece in the 3-jaw chuck so that about 75 mm protrudes from the jaws. Tighten the chuck with the key and return the key to its rack.

For convenience only, we are starting with the work protruding 75 mm. In this case it is quite safe. However, the rule, when turning in a chuck is to keep the work protruding only just far enough to complete the operations you have planned, thus making it rigid.

First bring the tool up to the work by using the apron and cross slide hand wheels. We are assuming that the correctly

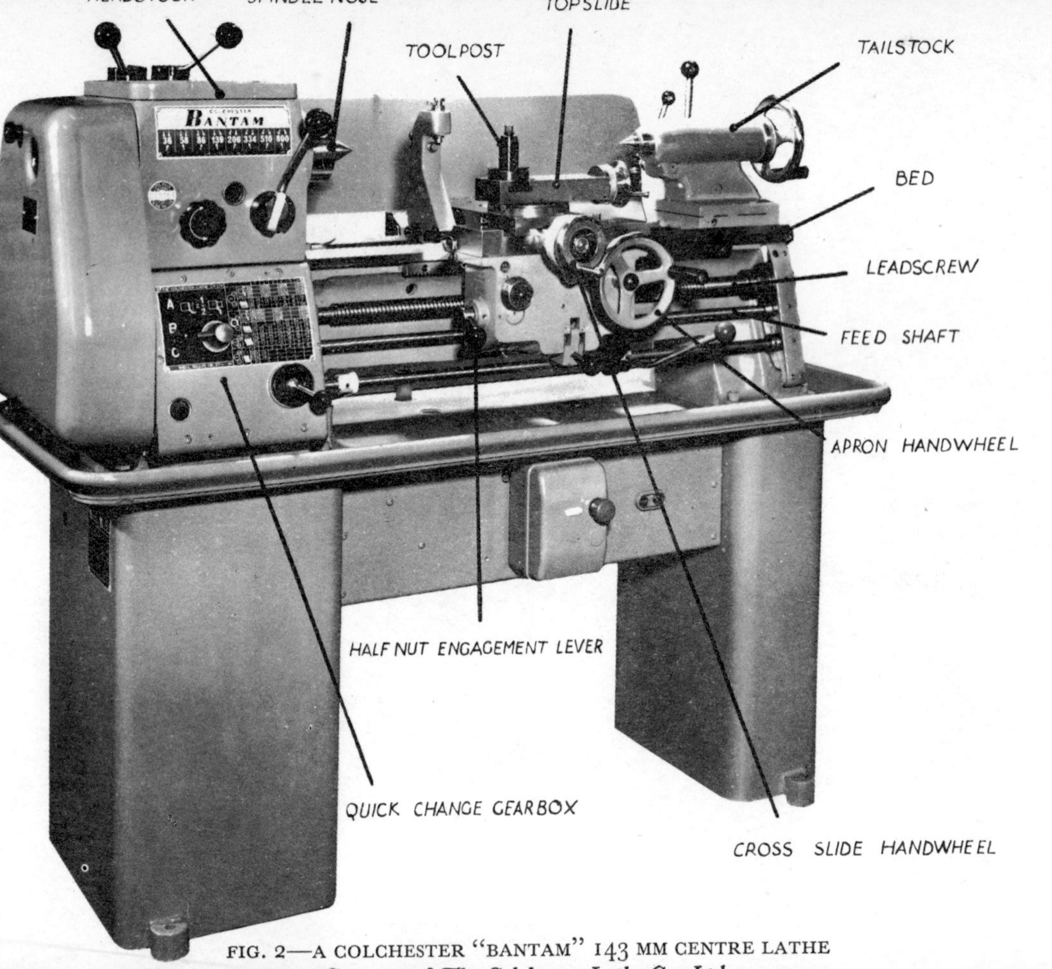

FIG. 2—A COLCHESTER "BANTAM" 143 MM CENTRE LATHE

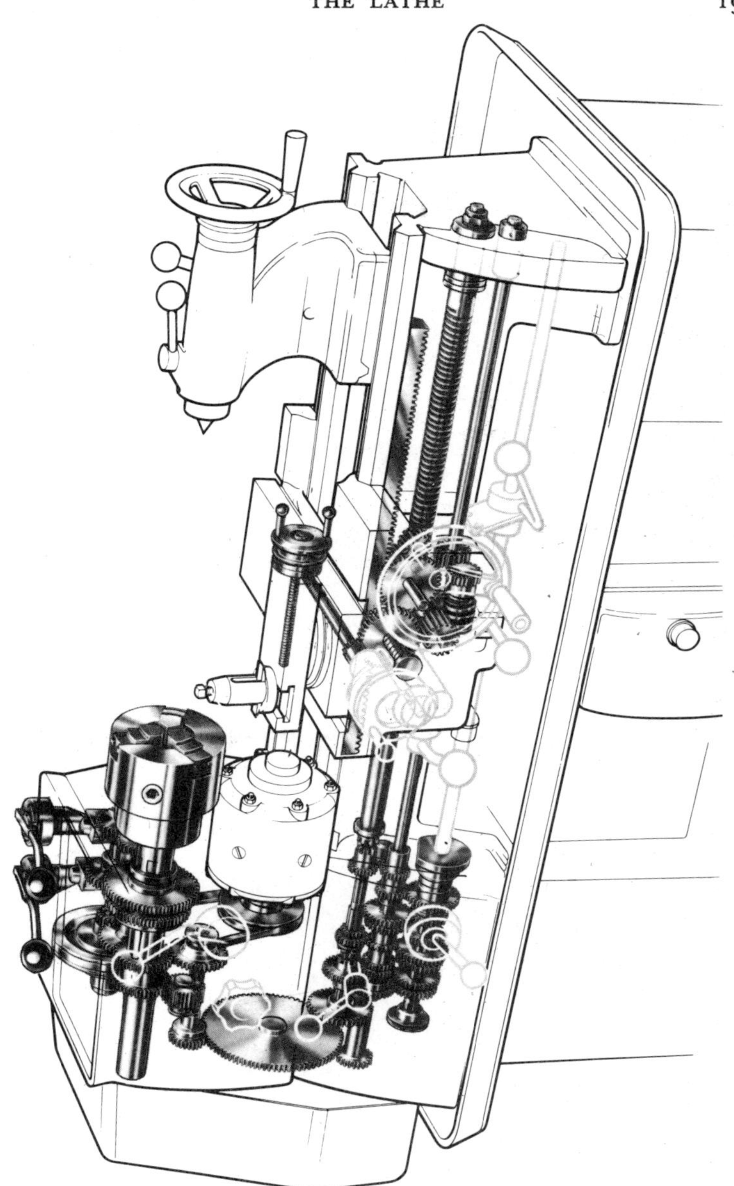

FIG. 3—VIEW SHOWING DETAILS OF TRANSMISSION ON 143 MM "BANTAM" LATHE

Courtesy of the Colchester Lathe Co. Ltd.

sharpened tool is set up as shown in figure 4. Switch on the machine at about 400 R.P.M. and, using the cross slide, start taking a facing cut by feeding the tool in gently. Try to keep the tool cutting and the feed as constant as you can right to the centre, then stop the machine. If the work is not properly faced take more cuts (0·75 mm at a time is enough) until it is properly faced.

The important thing to remember with all turning is: keep the tool cutting and do not let it rub. By rubbing we mean the act of leaving the tool against the work whilst the lathe is spinning. This blunts the tool more quickly than taking a cut.

Without altering the setting of the tool (this is the reason for having the tool this shape and at this angle) take a sliding cut as shown by using the apron handwheel, not the top slide, and try to keep the cut going smoothly. Stop the machine or withdraw the tool as soon as you get to the end of the cut.

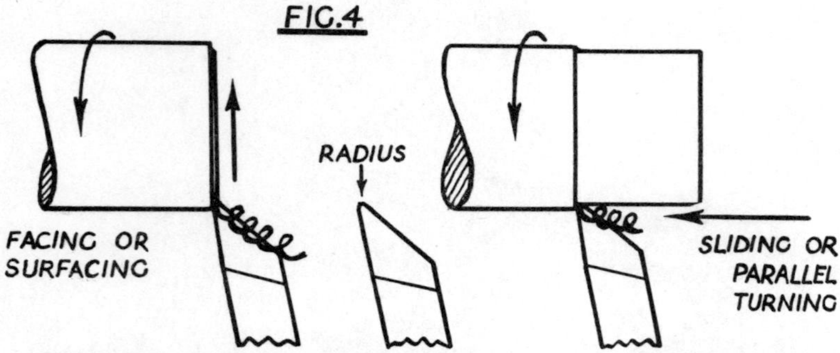

The machine in figure 2 is sturdy enough to reduce a 25 mm bar of mild steel to nothing in one cut, i.e. a 12·5 mm deep cut. But for this first trial a cut of about 1·5 mm, i.e. 3 mm on diameter is sufficient.

Never let the tool or any part of the lathe hit the chuck whilst it is spinning. This can cause serious damage.

Having got the "feel" of the machine, try the same facing and sliding cuts by using the self act or automatic feed. Since lathes vary in the method of feed engagement, the Operator's Hand Book must be consulted, or ask the teacher.

Generally in turning we use a wide range of cutting tools (fig. 5) but it is common practice to take the first heavy cuts

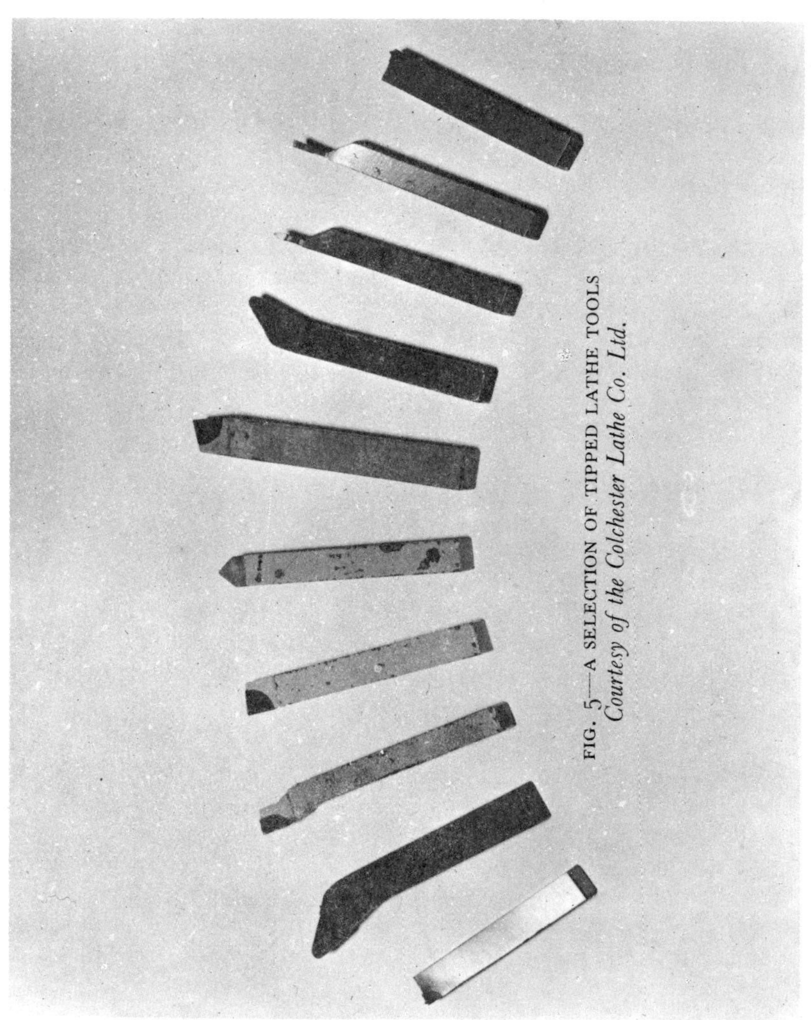

FIG. 5—A SELECTION OF TIPPED LATHE TOOLS
Courtesy of the Colchester Lathe Co. Ltd.

with a sturdy roughing tool then to finish with a tool accurately sharpened for the purpose.

A deep cut and a light regular feed are better than a light cut and a coarse feed. A coarse feed causes more abrasion at the cutting edge of the tool thus it becomes blunt more quickly.

Before starting on a piece of turning you must plan your operations carefully, otherwise you might find yourself with a partly finished component which you are unable to hold in the chuck, for further work, without damaging it.

Remember too when using a 3-jaw chuck that once the turned work has been taken out of the chuck it can seldom be put back to run absolutely true again however good the chuck. For this reason always try to do as many operations as you can at one setting.

The beginner now needs to know the different ways in which the work can be held and turned in the lathe.

METHODS OF HOLDING AND TURNING WORK

The 3-jaw Self Centring Chuck

This is shown in part section in figure 6. These chucks are provided with inside and outside jaws. The sets of jaws are numbered 1, 2, 3, and so is the body of the chuck.

It is most important that each jaw goes into its proper place, i.e. number 1 in slot number 1 and so on.

When inserting the jaws turn the chuck so that number 1 on the chuck is in the 12 o'clock position. With the chuck key turn the scroll so that the tail of the scroll just begins to show in slot No. 1. Now turn the scroll back slightly so that the tail just disappears and insert jaw No. 1, then turn the scroll so that the tail just engages the first tooth on the jaw. This can be tested by pulling the jaw: if it is properly engaged it will be held. Now turn the whole chuck so that No. 2 on the chuck is at 12 o'clock and insert jaw No. 2. Press the jaw against the scroll and rotate the scroll until the tail just engages the first tooth. Repeat this for jaw No. 3.

Note that apart from the number 1, 2 or 3 on each jaw there is also a long serial number which is the same as on the body

FIG. 6—CUT-AWAY VIEW OF 3 JAW CHUCK SHOWING SCROLL
Courtesy of F. Pratt Eng. Corp. Ltd.

of the chuck. The two sets of jaws should be kept with their proper chuck. They are not interchangeable with other chucks.

FOUR JAW INDEPENDENT CHUCK

Each jaw can be moved independently and is reversible. By adjusting each jaw separately irregular work can be held. Also round work can be set up to run quite true with the aid of a Dial Test Indicator (D.T.I.). Any slight movement of the

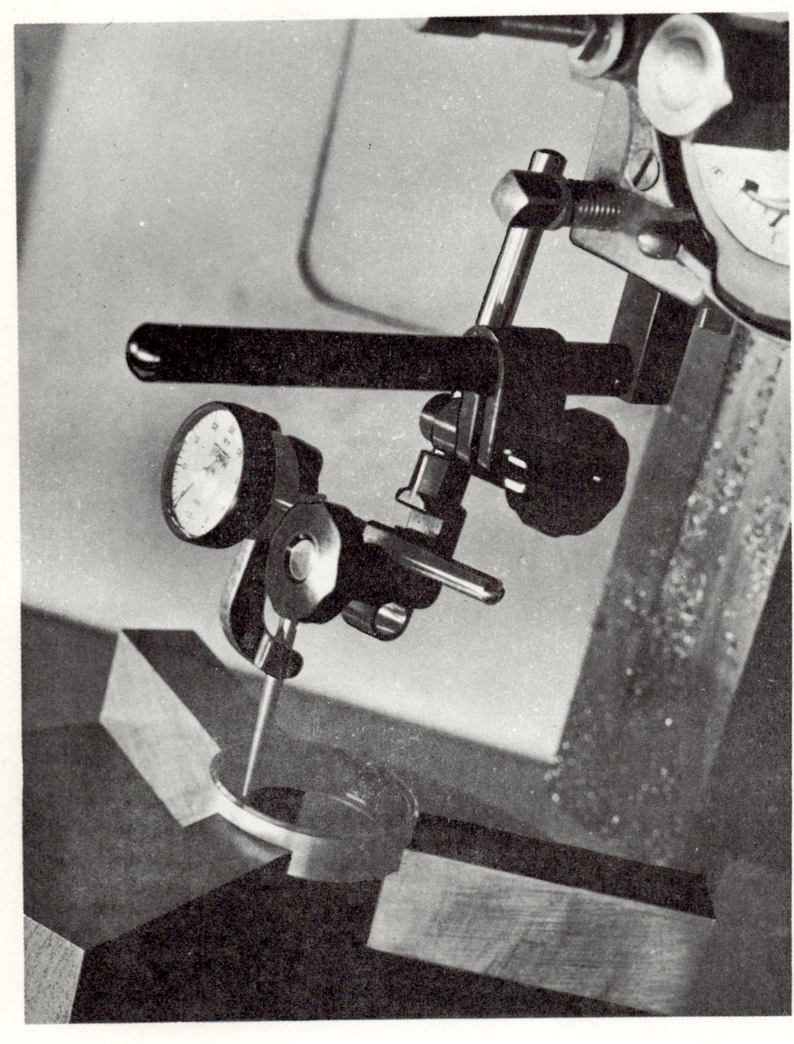

FIG. 6A—DIAL TEST INDICATOR
Courtesy of Thomas Mercer Ltd.

FIG. 7—USING INDEPENDENT 4 JAW CHUCK FOR HOLDING WORKPIECE
Courtesy of the Colchester Lathe Co. Ltd.

plunger or arm, which bears on the work, is shown on the dial of this instrument (fig. 6A).

Method of Setting up Round Work. Switch off the isolator. Set the work central by using the concentric rings on the face of the chuck (fig. 7). Turn the chuck by hand. With a D.T.I. check the work close to the jaws. By tightening or slackening the jaws opposite to each other—No. 1 opposite No. 3 and No. 2 opposite No. 4—it is possible to get the work to run true.

Now withdraw the D.T.I. and move it to check the end of the work furthest from the chuck. Any error at this end is removed by tapping the work with a hide mallet, but remember to withdraw the D.T.I., whilst actually tapping the work, otherwise it will be damaged. By using the mallet only, this end is made to run true. Next check the end of the work nearest the chuck. This will now be slightly out of true. True up by using the chuck key. Now check the end furthest from the chuck: use a mallet as before and make it run true. Repeat as often as necessary.

Remember: True the work near the chuck by using the chuck key only and the part furthest from the chuck with the mallet only.

By this method it is possible to get the work quite true over its whole length when checked with a D.T.I.

LATHE TOOLS

The grinding and setting up of a lathe tool is of primary importance and it takes not a little practice to become proficient in grinding these tools. Figure 8 shows a typical general purpose tool.

The lathe tools we use in the school workshop are mostly of high speed steel (H.S.S.) but we sometimes use carbon steel tools, particularly when we need to make form tools or special boring tools. Carbon steel tools are excellent but they are not as tough or long-lasting as H.S.S. and must be run at a slower speed. Tipped tools are also available. These consist usually of a small piece of tungsten carbide brazed to a carbon steel shank

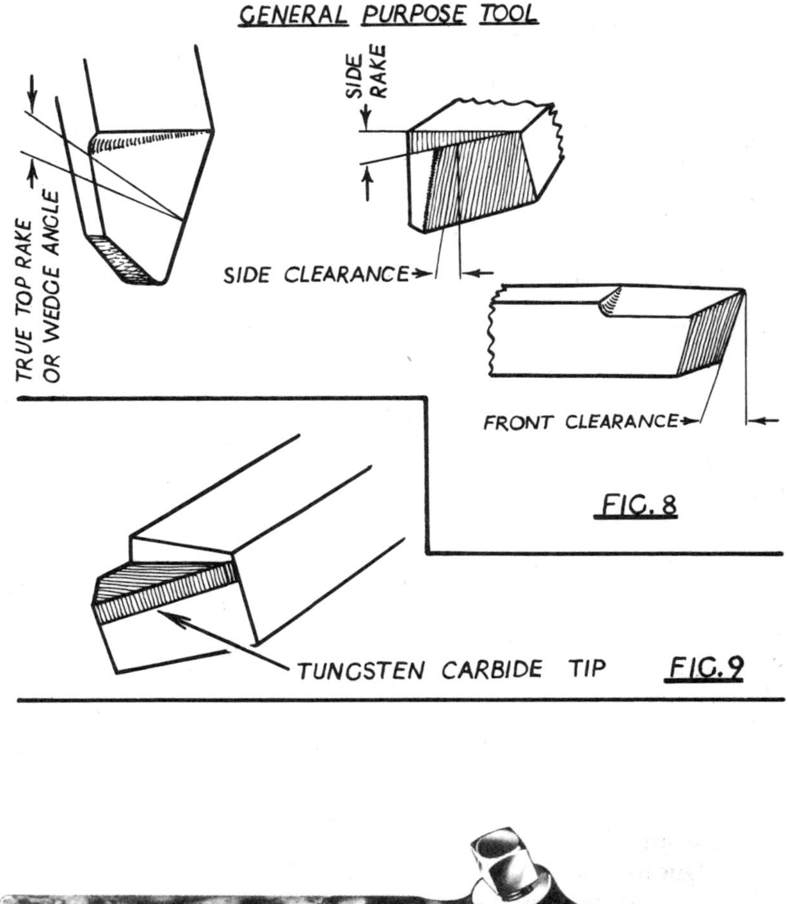

GENERAL PURPOSE TOOL

SIDE RAKE

TRUE TOP RAKE OR WEDGE ANGLE

SIDE CLEARANCE

FRONT CLEARANCE

FIG. 8

TUNGSTEN CARBIDE TIP

FIG. 9

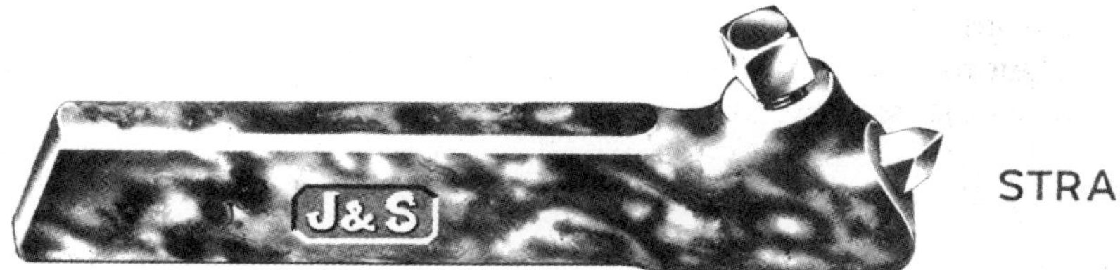

FIG. 10—STRAIGHT LATHE TOOL HOLDER
Courtesy of Jones and Shipman & Co.

(fig. 9). These tools are so hard that they need special diamond wheels to grind them. For this reason they are seldom used in school.

However, from whatever steel the tools are made the cutting and clearance angles must be made to suit the material being cut. The following table can be used as a guide when grinding tools:

Material	*Top Rake*	*Side and Front Clearance*
Aluminium	25°–35°	
Mild steel	23°–30°	
Carbon steel	15°–25°	5°–10°
Cast iron	7°–12°	
Bronze	5°–10°	

TABLE OF TOOL ANGLES

(Notice that the softer the material the greater the top rake.)

Lathe tools can be either in the form of tool bits which are held in a tool holder (fig. 10) or large solid tools (fig. 5) held directly in the tool post.

Figure 8 shows the tool ground for efficient performance with the cutting edge horizontal. However, it is not always possible to keep the cutting edge horizontal when the tool is set up, especially since manufacturers make tool holders which hold the tool at an angle.

The tool should always be set up so that the tip is at centre height. Figure 11 shows a tipped tool being adjusted to centre height against the point of the lathe centre, and figure 12 shows a parting tool set by the same method. Another good method is to lightly hold a thin 150 mm rule against the work with the tip of the tool (fig. 13). If the rule is upright the tool is central.

Figure 14 shows a roughing tool which is used for taking heavy cuts. The finishing tool has a radius on the tip. If this is used in conjunction with a fine feed the resultant finish will be

FIG. 11—ADJUSTING TOOL TO CENTRE HEIGHT USING QUICK CHANGE TOOL POST

Courtesy of the Colchester Lathe Co. Ltd.

FIG. 12—SETTING TOOL TO CORRECT CENTRE HEIGHT WITH THE USE OF PACKING AND BOAT

Courtesy of the Colchester Lathe Co. Ltd.

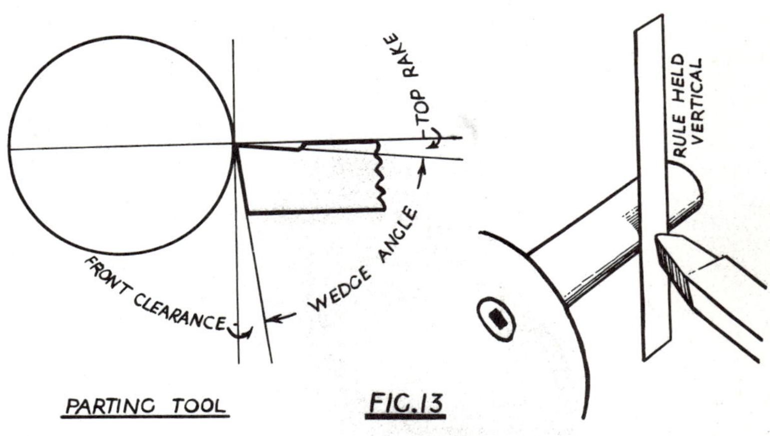
TOP RAKE
RULE HELD VERTICAL
WEDGE ANGLE
FRONT CLEARANCE
PARTING TOOL

FIG. 13

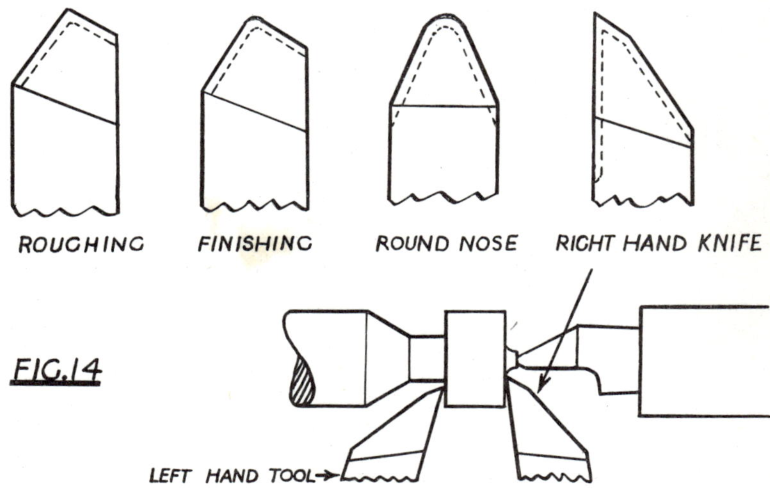
ROUGHING
FINISHING
ROUND NOSE
RIGHT HAND KNIFE
LEFT HAND TOOL

FIG. 14

smooth. The round nose tool can also be used for finishing or for making radii. The knife tool is used as shown.

A tool is either right hand or left hand. A right hand tool is used on the right of the piece being turned and the left hand tool on the left.

TOOL POSTS

Figure 15 shows three tool posts: on the left is the swivel type tool post; in the centre is shown a rear tool post (this is useful for parting off, the parting tool being held upside down); the third is a pillar type tool post (by means of the rocker or boat the height of the tool can be adjusted). Figure 16 shows a quick change tool post with its set of tool holders and wrenches. These are useful where various tools are being used on a component. Once the centre height of the tool is set they can be taken out and returned in a second and will always return to centre height. Figure 17 shows the swivel type four-way tool post.

FIG. 15—3 TYPES OF TOOL POSTS:
LEFT—*Swivel type tool block*
CENTRE—*Rear toolpost*
RIGHT—*Pillar type toolpost*
Courtesy of Colchester Lathe Co. Ltd.

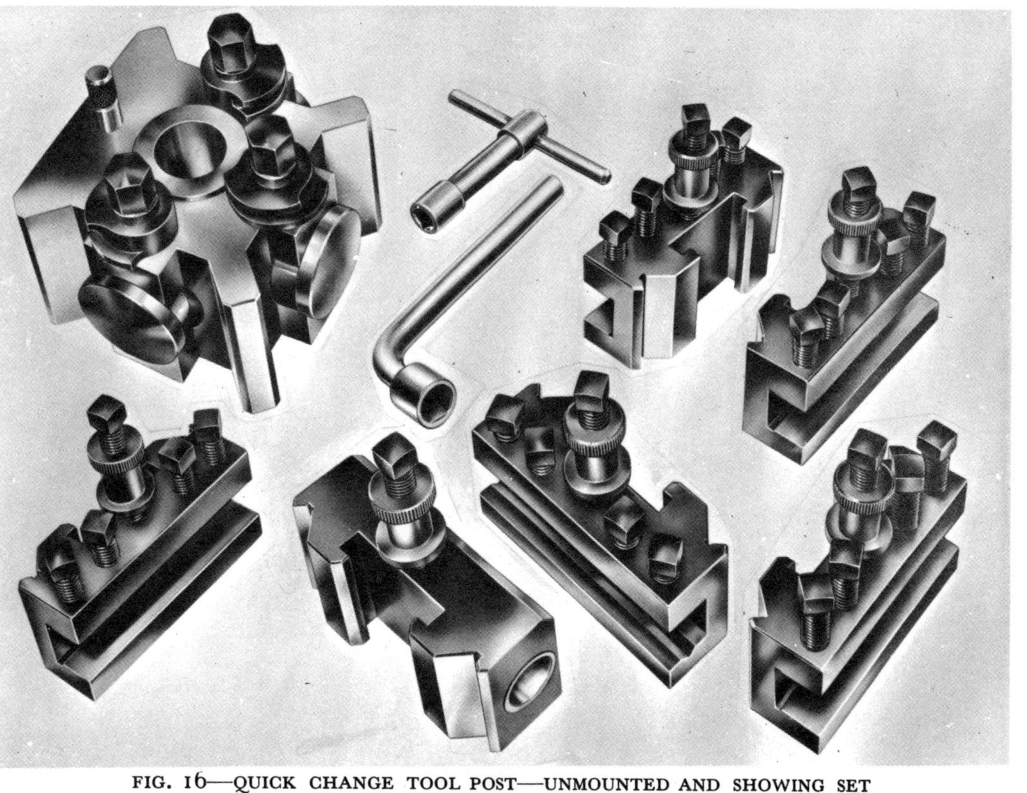

FIG. 16—QUICK CHANGE TOOL POST—UNMOUNTED AND SHOWING SET OF TOOLHOLDERS AND WRENCHES

Courtesy of the Colchester Lathe Co. Ltd.

CUTTING SPEED

The speed at which the work revolves when being turned is determined by 1. the diameter of the work, 2. the material being turned, 3. the kind of tool, i.e. H.S.S., carbon or tungsten tipped, 4. the rigidity of the machine, and 5. whether a coolant is being used or not.

It is difficult to lay down hard and fast rules because there are all these factors to be considered.

The following table of speeds will be found useful, but common sense based on experience must be applied.

TABLE OF CUTTING SPEEDS

	Aluminium	*Brass*	*Bronze*	*M/S*	*High carbon steel*	*Cast iron*	
Dry	120	90	20	28	15	20	Cutting speeds in metres per minute
With coolant	150	—	25	33	18	—	
Screw cutting	18	18	18	12	10	10	

The above table is for H.S.S. tools. For carbon steel tools these speeds must be halved. For tipped tools they can be trebled. Notice that brass and cast iron are machined without lubricant.

To calculate the speed at which a piece of work is being cut: given the diameter of the work and the speed in revs. per minute

$$\text{Cutting Speed} = \frac{\text{Diam. of work in mm} \times 3\tfrac{1}{7} \times \text{R.P.M.}}{1000}$$

e.g. 75 mm diameter work revolving at 140 R.P.M. Find the cutting speed.

$$\frac{75 \times 3\tfrac{1}{7} \times 140}{1000} = 33 \text{ metres per min.}$$

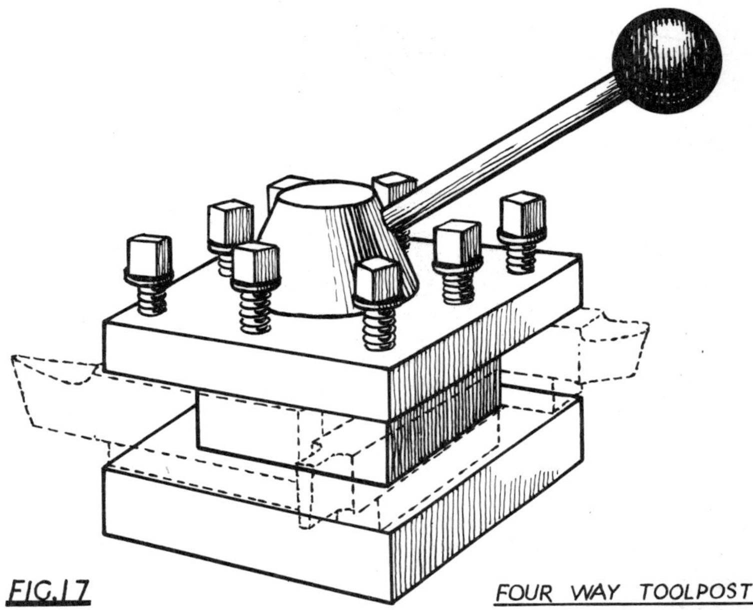

FIG. 17 FOUR WAY TOOLPOST

This speed of 33 metres per minute is also known as the surface or peripheral speed.

If the lathe when cutting makes an excessive noise, chatters or overheats, stop the machine and check the speed, the sharpness of the tool and the rigidity of the setting, i.e. the tightness of the chuck, the amount of play if a centre is being used and consider, if applicable, the use of a coolant. Check also the feed. Generally a lighter cut and a finer feed combined with a sharp tool and coolant (if applicable) will improve the work.

Coolants lubricate the tip of the tool and make the passage of the swarf over it easier; they also take away the heat from the work and the tool thus reducing the wear. Brass and cast iron form small chips and for this reason they do not abrade the top of the tool in the same way.

Soluble oil is the coolant most used in school for steel but there are many others available but they tend to be more expensive (see Chapter 16). Here are some recommended coolants:

TABLE OF COOLANTS

Metal	*Coolant*
Aluminium	Paraffin
Duralumin	Paraffin
Mild steel	Soluble oil
Carbon steel	Soluble oil
Cast iron	Dry
Brass	Dry

PROCESSES

Parting Off

This process causes some difficulty in school.

For successful parting off the lathe bearing should be good and the top slide and cross slide properly adjusted so that they are not too loose.

The tool must be accurately ground as shown in figure 13 and figure 18 with little top rake and front clearance: this is to keep the tip as strong as possible.

Have the tool protruding from the holder just enough to part through the work (and no more), and set it up perfectly central and at right angles to the axis of the work.

Try to plan the work so that the parting off cut is done as close to the chunk, i.e. the point of support, as possible.

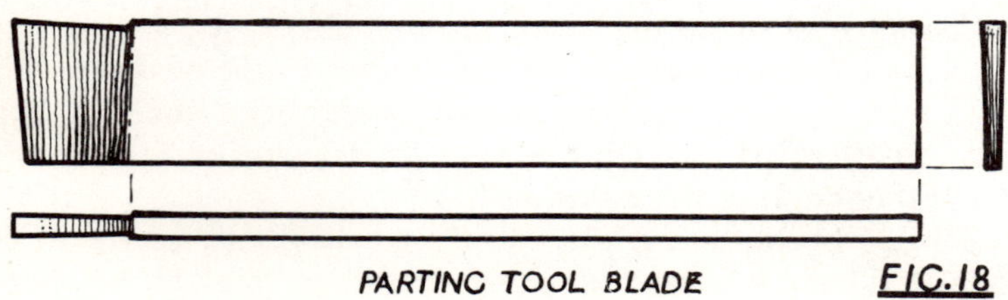

PARTING TOOL BLADE FIG. 18

FIG. 19—PARTING-OFF
Courtesy of the Colchester Lathe Co. Ltd.

FIG. 20—A DIAMOND PATTERN KNURL WITH KNURLING TOOL
Courtesy of the Colchester Lathe Co. Ltd.

Start the lathe and commence parting off. If it starts chattering do not withdraw but increase the speed of your feed. Keep the tool cutting but do not force it. Figure 19 shows pieces that have been parted off a 25 mm bar of M.S. without any coolant, for demonstration purposes, but a coolant will prolong the life of the tool and give a cleaner cut.

Parting off can be done at speeds just below those for ordinary turning.

Knurling

This can be either straight knurling or diamond. Figure 20 shows a diamond knurl: this is done with double wheels as shown.

Knurling imposes a considerable strain on the work and the lathe so be sure the work is held tightly in the chuck and that the knurling wheels are oiled.

For smaller lathes the knurling tool shown in figure 21 is recommended because the tool itself takes much of the strain.

FIG. 21—ADJUSTABLE KNURLING TOOLHOLDER
Courtesy of Jones and Shipman & Co.

Start with the wheels partly off the work as in figure 22 and apply enough pressure to start the pattern. Feed the knurling tool along using the apron hand wheel and return to the starting point, feed in the cross slide about 0·1 mm. Repeat as required.

The knurling is not complete until the diamonds are properly formed. Beware of over knurling. This causes pieces to be broken away from the knurled surface.

The edge of the knurling can be finished either with a chamfer or with a turned step as in figure 22.

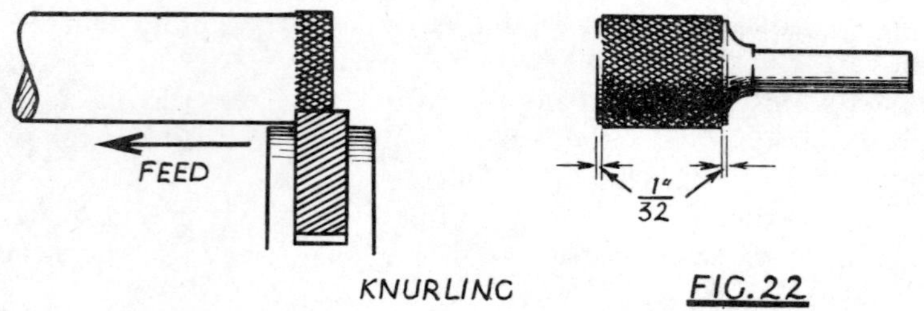

KNURLING FIG. 22

The speed for knurling a 25 mm diameter piece of mild steel is about 75 R.P.M. A coolant may be used according to the type of material being knurled. The speed for other materials and diameters can be judged from the speed for mild steel.

Drilling

This is done with the drill held in the tail-stock chuck. Always start by using a slocombe centre drill (figs. 23 and 24) Be sure to run the lathe fast enough. Centre drills are often broken because the speed is not high enough.

FIG. 23—SLOCOMBE CENTRE DRILL
Courtesy of Jones and Shipman & Co.

FIG. 24—TAILSTOCK CHUCK HOLDING CENTRE DRILL
Courtesy of the Colchester Lathe Co. Ltd.

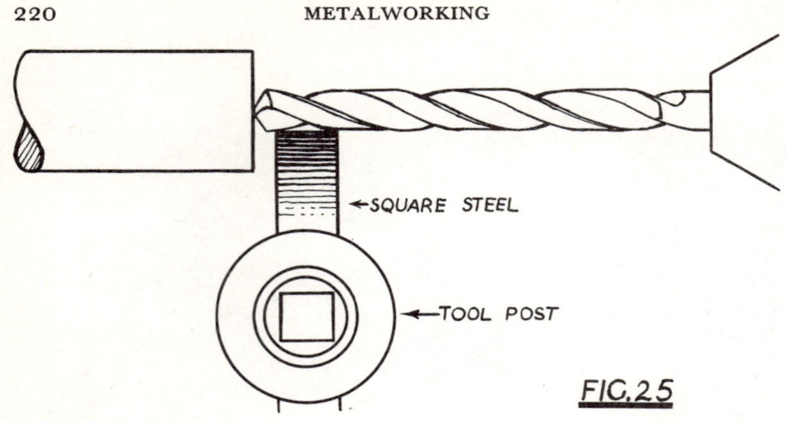

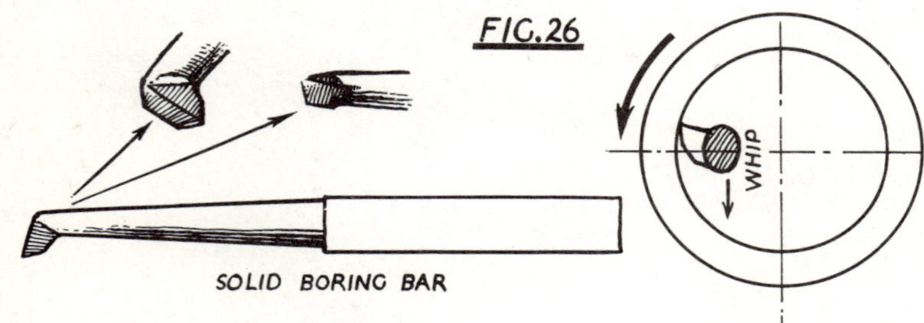

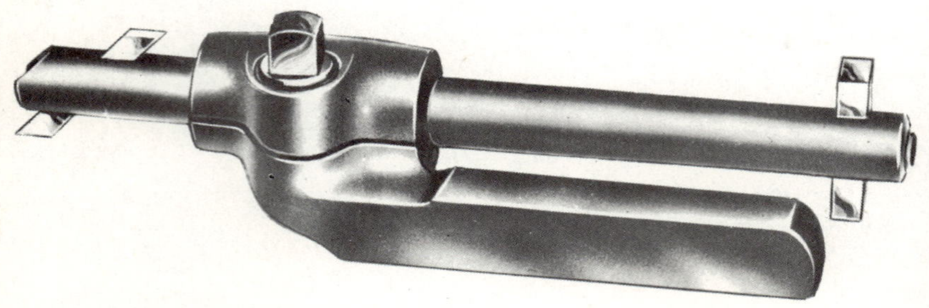

FIG. 27—BORING BAR AND TOOL BIT
Courtesy of Jones and Shipman & Co.

Start centre drilling gently with the quill clamping nut partly tightened, then slacken it off as the drilling proceeds. It is important to keep the centre drilling true, particularly if it is to be followed by other drills which must be concentric.

Drills can be kept steady by holding a piece of steel against the tip as shown in figure 25.

A large taper shank drill may be held in the Morse taper of the tailstock quill. A Morse taper sleeve may be necessary for this.

Boring

Boring can be done either with a solid boring bar as in figure 26 or a boring bar and tool bit as in figure 27.

The solid boring bar can be of H.S.S. steel or it can be forged in the workshop from carbon steel.

When setting up a boring tool keep it as short as possible, i.e. rigid. The tip of the tool can be set slightly above centre when boring parallel holes. By setting it high the tendency to "dig in" is reduced because as the tool "whips" downwards it will tend to clear itself (fig. 26). It is often necessary to increase the front clearance angle on the boring tool as shown.

Another method of boring, less used in school, is to have the boring tool revolving in the chuck and the work clamped on the cross slide.

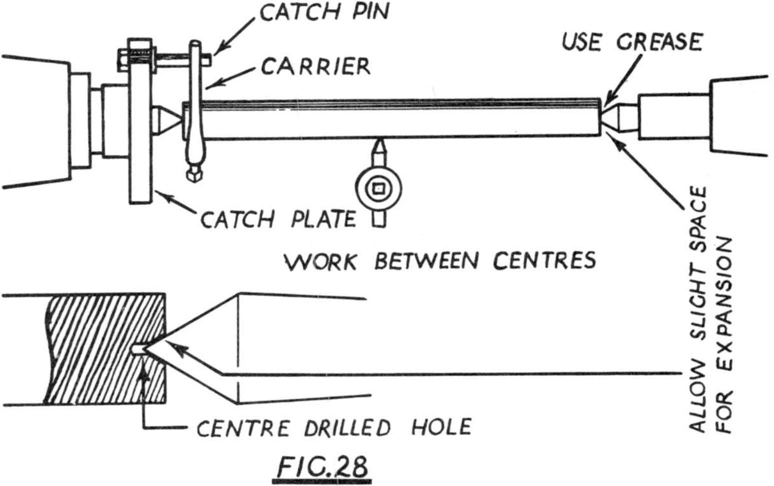

FIG. 28

FIG. 29—DRIVING WORK HELD BETWEEN CENTRES

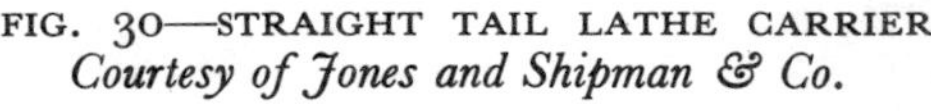
FIG. 30—STRAIGHT TAIL LATHE CARRIER
Courtesy of Jones and Shipman & Co.

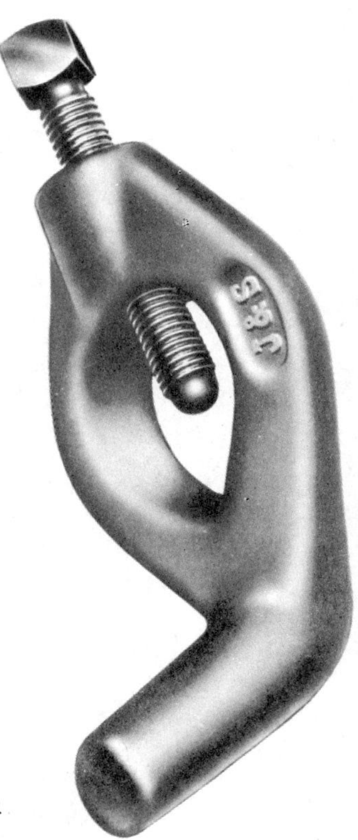

FIG. 31—BENT TAIL LATHE CARRIER
Courtesy of Jones and Shipman & Co.

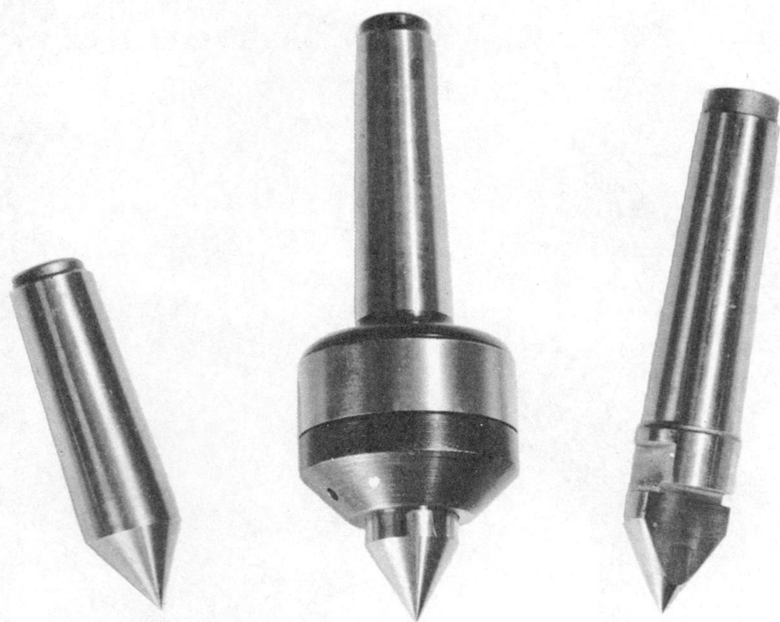

FIG. 32—3 TYPES OF CENTRES—LATHE CENTRE, ROTATING CENTRE, HALF CENTRE
Courtesy of the Colchester Lathe Co. Ltd.

Turning between Centres

Figures 28 and 29 show work set up between centres.

Before this can be done each end of the work to be turned must be properly centre drilled with a slocombe centre drill. The large cutting edges of a centre drill are ground to 60° to suit the lathe centres (fig. 28).

The work is driven by a catch plate on which there is a catch pin, which turns the carrier (fig. 30). A bent tail carrier (fig. 31) can be used with a catch plate which has a slot instead of a catch pin. The tail of the carrier fits into the slot.

Lathe centres are shown in figure 32: the right hand one is cut away. The centre one is a revolving centre and the left hand one is the standard model.

Before the centres are put in the lathe they must be thoroughly wiped with a cloth and the holes in the headstock and tailstock cleaned, also the sleeves if they are being used.

Often the centre which fits into the headstock spindle is soft so that it can be turned when it becomes out of true. It is important that the headstock centres run true. This can be checked with a D.T.I.

The tailstock or dead centres are hard. The cut away variety are also known as half centres and are useful for facing work with a right hand knife tool (fig. 14).

When setting up work using a dead centre there must be a slight amount of play between the work and the centre, i.e. it must be able to revolve freely. For this reason the back centre must be kept greased and great care taken to avoid the work overheating at the centre owing to friction caused by the work expanding as a cut is taken.

This friction can be avoided by using a revolving centre but care must be taken with long work which is likely to expand more than short work.

Revolving centres turn at the same speed as the work.

When starting to turn between centres first take a light cut along the full length of the work and check both ends with a micrometer. If the work is tapered the tailstock must be adjusted; this is done by first slackening the clamping screws and then setting the top part of the tailstock over by using the side screws. This varies from lathe to lathe.

Use of Mandrels

Figure 33 shows a mandrel. These are made from hardened tempered and ground steel. They have a slight taper of about

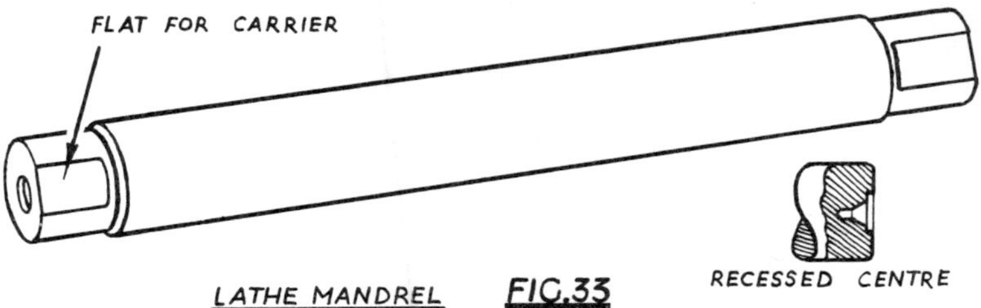

LATHE MANDREL FIG.33

FIG. 34—FIXED OR STATIONARY STEADY
Courtesy of the Colchester Lathe Co. Ltd.

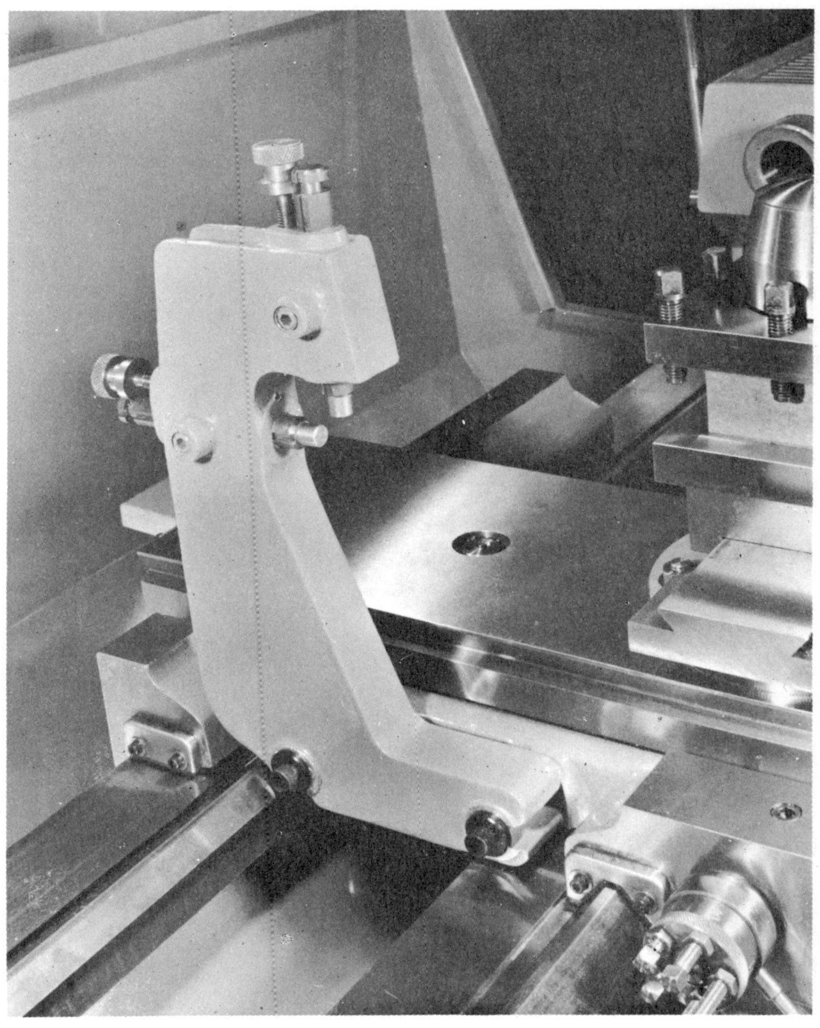

FIG. 35—TRAVELLING STEADY
Courtesy of the Colchester Lathe Co. Ltd.

0·075 mm over a 150 mm length. Each end is centre drilled and recessed to protect the edges of the centre from damage. A flat is provided for the screw of the carrier. Mandrels can be bought in sizes from 4·5 mm up to 37 mm diameter.

Work which has been previously bored or reamed is pressed on to these and held by friction then turned between centres. Gear wheel blanks are often done in this way.

Use of Steadies

Long work between centres or long work which cannot be supported with the tailstock centre can be supported with a steady.

There are two kinds of steady. Figure 34 shows a fixed steady. Figures 35 and 36 show travelling steadies.

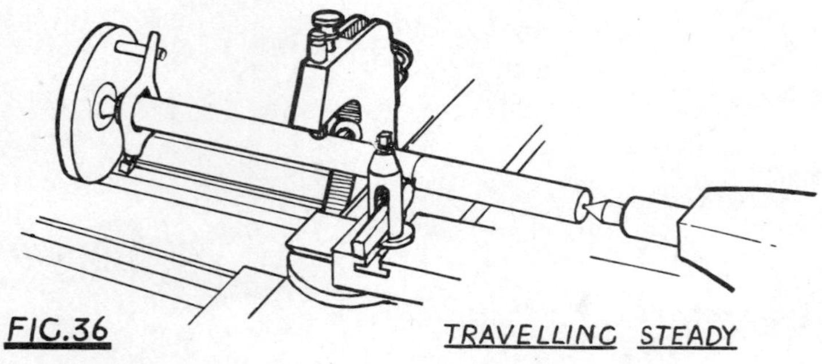

FIG. 36 TRAVELLING STEADY

When setting up a steady adjust the points of support for the work, which are made of phosphor bronze, so that they just bear against the work and then lock them with the screws provided. Lubricate the points of support and turn the lathe by hand to be sure they are not too tight.

The work must be running true before the steady is adjusted to it. Never force work to run true with a steady as this strains the steady, causes the work to be turned out of round and can cause other parts to be eccentric if turned, when the steady is removed.

The travelling steady is particularly useful when cutting long slender threads.

FIG. 37—TAPER TURNING USING COMPOUND SLIDE
Courtesy of the Colchester Lathe Co. Ltd.

Taper Turning

The top slide is used for most short tapers as in figures 37 and 38.

If the angle is not given on the drawing it can be calculated as in the example in figure 38.

$$\text{Tan } \theta = \frac{\text{opposite}}{\text{adjacent}} = \frac{7{\cdot}5 \text{ mm}}{30 \text{ mm}} = 0{\cdot}25$$

$$\text{Tan } 0{\cdot}25 = 14^\circ \text{ approx.}$$

The tool itself set at an angle can be used for very short tapers as in figure 39.

Long slight tapers can be made with the work between centres and the tailstock centre set over as shown in figure 40.

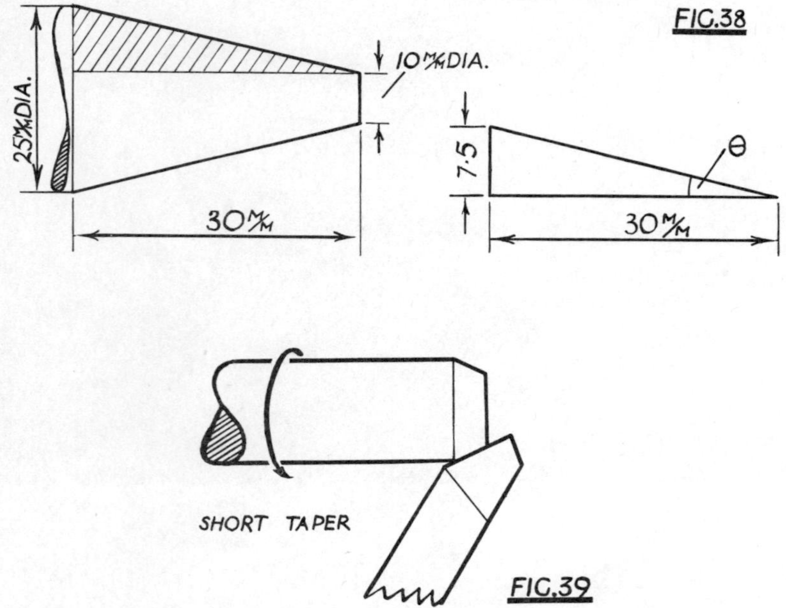

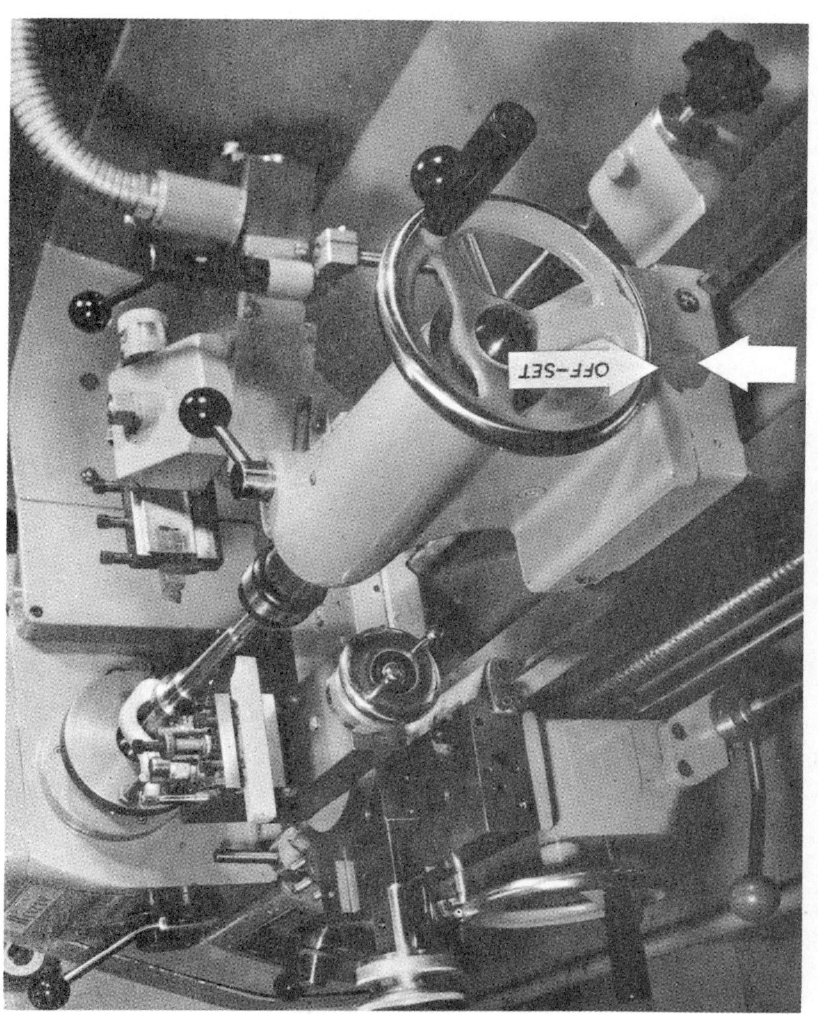

FIG. 40—THE "OFF-SET" TAILSTOCK METHOD OF TAPER TURNING
Courtesy of the Colchester Lathe Co. Ltd.

Figure 41 shows a method of calculating the amount of "set over" or "off-set".

If we assume the component at the top of figure 41 is to be made from 25 mm diameter bright drawn mild steel an accurate way to set over the tailstock is shown. First set the work up between centres, then by calculation reduce the base of the triangle to a length which can be accommodated on the top slide. Be sure the top slide is set to cut parallel. With a D.T.I. fixed in the tool post wind the top slide over to the left and return it slightly to eliminate the back lash and set the micrometer collar to zero. Wind the cross slide in so that the D.T.I.

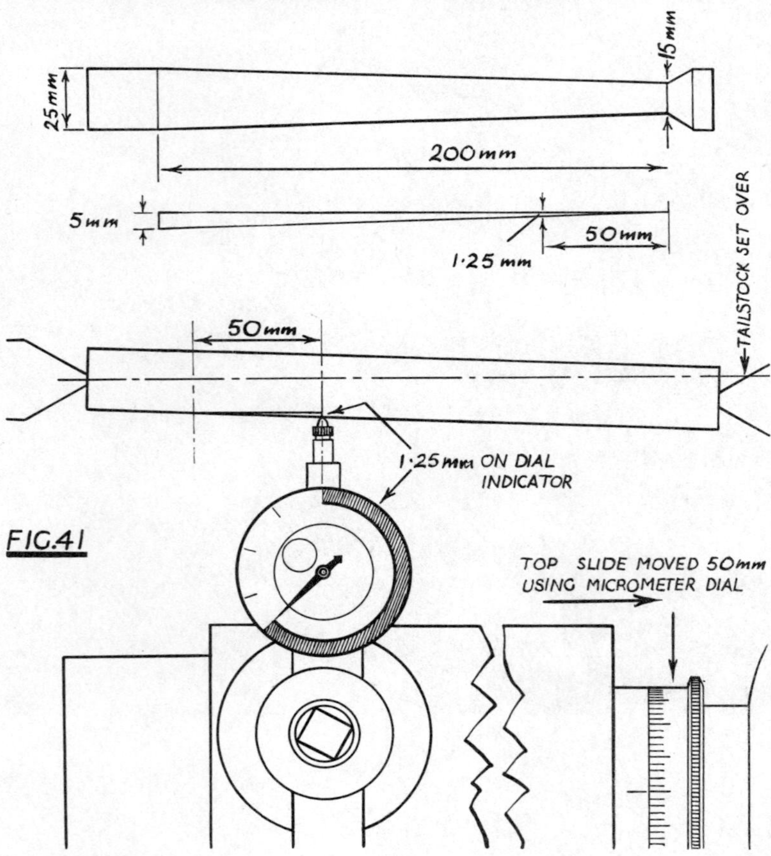

FIG.41

FIG. 42—TAPER TURNING USING TAPER TURNING ATTACHMENT
Courtesy of the Colchester Lathe Co. Ltd.

starts reading, then zero it. Now wind the top slide back 50 mm (carefully counting the turns). Check the reading on the D.T.I. If it is less than 1·25 mm the tailstock must be set over more and vice versa. Repeat until the D.T.I. reads exactly 1·25 mm when it is traversed 50 mm.

Always check beforehand that the D.T.I. is well able to accommodate the range of reading that you require.

A better way to turn long tapers is to use a taper cutting attachment as shown in figure 42. Greater angles can be turned by this means and turning and boring can be done. The cross slide nut must be disengaged and the extension piece clamped by the nut over the taper cutting attachment. The top slide must be turned through 90° (not shown in fig. 42) so that the tool can be "fed in". When this attachment is set over at an angle and the saddle is traversed the tool will run parallel to the slide of the taper cutting attachment and so cause the tool to cut a taper. (The cross slide nut need not be disengaged on lathes with special splined cross slides.)

The taper turning attachment is marked at one end in degrees.

Spiggots

These are generally slightly tapered and the work is pressed on and held by friction (figs. 43 and 44). They are used for

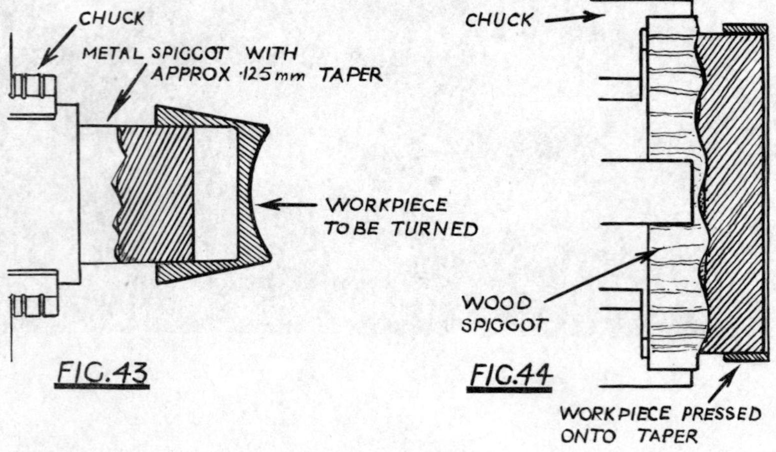

FIG. 43

FIG. 44

FIG. 45—TYPICAL COMPONENT FOR FACEPLATE WORK SHOWN FIXED TO ANGLE BRACKET WITH BALANCE WEIGHTS ON FACEPLATE
Courtesy of the Colchester Lathe Co. Ltd.

holding work which would otherwise be difficult to hold. In Figure 44 the spiggot is being used for turning a small amount off a gilding metal bezel. In figure 43 the cover of a small circular box is being held for turning.

Face Plate Work

A face plate is shown in position on the lathe in figure 45. Because the weight is not evenly distributed balance weights have been attached.

The face plate is often used for work which would be difficult or impossible to hold by other means. It is frequently used on castings where one machined face is clamped flat on to the face plate by means of the holes or slots in the plate.

When setting work on the face plate it is often easier to set it up in its approximate position with the face plate on a bench before it is put on the machine. Then it can be trued with the aid of a D.T.I. or a pointer as in figure 46.

Paper between the work and the face plate improves the grip. Care must be taken not to distort work when the clamps or holding screws are tightened.

Screwcutting

Screw threads have been mentioned in Chapter 3. Here we are concerned with cutting a thread on the lathe using the lead screw to move the cutting tool in a certain relationship to the revolutions of the headstock. This relationship or

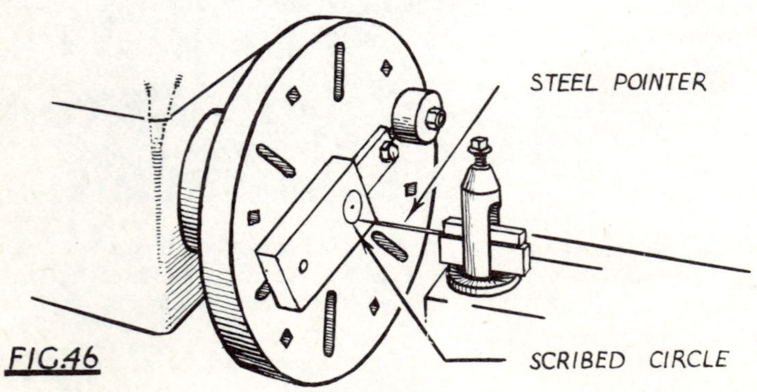

FIG.46

FIG. 47—GUARD REMOVED SHOWING SIMPLE TRAIN OF GEARS
Courtesy of the Colchester Lathe Co. Ltd.

ratio is obtained by gearing the headstock spindle to the leadscrew. On most modern lathes this is done by selecting the gears on what is known as a Norton gearbox.

The lathe in figure 2 has a quick-change gearbox. However, many lathes still use change wheels. Whatever sort of lathe is used you should understand how to calculate the gears or change wheels. Figure 47 shows a lathe with the guard removed to reveal the gears which connect the headstock spindle with the leadscrew.

On a simple gear train (fig. 48) if the gear on the headstock spindle or stud wheel is the same size as the gear on the leadscrew then the ratio between them will be 1:1, i.e. the headstock spindle will revolve at the same speed as the leadscrew. The formula used for calculating change wheels is as follows:

$$\frac{\text{Pitch of thread to be cut}}{\text{Pitch of lead screw}} = \frac{\text{Drivers}}{\text{Driven}}$$

If we want to cut a thread with a quarter of the pitch of the lead screw then the ratio is 1:4 and we should use a driving wheel a quarter of the size of the leadscrew gear. The gear train would be as in figure 48. The intermediate or idler gearwheel

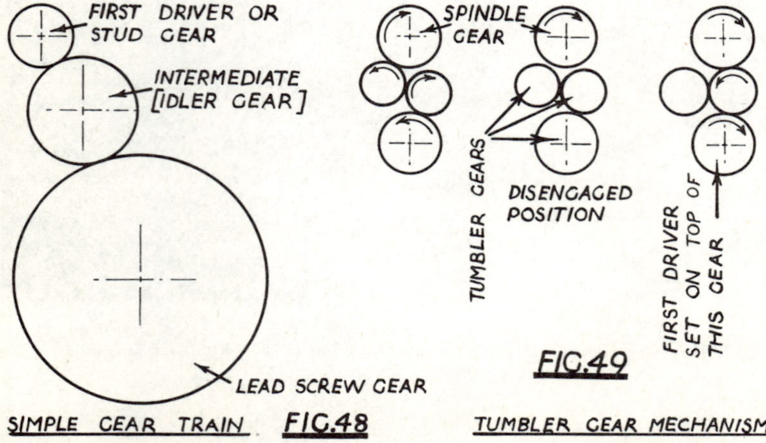

SIMPLE GEAR TRAIN FIG.48

FIG.49 TUMBLER GEAR MECHANISM

merely transmits motion and keeps the driver and driven wheels going in the same direction.

Lathes are supplied with change wheels: these usually have teeth ranging in number from 20 to 120 depending on the type of gear box on the machine. A lathe with an imperial lead screw can be set up to cut metric threads by using a 127 wheel as explained later.

The direction of the leadscrew can be reversed for cutting left hand threads, by tumbler gears (fig. 49). These gears are not taken into account when calculating the change wheels because having a ratio of 1:1 they cause the stud and headstock spindle to move in unison.

Example 1

To cut a thread with a 5 mm pitch on a lathe having a 6 mm pitch lead screw:

$$\frac{\text{Driver}}{\text{Driven}} = \frac{\text{Pitch of thread to be cut}}{\text{Pitch of lead screw}} = \frac{5}{6} \times \frac{10}{10} = \frac{50}{60}$$

i.e. a 50 tooth gear on the spindle or stud and a 60 tooth gear on the lead screw meshed with any suitable intermediate gear.

Example 2

To cut a thread with a 3·5 mm pitch on a lathe having an 8 mm pitch lead screw:

$$\frac{\text{Drivers}}{\text{Driven}} = \frac{\text{Pitch of thread to be cut}}{\text{Pitch of lead screw}}$$

$$= \frac{3{\cdot}5}{8} = \frac{35}{80} = \frac{7}{8} \times \frac{5}{10} = \frac{70}{80} \times \frac{50}{100}$$

These gears must be set up in a compound train as shown in figure 50.

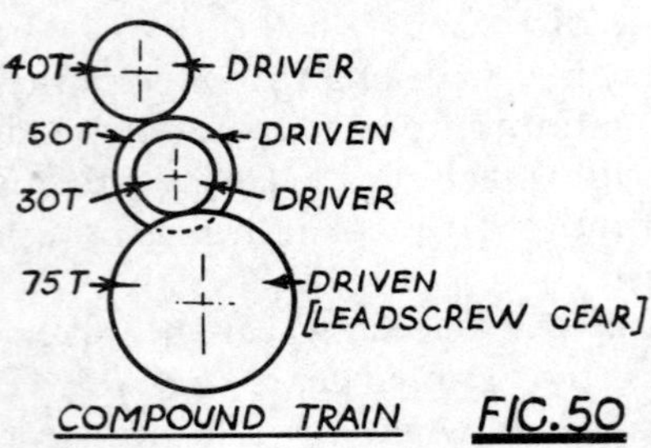

FIG.50

Metric Threads Cut on an English Lathe

There are approximately 25·4mm in 1″. A large lathe having a leadscrew of 1″ pitch with a 1 : 1 ratio set up on the gears would cut a thread with a pitch of 25·4mm. A 10:1 ratio would give a pitch of 254mm. This would be $\frac{10}{1}\frac{\text{Driver}}{\text{Driven}}$ To cut a pitch of 1mm the ratio would be: $\frac{10}{1} \times \frac{1}{254} = \frac{5}{127}$ But this is for a lathe with a 1″ pitch leadscrew. A 4 t.p.i. leadscrew would have to turn 4 times as fast to cut the same thread.

This can be set down as

$\frac{\text{Drivers}}{\text{Driven}} \frac{5 \times 4}{127}$ cuts 1mm pitch thread

If we wanted to cut a 5mm pitch thread the leadscrew would need to turn 5 times as fast, so we would multiply the drivers by 5.

$$\frac{5 \times 4 \times 5}{127} = \frac{\text{Drivers}}{\text{Driven}} = \frac{100}{127}$$

The rule then is:

$$\frac{5 \times \text{t.p.i. of leadscrew} \times \text{pitch to be cut in mm}}{127} = \frac{\text{Drivers}}{\text{Driven}}$$

Note: When setting up any train of gears adjust them so that there is a little play between the teeth of the meshing gears.

Screw Cutting Method

The work must first be turned to the correct diameter and for ease of cutting the thread it is best, though not always possible, if it is turned down to the core diameter at one end and relieved with a groove at the other end as in figure 51. Long work must be supported with a centre.

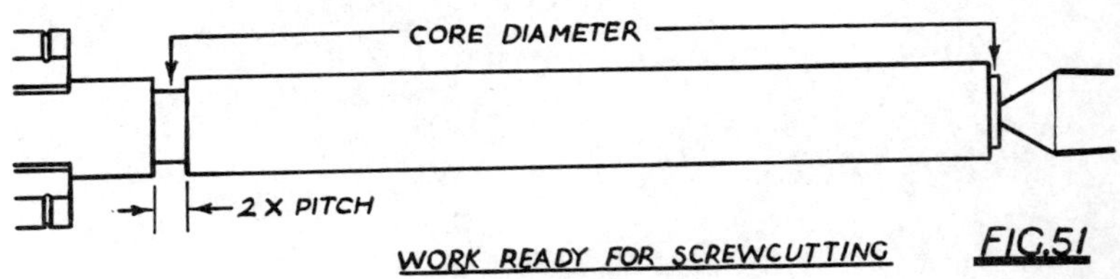

WORK READY FOR SCREWCUTTING FIG.51

The tool must be set up not only centrally but also square to the work. The tool for vee threads is set up with a thread angle or screwcutting gauge as in figure 52.

The tools are ground to the correct angle using the screw-cutting gauge and the radius at the tip of the tool can be stoned to suit the radius on the screw pitch gauge (see Chapter 3, fig. 16). Clearance and top rake as for other lathe tools is required depending on the material being cut. Remember that the rake alters the flank angles of the thread.

Assuming that the correct change wheels are set up and that the top slide is parallel to the bed of the lathe, wind the cross slide in until the tip of the tool just touches the work. Now carefully set the micrometer collar on the cross slide to zero. Move the saddle to the right so that the tool is just clear of the end of the work. This is assuming we are cutting a right hand thread. Start the machine on a slow speed—the slower the better for a beginner—but the speed can be increased later (see table of cutting speeds).

FIG. 52—SETTING THREADING TOOL WITH A THREAD ANGLE OR SCREW CUTTING GAUGE

Courtesy of the Colchester Lathe Co. Ltd.

FIG. 53—CUTTING A METRIC THREAD ON A COLCHESTER BANTAM LATHE
Courtesy of Colchester Lathe Co. Ltd.

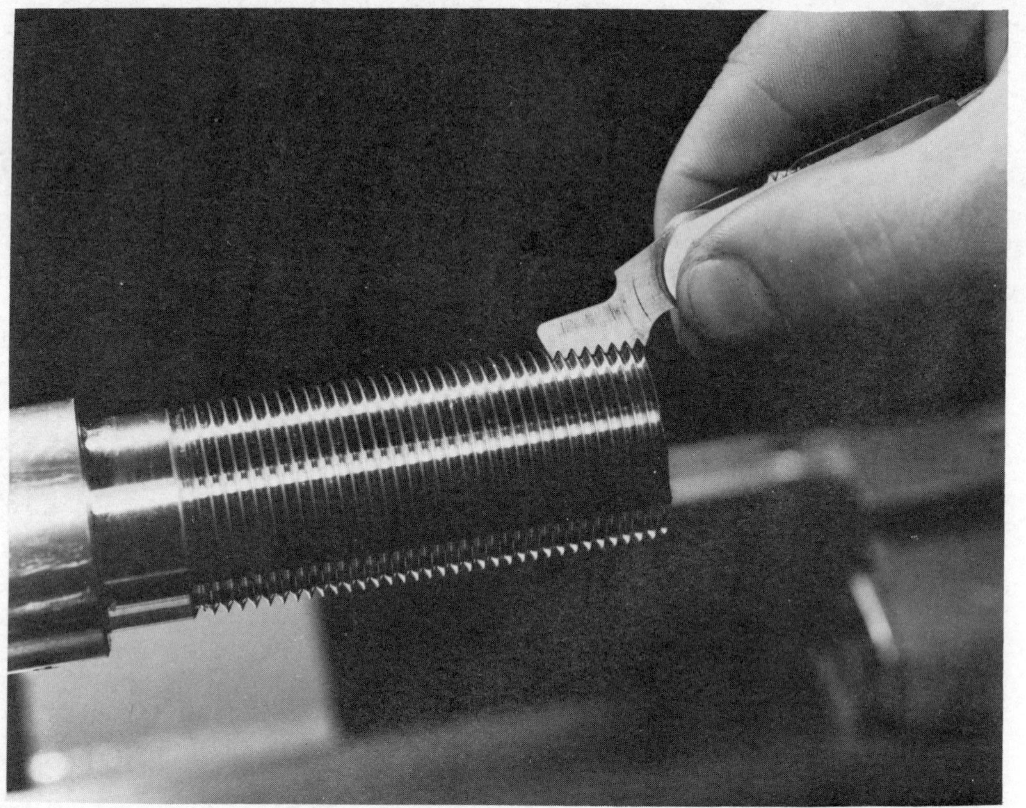

FIG. 55—CHECKING PITCH OF T.P.I. USING PITCH GAUGE
Courtesy of Colchester Lathe Co. Ltd.

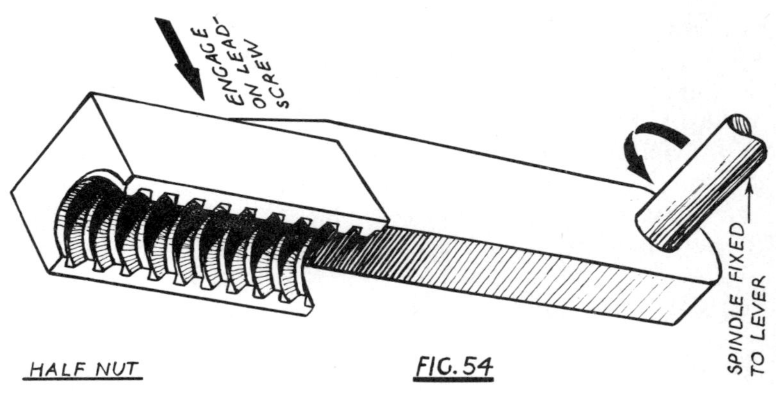

FIG. 54

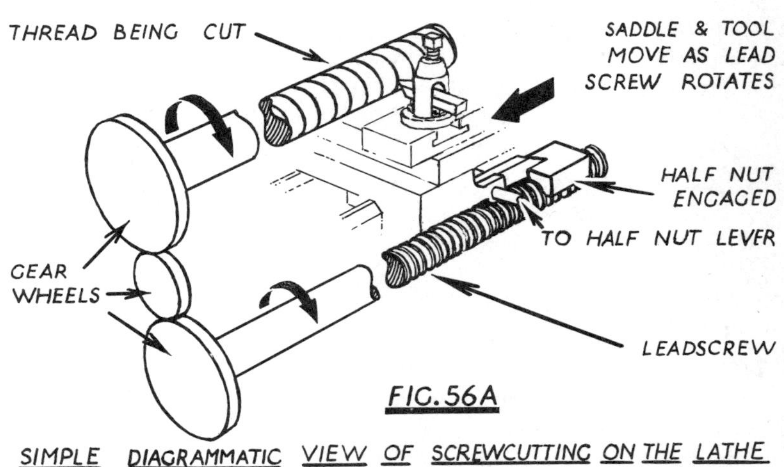

FIG. 56A

SIMPLE DIAGRAMMATIC VIEW OF SCREWCUTTING ON THE LATHE

Carefully operate the half nut lever until the half nuts are properly closed over the lead screw. The saddle will now move and the tip of the tool will just start to cut the thread. When the tool enters the groove at the left-hand end, stop the machine. Withdraw the tool and reverse the machine until the tool is just past the right-hand end of the workpiece. Stop the machine. Wind the cross slide handle in to take a cut of about 0·05 mm, and note the reading on the micrometer collar. Remember, always wind in to the number you want on the cross slide micrometer collar to eliminate the play between the cross slide nut and thread (backlash). Start the machine and take the cut. Proceed as before and continue taking cuts. After about six cuts the top slide can be moved about 0·025 mm forward or back in conjunction with the cross slide. This is known as 'side-cutting' and is done to relieve the pressure on the tool and to get a better finish. When the tool touches the core diameter the thread is deep enough.

Although the basic profile of the ISO triangular screw thread (see Fig. 38, page 59) has a flat at the crest and the root, in practice, the crests of the bolts may be rounded inside the maximum outline. The internal thread (nut) is also, in practice, rounded at the root beyond the width of P/8. To obtain a well finished thread, a chaser may be used, Figure 57. The thread chasers can either be set up in the tool post or can be used by hand on a suitable rest.

Another method of cutting a thread is to set the top slide at an angle of half the thread angle or one degree less for a better finish, i.e. 29° (fig. 58). At the end of each cut the cross slide must be returned to zero or to a stop and the amount of cut taken with the top slide only.

When cutting threads use the appropriate coolant as this will improve the finish.

Dieing and Tapping in the Lathe

Threads can be cut on the lathe by using a die holder lightly supported by the tailstock quill whilst the lathe is turned by hand (always switch off the machine at the isolator).

A very reliable way to die threads is to hold the die in a tailstock die holder (fig. 59). These are reversible and can

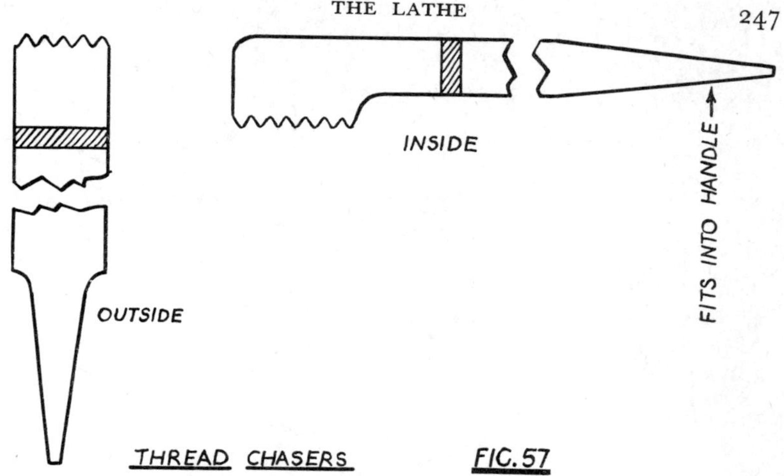

THREAD CHASERS FIG. 57

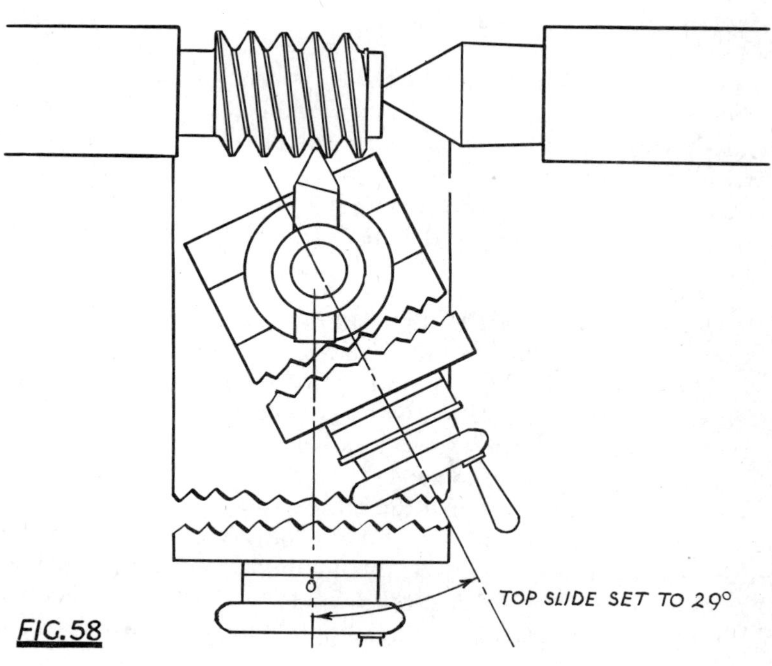

FIG. 58

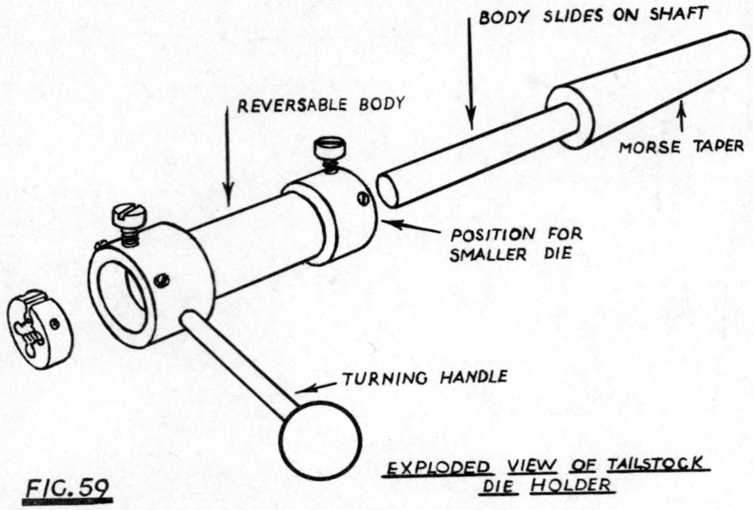

FIG. 59

hold a large die at one end and a small one at the other. The stem is parallel and the body part slides over it. The Morse taper fits into the tailstock quill. The work is held in the chuck and the tailstock with the die holder is brought up to the work. The chuck key can be put in the chuck to rotate it with the left hand whilst the handle of the die holder is rotated against it with the right hand. Slight pressure is needed to start the die cutting, but once it starts cutting it will move down the thread being kept quite true by the stem. Use the proper coolant for best results.

Tapping in the Lathe. This can be done providing the tap has a centre hole in the shank end.

The lathe is turned by hand with the tap supported by the tailstock centre and turned with a spanner or a tap wrench. As the tap starts cutting the thread so the tailstock centre is wound in to keep it supported. Care must be taken not to force the tailstock centre against the tap.

Smaller taps can be held in the tailstock chuck especially for tapping brass. However, this method is not recommended, except for starting off a tapped hole, because it is difficult to judge how much force is being applied to the tap.

Spinning. Spinning is a method of making hollow vessels on a lathe using a former over which the work is pressed, whilst rotating at high speed, with a smooth, hard and highly polished tool.

In factories spinning is done on high speed spinning lathes.

However, small work can be spun on any school lathe, but generally the larger lathes are better because the bearings stand the thrust imposed on them better.

Spinning is often said to be dangerous, but in fact it is no more dangerous than wood turning providing it is supervised by the teacher.

Copper and aluminium are two metals which, because of their softness, can be readily spun. 0·9 mm is a good thickness for copper and 1·63 mm, 1·22 mm or 0·9 mm for aluminium. Brass and gilding metal can also be spun but need more frequent annealing.

Deep shapes are best done in two stages, i.e. two spinning chucks are used. This reduces the tendency for the metal to wrinkle or become too thin. Figure 60 shows two chucks which can be held in a 3-jaw chuck. These can be made from close grained wood such as maple or beech. Often boards have to be glued together to make up the required thickness.

The disc to be spun must be properly annealed and clamped centrally against the end of the former or chuck with a pressure

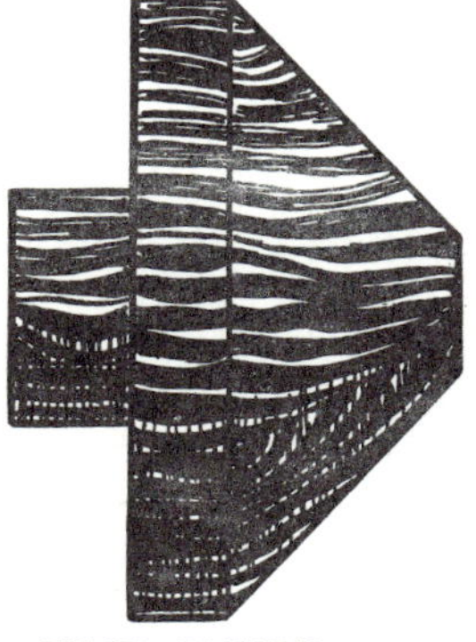

SECOND CHUCK

FIRST CHUCK

SPINNING CHUCKS FIG.60

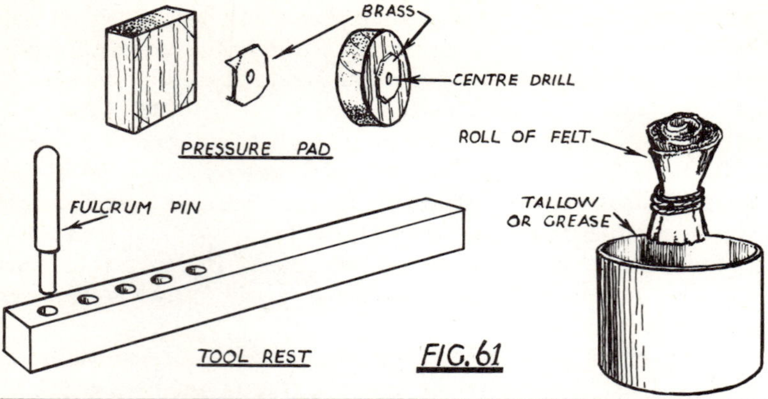

BRASS
CENTRE DRILL
PRESSURE PAD
ROLL OF FELT
FULCRUM PIN
TALLOW OR GREASE
TOOL REST

FIG. 61

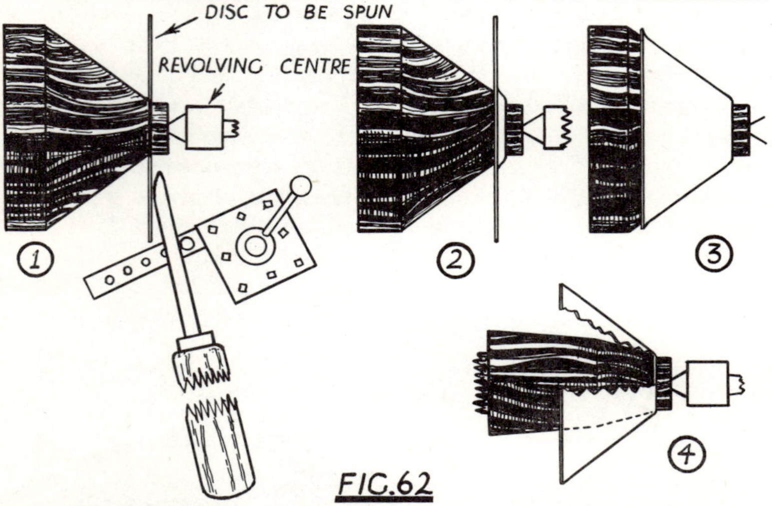

DISC TO BE SPUN
REVOLVING CENTRE
1
2
3
4

FIG. 62

SPINNING TOOL
500 mm
200 mm
600 mm
BACK STICK
SPINNING TOOL
15 M/M
PLANISHING TOOL

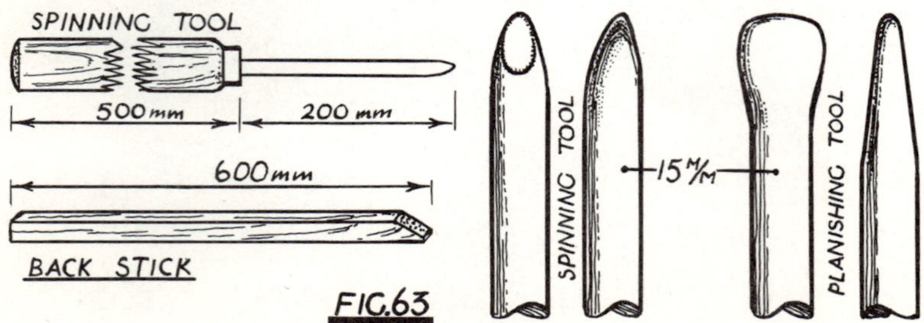

FIG. 63

pad (fig. 61) held by a revolving centre (fig. 62). (The size of the disc is calculated as for raising.) The pressure pad should be only slightly smaller than the small diameter of the chuck and should be reinforced with a piece of metal which is centre-drilled as in figure 61.

The tool (fig. 63) is supported on a tool rest (fig. 61) which can be held in the tool holder. The tool is levered against the fulcrum pin which can be moved into any of the holes provided. To counteract the thrust the saddle should be tightened. The disc must be lubricated with grease, soap or tallow to prevent it becoming scored.

Start spinning by pressing the rounded side of the tool against the revolving metal close to the pressure pad. Keep the tool moving from the centre outwards and then back towards the centre over a small area at first. As the metal is spun down to the chuck the fulcrum pin should be moved to the left so that better leverage can be obtained. If the metal starts to wrinkle press the spinning disc between the tool and the back stick (figs. 63 and 64). Always "coax" the metal with quick, smooth strokes of the tool. Do not let the tool stand still on the disc because this will harden the metal. Too much force will cause grooves.

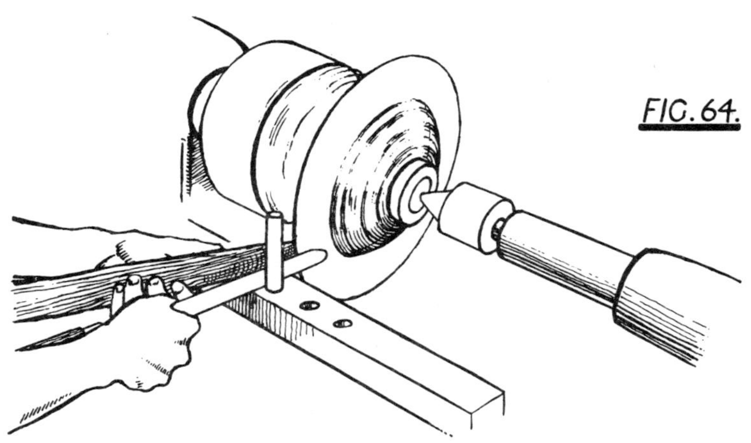

FIG. 64.

As the spinning progresses the work will need annealing from time to time.

Finish the work with the planishing tool. This is used in the same way as the spinning tool but a smoother surface can be obtained by its use.

The speed for spinning can be about 1000 R.P.M., although in industry much higher speeds are used.

14

Shaping and Milling

SHAPING

The Shaping Machine

The shaping machine is used for making flat surfaces, keyways and slots. Although it uses a single point tool similar to a turning tool, and cuts only on the forward stroke, it removes metal very quickly.

The machine is made of cast iron. The heavy ram on the top moves backwards and forwards in slideways and the length and speed of the stroke can be adjusted to suit the work being machined. The return or non-cutting stroke is quicker than the forward or cutting stroke. The reason is that the crank pin travels a greater distance on the cutting stroke than on the return stroke as shown in figure 1, which also shows how the

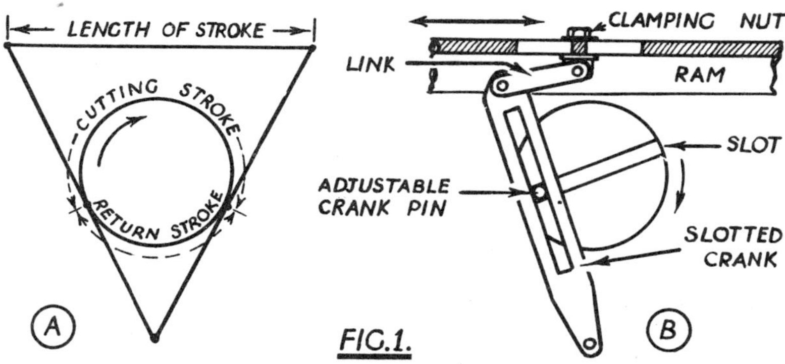

FIG.1.

length of stroke is adjusted. The table can be raised or lowered and moved at right angles to the movement of the ram. Figure 2 shows the shaping machine.

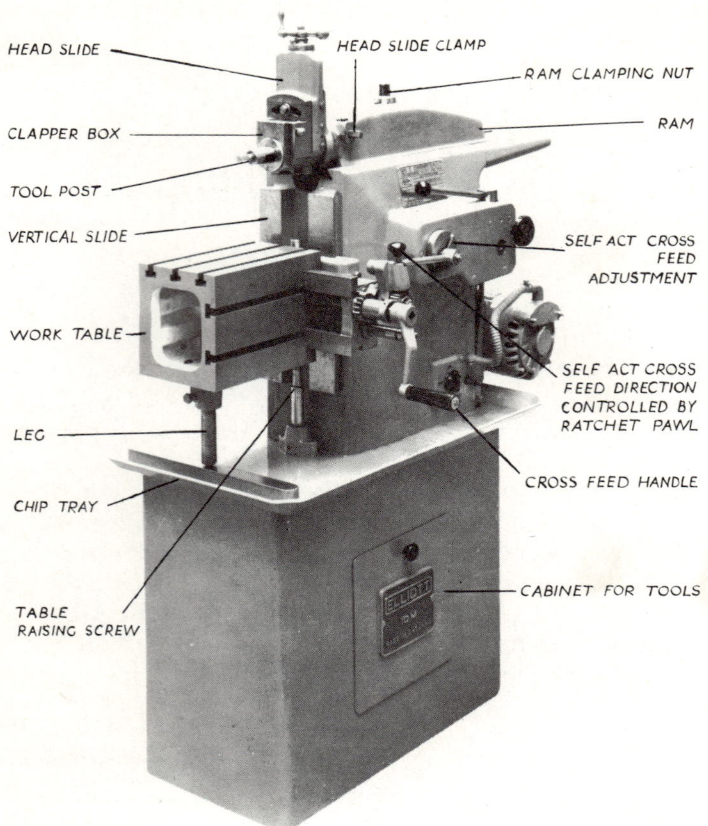

FIG. 2—SHAPING MACHINE
Courtesy of B. Elliott (machinery) Ltd.

The work can be held in a vice or clamped on to the table as in figures 3 and 4. After the work has been positioned and the stroke adjusted so that it clears the work by about 25 mm both on the cutting and return stroke, the tool can be brought down to the work with the head slide handwheel. When the machine is set in motion the clapper box allows the tool to lift on the return stroke thus reducing friction. The clapper box is so called because of the clapping sound it makes. The feed ratchet mechanism, when it is engaged, feeds the table across on each return stroke (fig. 3). When cutting a vertical face the clapper box as well as the tool must be set over so that the arc made by the tool on the return stroke clears the vertical face of the work (fig. 4).

SHAPING TOOLS

These are similar to lathe tools but are more robust in order to withstand the shock of the intermittent cutting action. The front clearance angle should be slightly more than for a lathe tool to allow clearance on the return stroke. 10°–12° is usual. Figure 5 shows three typical shaping tools.

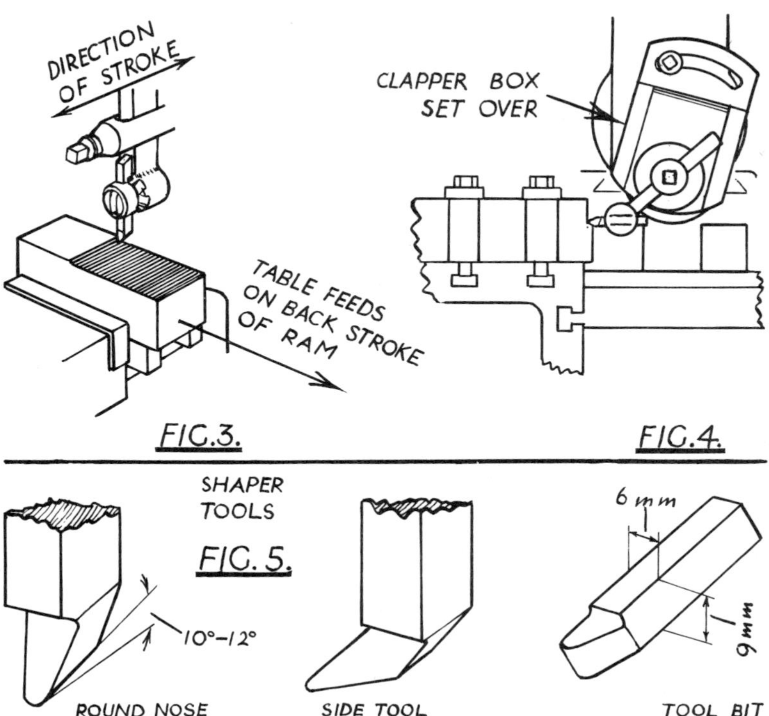

MILLING

The Milling Machine

In the school workshop the milling machines are either "vertical" or "horizontal". The kind of machine which can be converted either to horizontal or vertical cutting is, for reasons of economy, often used (fig. 1). The horizontal attachment is shown in position in figure 2.

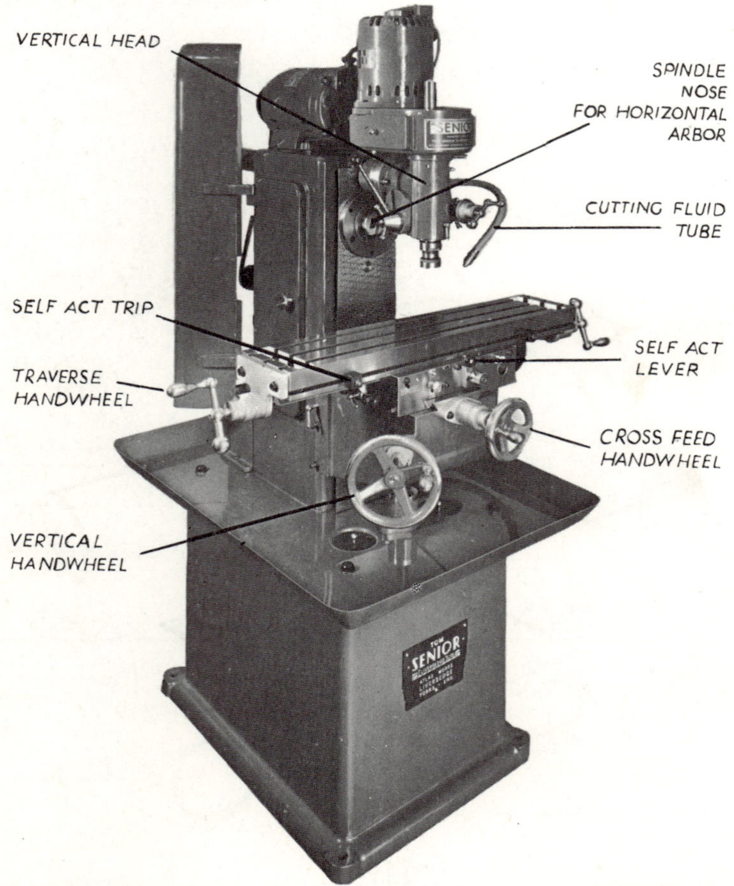

FIG. 1—MILLING MACHINE WITH VERTICAL ATTACHMENT
Courtesy of Tom Senior (Liversedge) Ltd.

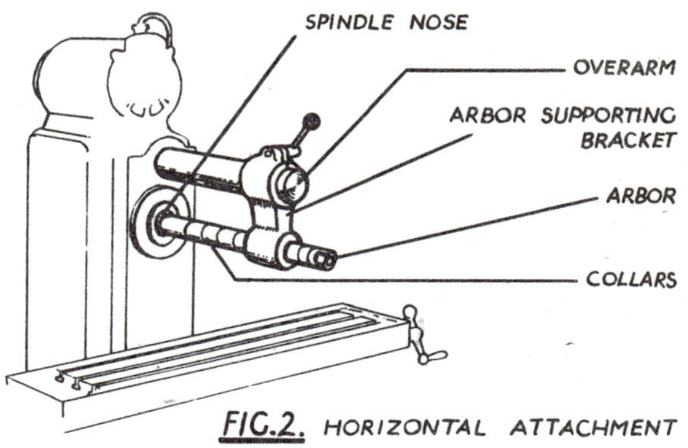

FIG.2. HORIZONTAL ATTACHMENT

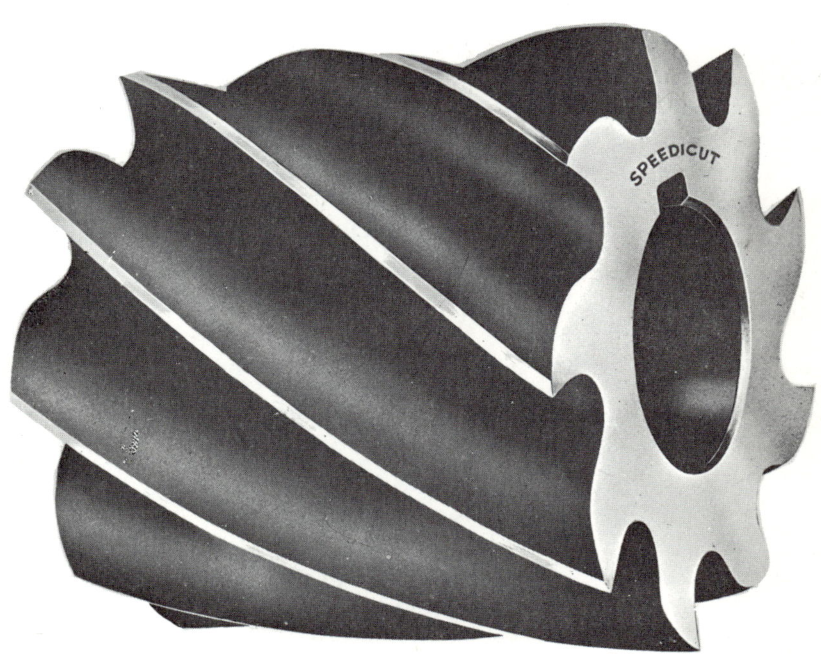

FIG. 3—CYLINDRICAL CUTTER OR SLAB MILL
Courtesy of Firth Brown Tools Ltd.

In industry this machine and variations of it are used for many specialised jobs such as gear cutting, spline cutting, helical milling etc. In fact milling on its own is a specialised study and the interested reader is advised to read one of the many books entirely devoted to this subject. The milling operations discussed here are the simple ones of making flat surfaces and slots.

Milling Cutters

The cylindrical Milling Cutter. This is shown in figure 3. This is also known as a slab mill and it is used for making flat surfaces. Figure 4 shows the cutter set up on the horizontal arbor. These cutters are available in various diameters and widths.

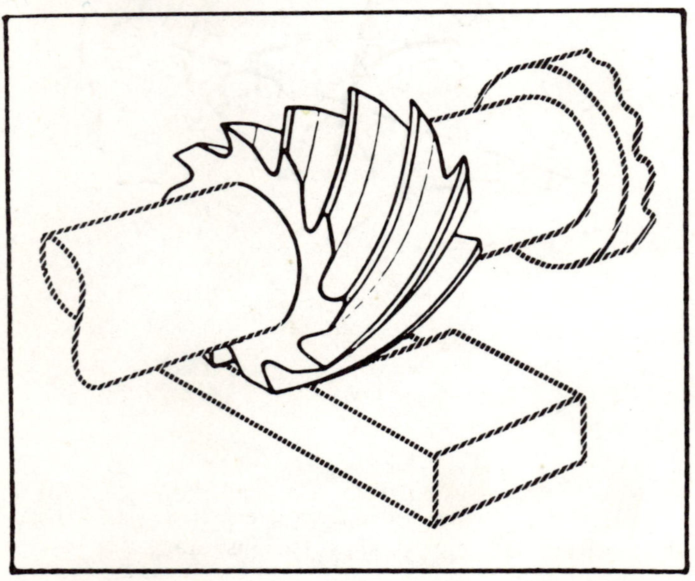

FIG. 4—CYLINDRICAL CUTTER "SET-UP" ON THE ARBOR
Courtesy of Firth Brown Tools Ltd.

FIG. 5—SIDE AND FACE CUTTER
Courtesy of Firth Brown Tools Ltd.

Side and Face Cutter (fig. 5). This has teeth on the side and face and is useful for cutting grooves as shown in figure 6. These cutters are available in various diameters and up to 35 mm wide.

Slitting Saw (fig. 7). The teeth are usually only on the periphery. It is used for making narrow slots and for cutting

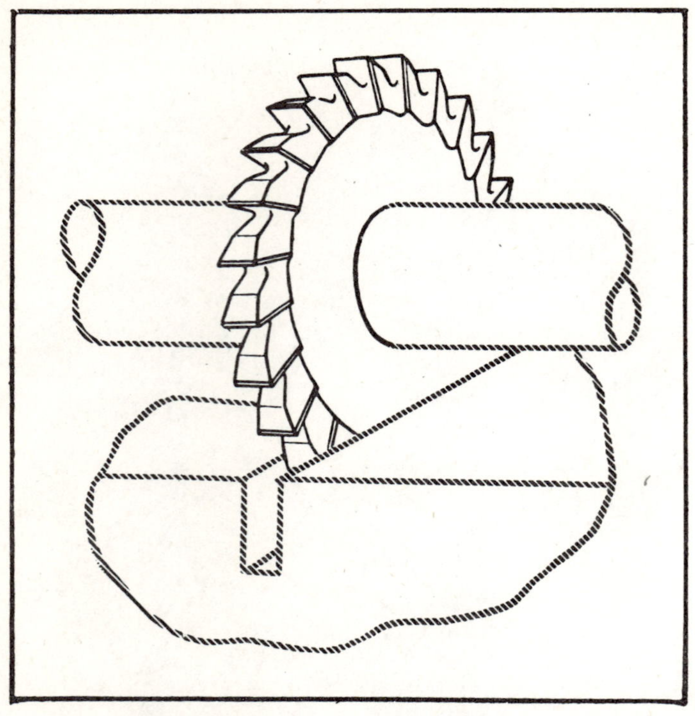

FIG. 6—SIDE AND FACE CUTTER "SET-UP" ON THE ARBOR
Courtesy of Firth Brown Tools Ltd.

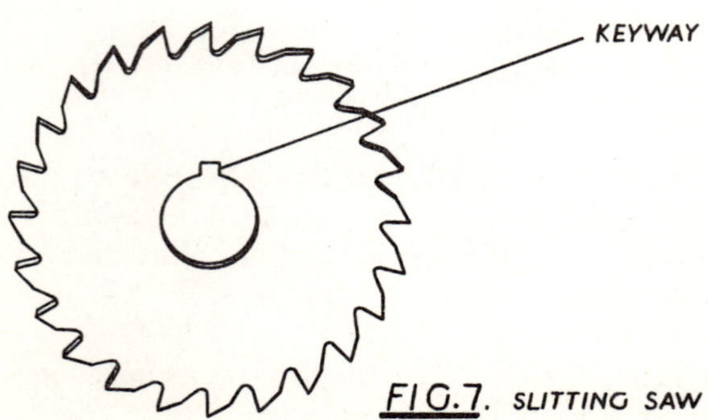

FIG. 7. SLITTING SAW

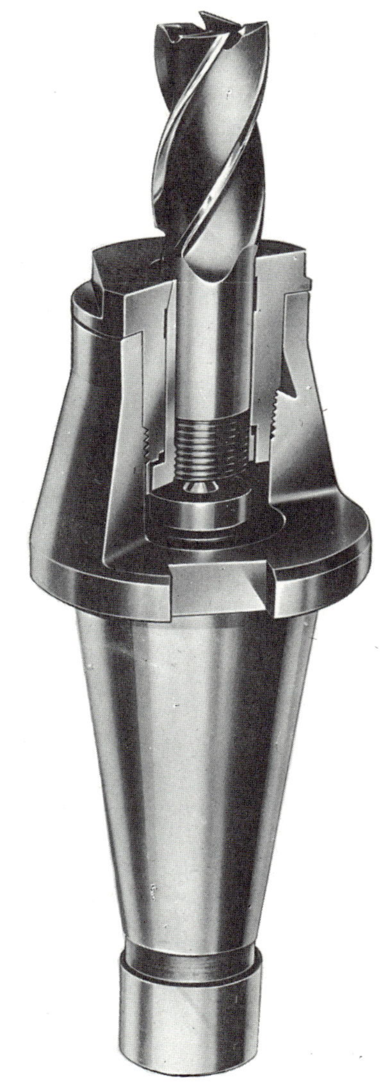

FIG. 8—"AUTOLOCK" END MILL CHUCK
Courtesy of Clarkson (engineers) Ltd.

through metal. These saws are available in various diameters and widths from 0·3 mm to 6 mm.

End Mills. These have either parallel, Morse taper or screwed shanks. Figure 8 shows an end mill chuck which has been part sectioned to show how a screwed shank end mill is held. Parallel and morse taper shank end mills must be used in their proper chucks. End mills vary in length and in diameter from 3 mm diameter to 50 mm and are used for cutting slots, keyways and for making flat surfaces.

Methods of Holding Work

There are scores of ways of holding work for milling, but whatever method is used the work should be as rigid as possible. Figure 9 shows three pieces of work set up. Parallel strips and the dial indicator are invaluable aids to setting up.

Milling Procedure

When using the horizontal miller always feed the work against the rotation of the cutter as shown in figure 10. This is known as "upcut milling". On large specially designed mach ines cutting can be done in the other direction, but it should not be tried on the school machine because the cutter tends to "grab" the work.

Use a coolant, where applicable, which is fed on to the cutter through the tube provided: but never apply coolant with a brush. This is dangerous.

When using the vertical miller the work should again be "fed" against the direction of the end mill (fig. 11). When milling out a slot (fig. 12) first drill holes to the depth of the slot but slightly smaller in diameter. These holes can be drilled on the milling machine and the micrometer dial used for obtaining the correct depth. The end mill then removes the webs between the holes. In this case the end mill cuts on both sides of the slot, i.e. upcut milling on one side and downcut milling on the other. If this slot is attempted without first drilling, the cutter will almost surely break because the cutters used in school are not designed to cut to any appreciable depth on the end.

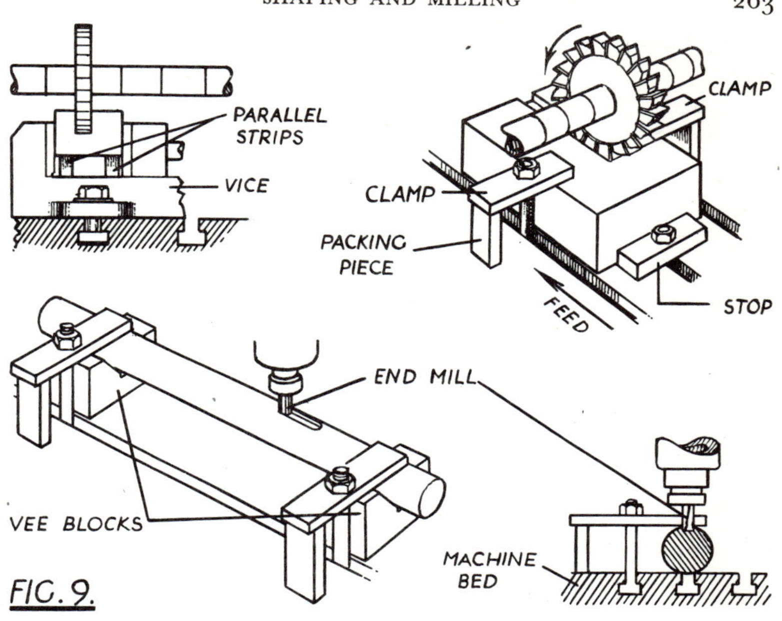

FIG. 9.

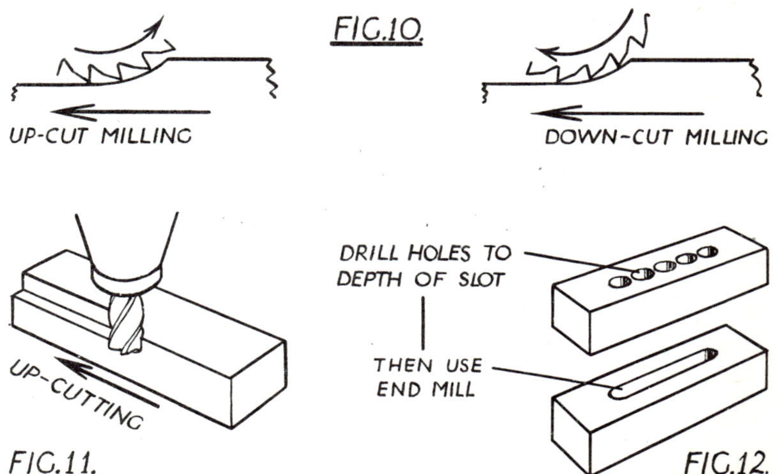

FIG.10.

FIG.11.

FIG.12.

Speeds and Feeds

The speed at which to run the cutter can be obtained by using the following formula:

$$\text{Revs. per minute} = \frac{1000 \times \text{Surface speed in metres per min.}}{\pi \times \text{Diameter of cutter in millimetres}}$$

The surface speed at which the metal can be cut is found by referring to a table similar to that on page 212. However, so much depends on the rigidity of the machine, the condition of the bearings and the sharpness of the cutter, that any theoretical speed obtained by using this formula must be modified accordingly.

When cutting (assuming that both the speed and feed are constant) each tooth of the milling cutter will remove a small chip of metal. The rate at which the work is fed into the cutter and the number of teeth on the cutter and its speed will alter the thickness of each chip.

For school work, using the horizontal machine, if we allow each tooth of the cutter to remove about 0·025 mm when cutting mild steel, we shall be on the "safe side". The rate of feed on the automatic traverse is usually stated in terms of mm per revolution of the cutter. So if this stated figure is divided by the number of teeth in the cutter we arrive at how much each tooth is taking off.

For vertical milling a much finer feed must be used, particularly when small cutters are being used.

15

Grinding and Polishing

GRINDING

The type of machine used for off-hand grinding in school may be of the bench type (fig. 1) or pedestal type: or it may be a combined buff and grinder, either pedestal or bench type with a polishing mop on one end of the spindle and a grinding wheel on the other.

Grinding wheels consist of particles of abrasive material, such as aluminium oxide or silicon carbide, which are held

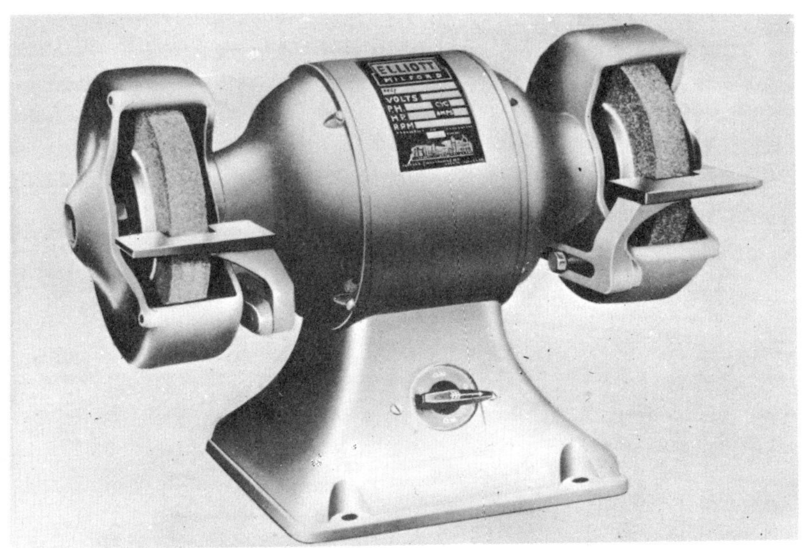

FIG. 1—BENCH GRINDER
Courtesy of B. Elliott (machinery) Ltd.

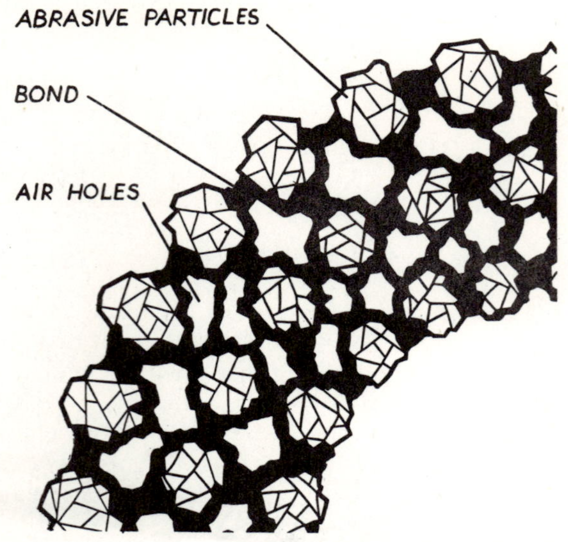

FIG. 2—MAGNIFIED PORTION OF GRINDING WHEEL
Courtesy of Carborundum Co. Ltd.

together by a bonding agent. Figure 2 shows a magnified portion of a wheel showing the abrasive particles held in the bonding material. The grade of the wheel refers to the strength of this bonding agent.

The abrasive particles are known as the grit, and these are graded by passing through a screen, e.g. 46 grit will pass through a screen having 46 meshes to the linear inch*.

We must therefore consider the grit and the grade of the wheel. Generally speaking when a piece of metal is being ground the abrasive particles become blunt after a time. If the wheel is right for the material being ground, the grade (i.e. the bonding material) of the wheel should be soft enough to allow the blunt particles to break away thus exposing fresh sharp particles. It follows then that when grinding a hard metal the particles will become blunt more quickly so they must be allowed to break away more quickly. This means that the

* Carborundum Co. Ltd. does not envisage a change to metric units within the foreseeable future.

harder the metal being ground, the softer the grade must be and vice versa.

When ordering a wheel at least five points must be mentioned: diameter, thickness, size of hole, grit and grade. A maker's catalogue should be consulted.

Wheel Dressing

After long use the wheel goes out of true and the edges become radiused and if the wrong material has been ground the wheel also becomes glazed (the equivalent of pinning on files). A wheel dresser of the kind shown in figure 3, known as

FIG. 3—HUNTINGTON TYPE WHEEL DRESSER
Courtesy of Jones and Shipman & Co.

the Huntington type wheel dresser, is held firmly on the rest with the star wheels against the periphery of the wheel. As the wheel rotates the abrasive particles on the periphery are removed. The dresser should be held firmly and moved slightly from side to side to cover the width of the wheel. After truing the wheel , the tool rest should be adjusted so that the gap is about 1·5 mm.

Goggles or an eye shield must always be used when grinding.

Cutter Grinding

Milling cutters, when they become blunt, are ground on a cutter-grinding machine. The cutter to be ground is pushed on

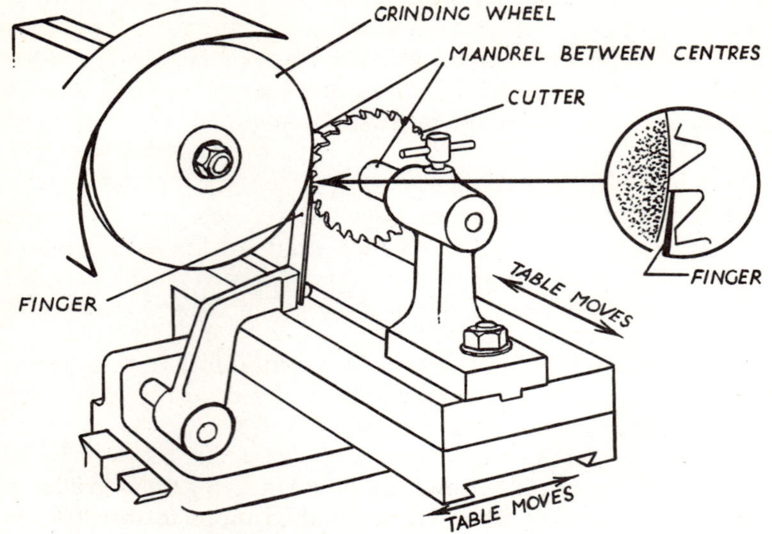

FIG. 4. DETAIL OF CUTTER GRINDING MACHINE

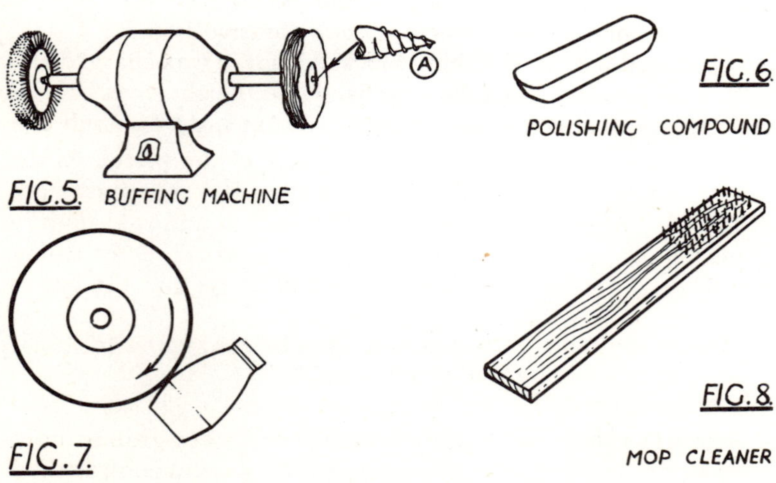

FIG. 5. BUFFING MACHINE

FIG. 6. POLISHING COMPOUND

FIG. 7.

FIG. 8. MOP CLEANER

to a tapered mandrel which is then set up on the machine between centres (fig. 4). Each tooth of the cutter is rested on the finger which is stationary and the cutter is drawn across the periphery of the grinding wheel. Each tooth in turn is taken across the grinding wheel in the same manner. Many complex grinding operations with a high degree of accuracy can be done on these small machines. The makers supply full instructions with each machine.

POLISHING

Polishing done on the buffing machine is similar in principle to that done by hand. The polishing materials are used in order of their fineness finishing with the finest one.

A buffing machine is shown in figure 5. The mops screw on to the tapered point shown at figure 5A. Various grades of mops are available from coarse stitched mops to soft "swansdown". Similarly abrasive compounds in 1 lb blocks (fig. 6) are in various grades. The block is pressed against the spinning mop so that the friction and heat causes some of the abrasive compound to adhere to the mop. This is now ready to polish the work which should be pressed against the mop as shown in figure 7. Each grade of mop should be used for one grade of abrasive only, so that when a finer abrasive is used, a softer mop is used with it. Polishing blocks consist of wax charged with abrasive powder. The following list shows the abrasives in order of coarseness and the type of mop recommended for each one:

Polishing Compound	*Mop*
Carbrax	Stapol
Tripoli	Stitched calico
Crocus	Unstitched calico
Rouge	Swansdown

Clean the mop from time time to remove the old abrasive. This can be done by firmly holding a piece of wood, from which nails are protruding (fig. 8) against the mop whilst it is spinning. Recharge the mop with the correct abrasive when it is clean.

Safety

Never hold work in rag. It might get caught up. Never polish lengths of chain—these are dangerous if they become entangled. Polish thin pieces of metal by holding them flat on a suitable piece of wood.

16

Lubricants and Cutting Fluids

LUBRICANTS

Machines are lubricated to reduce friction between moving parts. The oil film prevents metal to metal contact. Grease is used on moving parts usually where there is not too much heat and where, sometimes, the bearing is sealed, but generally oil is the more widely used. Moving parts under heavy pressure are often lubricated with E.P. (Extreme Pressure) oil.

CUTTING FLUIDS

Cutting fluids should:

remove heat rapidly and thus reduce distortion
wet the metal efficiently so that cooling may be effective
have good lubricating properties thus reducing power consumption
reduce welding of chip to tool
improve surface finish
reduce tool wear
protect workpiece and machine from corrosion
permit increased speeds of production
wash away chips and swarf.

Cutting oils can be classified as follows:

1. *Aqueous Cutting Fluids*
   water
   aqueous solutions

2. *Neat Cutting Oils*
   mineral oils
   mineral/lard (compounded) oils
   fatty oils
   extreme pressure (E.P.) oils

3. *Aqueous Emulsions of Soluble Cutting Oils*

Water on its own has very good cooling powers but it has two disadvantages: 1. it rapidly rusts steel, 2. it does not wet metal efficiently. Modern soluble oils (10% emulsifiable oil, 90% water) overcome these disadvantages and they also give a measure of lubrication. Thus the greater the oil content of a soluble oil emulsion the better it will lubricate but the less it will cool, and vice versa.

For further information on this subject read the booklet mentioned at the back of this book.

Tables

B.S. 3643

ISO METRIC SCREW THREADS

Selected 'coarse' and 'fine' Series for Screws, Bolts, Nuts and other common threaded fasteners

(dimensions in millimetres)

1	2	3	4
Basic major diameters		Pitches	
First choice	*Second choice*	*Coarse Series*	*Fine Series*
1.6	—	0·35	—
—	1·8	0·35	—
2	—	0·4	—
—	2·2	0·45	—
2·5	—	0·45	—
3	—	0·5	—
—	3·5	0·6	—
4	—	0·7	—
—	4·5	0·75	—
5	—	0·8	—
6	—	1	—
—	7	1	—
8	—	1·25	1
10	—	1·5	1·25
12	—	1·75	1·25
—	14	2	1·5
16	—	2	1·5
—	18	2·5	1·5
20	—	2·5	1·5
—	22	2·5	1·5
24	—	3	2
—	27	3	2
30	—	3·5	2
—	33	3·5	2
36	—	4	3
—	39	4	3

Note: The diameters given in Column 1 should be used in preference to those in Column 2.

BRITISH STANDARD TWIST DRILL SIZES

Superseding drill gauge and letter sizes

Drill gauge and letter sizes of twist drills are now obsolete and should not be used in new designs. To assist users in securing the drill sizes required, the equivalent standard sizes are given below in bold type.

Old drill gauge and letter size		*British Standard (international) series*			*Old drill gauge and letter size*		*British Standard (international) series*		
OLD SIZE	*Decimal equivalent*	**NEW SIZE**		*Decimal equivalent*	**OLD SIZE**	*Decimal equivalent*	**NEW SIZE**		*Decimal equivalent*
	in	*mm*	*in*	*in*		*in*	*mm*	*in*	*in*
80	0·0135	**0·35**		0·0138	45	0·0820	**2·10**		0·0827
79	0·0145	**0·38**		0·0150	44	0·0860	**2·20**		0·0866
78	0·0160	**0·40**		0·0157	43	0·0890	**2·25**		0·0886
77	0·0180	**0·45**		0·0177	42	0·0935		**3/32**	0·0938
76	0·0200	**0·50**		0·0197	41	0·0960	**2·45**		0·0965
75	0·0210	**0·52**		0·0205	40	0·0980	**2·50**		0·0984
74	0·0225	**0·58**		0·0228	39	0·0995	**2·55**		0·1004
73	0·0240	**0·60**		0·0236	38	0·1015	**2·60**		0·1024
72	0·0250	**0·65**		0·0256	37	0·1040	**2·65**		0·1043
71	0·0260	**0·65**		0·0256	36	0·1065	**2·70**		0·1063
70	0·0280	**0·70**		0·0276	35	0·1100	**2·80**		0·1102
69	0·0292	**0·75**		0·0295	34	0·1110	**2·80**		0·1102
68	0·0310		**1/32**	0·0312	33	0·1130	**2·85**		0·1122
67	0·0320	**0·82**		0·0323	32	0·1160	**2·95**		0·1161
66	0·0330	**0·85**		0·0335	31	0·1200	**3·00**		0·1181
65	0·0350	**0·90**		0·0354	30	0·1285	**3·30**		0·1299
64	0·0360	**0·92**		0·0362	29	0·1360	**3·50**		0·1378
63	0·0370	**0·95**		0·0374	28	0·1405		**9/64**	0·1406
62	0·0380	**0·98**		0·0386	27	0·1440	**3·70**		0·1457
61	0·0390	**1·00**		0·0394	26	0·1470	**3·70**		0·1457
60	0·0400	**1·00**		0·0394	25	0·1495	**3·80**		0·1496
59	0·0410	**1·05**		0·0413	24	0·1520	**3·90**		0·1535
58	0·0420	**1·05**		0·0413	23	0·1540	**3·90**		0·1535
57	0·0430	**1·10**		0·0433	22	0·1570	**4·00**		0·1575
56	0·0465		**3/64**	0·0469	21	0·1590	**4·00**		0·1575
55	0·0520	**1·30**		0·0512	20	0·1610	**4·10**		0·1614
54	0·0550	**1·40**		0·0551	19	0·1660	**4·20**		0·1654
53	0·0595	**1·50**		0·0591	18	0·1695	**4·30**		0·1693
52	0·0635	**1·60**		0·0630	17	0·1730	**4·40**		0·1732
51	0·0670	**1·70**		0·0669	16	0·1770	**4·50**		0·1772
50	0·0700	**1·80**		0·0709	15	0·1800	**4·60**		0·1811
49	0·0730	**1·85**		0·0728	14	0·1820	**4·60**		0·1811
48	0·0760	**1·95**		0·0768	13	0·1850	**4·70**		0·1850
47	0·0785	**2·00**		0·0787	12	0·1890	**4·80**		0·1890
46	0·0810	**2·05**		0·0807	11	0·1910	**4·90**		0·1929

BRITISH STANDARD TWIST DRILL SIZES

Superseding drill gauge and letter sizes

Drill gauge and letter sizes of twist drills are now obsolete and should not be used in new designs. To assist users in securing the drill sizes required, the equivalent standard sizes are given below in bold type.

Old drill gauge and letter size		*British Standard (international) series*			*Old drill gauge and letter size*		*British Standard (international) series*		
OLD SIZE	*Decimal equivalent*	**NEW SIZE**		*Decimal equivalent*	**OLD SIZE**	*Decimal equivalent*	**NEW SIZE**		*Decimal equivalent*
	in	*mm*	*in*	*in*		*in*	*mm*	*in*	*in*
10	0·1935	**4·90**		0·1929	K	0·2810		$\frac{9}{32}$	0·2812
9	0·1960	**5·00**		0·1968	L	0·2900	**7·40**		0·2913
8	0·1990	**5·10**		0·2008	M	0·2950	**7·50**		0·2953
7	0·2010	**5·10**		0·2008	N	0·3020	**7·70**		0·3031
6	0·2040	**5·20**		0·2047	O	0·3160	**8·00**		0·3150
5	0·2055	**5·20**		0·2047	P	0·3230	**8·20**		0·3228
4	0·2090	**5·30**		0·2087	Q	0·3320	**8·40**		0·3307
3	0·2130	**5·40**		0·2126	R	0·3390	**8·60**		0·3386
2	0·2210	**5·60**		0·2205	S	0·3480	**8·80**		0·3465
1	0·2280	**5·80**		0·2283	T	0·3580	**9·10**		0·3583
A	0·2340		$\frac{15}{64}$	0·2344	U	0·3680	**9·30**		0·3661
B	0·2380	**6·00**		0·2362	V	0·3770		$\frac{3}{8}$	0·3750
C	0·2420	**6·10**		0·2402	W	0·3860	**9·80**		0·3858
D	0·2460	**6·20**		0·2441	X	0·3970	**10·10**		0·3976
E	0·2500		$\frac{1}{4}$	0·2500	Y	0·4040	**10·30**		0·4055
F	0·2570	**6·50**		0·2559	Z	0·4130	**10·50**		0·4134
G	0·2610	**6·60**		0·2598					
H	0·2660		$\frac{17}{64}$	0·2656					
I	0·2720	**6·90**		0·2717					
J	0·2770	**7·00**		0·2756					

A Newton is the force that will give a mass of 1 Kg an acceleration of 1 metre per second, per second.

Where to Buy Tools and Materials

STERLING SILVER

Johnson Matthey & Co. Ltd., Hatton Garden, London E.C.1. Also at Vittoria Street, Birmingham 1, and 75 Eyre Street, Sheffield 1.

Sheffield Smelting Co. Ltd., Royds Mill Street, Sheffield. Also at St. Paul's Square, Charlotte Street, Birmingham 3, and 1 Berry Street, Clerkenwell, London, E.C.1.

U.S.A.

Goldsmiths Bros., Smelting & Refining Co., 74 West 46th Street, New York, N.Y. (write for nearest distributor).

Handy & Harman, 82 Fulton Street, New York 7, N.Y. Also at 330 N. Gibson, El Monte, California.

METALS

Brinksway Bank Mill, Stockport, 16a Prospect Row, Birmingham, and 14 Prudhoe Street, Newcastle-upon-Tyne.

J. Smith & Son (Clerkenwell) Ltd., 50 St. John's Square, London E.C.1.

Aston Aluminium Warehouse Co. Ltd., Fenham Road, Aston, Birmingham.

Joseph Blair Ltd., 5–19 Church Lane, High Street, Belfast.

U.S.A.

American Handicrafts Company, 33–35 East 14th Street, New York, N.Y.

Allcraft Tool & Supply Co. Inc., 11 East 48th Street, New York, N.Y.

Broadhead & Garrett, 5660 East 71st Street, Cleveland, Ohio.

R & B Artcraft, 11019 South Vermont, Los Angeles 44, California. Also at 3276 El Cajon Blvd, San Diego, California.

T. E. Conklin Brass & Copper, 54 Lafayette St., New York, N.Y. (deal only in large quantities or wholesale—will sell to schools).

Revere Copper & Brass, Inc., 230 Park Avenue, New York 17, N.Y. (deal only in large quantities or wholesale—will sell to schools).

Reynolds Metals Co., Richmond 18, VA.—Ask for booklet for use in schools.

TOOLS

Buck & Hickman Ltd., 2 Whitechapel Road, London E.1 (all tools in stock).

William Whitehouse & Co. (Atlas Forge) Ltd., Atlas Works, Old Hill, Staffordshire (sell only art metalwork stakes and tools).

Charles Cooper, Wall House, Hatton Wall, Hatton Garden, London E.C.1 (small tools for art metalwork).

Firth Brown Tools Ltd., Speedicut Works, Carlisle Street East (PO Box 59), Sheffield 4 (all types of cutting tools).

Sheffield Twist Drill & Steel Co. Ltd., Summerfield Street, Sheffield 11 (all types of cutting tools).

Moore & Wright (Sheffield) Ltd., Sheffield (all types of hand tools).

U.S.A.

Browne & Sharpe Mfg. Co., Providence, Rhode Island (machine tools and hand tools).

South Bend Lathe Works, South Bend 22, Indiana (lathes and information on turning).

Ernest Linick & Co., 5 Wabash Avenue, Chicago, Illinois.

Norton Company, 1 New Bond Street, Worcester, Massachusetts.

ETCHING MATERIALS

Boots Pure Drug Co., Nottingham, England (supply most of the materials for making up resists etc.).

Johnson of Hendon Ltd., Hendon Way, Hendon, London N.W.4 (iron perchloride).

Cornelissen & Sons, Art Colourmen, 22 Great Queen Street, London W.C.2 (have complete range of tools and materials).

Admel International Ltd., Abbey House, Victoria Street, London S.W.1 (transfer lettering).

Letraset (Export) Ltd., St George's House, 195–203 Waterloo Road, London S.W.1 (transfer lettering).

Hunter Penrose Littlejohn Ltd., Engravers' Suppliers, Spa Road, London, S.E.16.

U.S.A.

E. C. Muller, Engravers' Tools, 61–63 Frankfort Street, New York, N.Y.

The Cronite Co. Inc., 35 Park Place, New York 7, N.Y.

William Dixon Co., Newark, New Jersey.

ENAMELLING MATERIALS

The Vitreous Enamel Development Council, 28 Welbeck Street, London W.1, will be pleased to give advice and information.

W. G. Ball Ltd., Anchor Road, Longton, Stoke-on-Trent.

W. J. Hutton (Enamels) Ltd., 285 Icknield Street, Birmingham 18. Also at 30 Gt. Hampton Row, Birmingham 19 (stock all the requirements for school enamelling).

U.S.A.

Carpenter & Wood, Providence, Rhode Island.

C. R. Hill Company, 35 West Grand River, Detroit, Michigan.

B. F. Drakenfield & Co., 45 Park Place, New York 7, N.Y.

Thomas Thompson, 1203 Deerfield Road, Highland Park, Illinois.

POLISHING, COLOURING, LACQUERING AND PLATING MATERIALS

W. Canning & Co. Ltd., 37 Green Hill Crescent, Hollywell Industrial Estate, Watford, Herts.

U.S.A.

Allcraft Tool & Supply Co. Inc., 15 West 45th Street, New York, N.Y.

Hoover & Strong Inc., 111 W. Tupper St., Buffalo 1, N.Y.

PLASTIC COATING

Telcon Plastics, Farnborough Works, Green Street Green, Orpington, Kent.

Books for Reference and Further Reading

W. A. J. Chapman, *Workshop Technology*, Part I, Arnold.

W. A. J. Chapman, *Workshop Technology*, Part II, Arnold.

W. A. J. Chapman, *Workshop Technology*, Part III, Arnold.

E. C. Rollason, *Metallurgy for Engineers*, Arnold.

Paul Benham, *Foundrywork Design & Practice*, John Murray.

Blacksmith's Craft, The Rural Industries Bureau.

Herbert Maryon, *Metalwork and Enamelling*, Dover.

Polly Rothenberg, *Metal Enamelling*, Geo. Allen & Unwin.

Oppi Untracht, *Enamelling on Metal*, Greenberg, New York, N.Y.

Oscar Almeida, *Metalwork & Its Decoration by Etching*, Mills & Boon.

Aluminium Foundry Work for Schools and *Anodising Kit for Schools*, Aluminium Development Association, 33 Grosvenor Street, London W.1. Write for information on other topics.

Cutting Oils: Shell-Mex & BP Ltd., 195 Knightsbridge, London S.W.7.

Information regarding hall-marking and advice on fine casting of gold and silver may be obtained from:
The Worshipful Company of Goldsmiths, Goldsmiths' Hall, Foster Lane, London, E.C.2.

Index